HONG KONG
ENCOUNTER

PIERA CHEN
ANDREW STONE

Hong Kong Encounter

Published by Lonely Planet Publications Pty Ltd
ABN 36 005 607 983

Australia Head Office, Locked Bag 1, Footscray, Vic 3011
☎ 03 8379 8000 fax 03 8379 8111
talk2us@lonelyplanet.com.au

USA 150 Linden St, Oakland, CA 94607
☎ 510 250 6400
toll free 800 275 8555
fax 510 893 8572
info@lonelyplanet.com

UK 2nd fl, 186 City Rd
London EC1V 2NT
☎ 020 7106 2100 fax 020 7106 2101
go@lonelyplanet.co.uk

The first edition was written by Steve Fallon and the second edition by Andrew Stone. This edition was commissioned in Lonely Planet's Oakland office and produced by: **Commissioning Editors** Catherine Craddock-Carrillo, Emily Wolman **Coordinating Editor** Angela Tinson **Coordinating Cartographer** Brendan Streager **Layout Designer** Wibowo Rusli **Managing Editors** Liz Heynes, Kirsten Rawlings **Managing Cartographer** Alison Lyall **Managing Layout Designer** Jane Hart **Assisting Editor** Cathryn Game **Cover Research** Sabrina Dalbesio **Internal Image Research** Rebecca Skinner **Thanks to** Helen Christinis, Lisa Knights, Annelies Mertens, Sunny Or, Naomi Parker

ISBN 978 1 74179 705 3

Printed in China.

HOW TO USE THIS BOOK

Colour-Coding & Maps

Colour-coding is used for symbols on maps and in the text that they relate to (eg all eating venues on the maps and in the text are given a green knife and fork symbol). Each neighbourhood also gets its own colour, and this is used down the edge of the page and throughout that neighbourhood section.

Prices

Multiple prices listed with reviews (eg $10/5 or $10/5/20) indicate adult/child, adult/concession or adult/child/family.

Send us your feedback We love to hear from readers – your comments help make our books better. We read every word you send us, and we always guarantee that your feedback goes straight to the appropriate authors. The most useful submissions are rewarded with a free book. To send us your updates and find out about Lonely Planet events, newsletters and travel news visit our award-winning website: ***lonelyplanet.com/contact***.

Note: We may edit, reproduce and incorporate your comments in Lonely Planet products such as guidebooks, websites and digital products, so let us know if you don't want your comments reproduced or your name acknowledged. For a copy of our privacy policy visit ***lonelyplanet.com/privacy***.

PIERA CHEN

Hong Kong writer Piera has been visiting Macau since she was six years old. Half of her family was born there and the other half just thought that sipping Mateus rosé while sitting on the old sea-wall was incredibly romantic. Later, while working in Hong Kong, it was poetry readings, *fado* concerts and, most of all, a masterfully executed *pato de cabidela* (duck stewed in its own blood) that kept luring her back. Piera has also written the Hong Kong and Macau chapters of the 12th edition of Lonely Planet's *China*, and co-authored the 14th *Hong Kong & Macau* city guide.

PIERA'S THANKS

I extend my warmest gratitude to people who are passionate about their cities – from Macau, Carlos Marreiros and Francisco Chan; and from Hong Kong, Jozev and Yvonne Ieong. Special thanks also goes to Janine Cheung, Sherman Chan, Susanna Eusantos and, most of all, my husband, Sze Pang-cheung, for his love and assistance.

THE PHOTOGRAPHER

Greg Elms completed a Bachelor of Arts in Photography at the Royal Melbourne Institute of Technology, then embarked on a travel odyssey across Australia, Southeast Asia, India, Africa, Europe and the Middle East. He has been the photographer for numerous award-winning books, and has worked for magazines, ad agencies, designers and, of course, book publishers such as Lonely Planet.

Our readers Many thanks to the travellers who wrote to us with helpful hints, useful advice and interesting anecdotes. Luke Armstrong, Nelson Chen, James Cridland, Denis Howe, Penny Lattey, Ryan Macdicken, Joris van der Meer, Helen Or, Devon Peavoy, Jacalyn Soo, Lois Warner, Rachel Willcocks, Susan Williams, Anke Werschnik.

Cover photograph Sightseeing junk on Victoria Harbour, Manfred Gottschalk/Lonely Planet Images. **Internal photographs** p52, p72, p111, p153 by Piera Chen, p85 by Andrew Stone; p16 myLAM/Alamy. All other photographs by Lonely Planet Images, and by Greg Elms except p6 (bottom) Tim Hughes; p6 (top), p57 John Hay; p24 Manfred Gottschalk; p26 Holger Leue; p28 Alain Evrard; p31 Dallas Stribley; p32 (top) Andrew Burke; p47 Krzysztof Dydynski; p13, p27, p50, p97, p98, p138 Michael Coyne; p8, p160, p173 Phil Weymouth; p17, p32 (bottom), p88, p114, p128, Richard I'Anson.

Take in the sights aboard one of Hong Kong's unique double-decker trams (p13)

CONTENTS

Why is our travel information the best in the world? It's simple: our authors are passionate, dedicated travellers. They don't take freebies in exchange for positive coverage so you can be sure the advice you're given is impartial. They travel widely to all the popular spots, and off the beaten track. They don't research using just the internet or phone. They discover new places not included in any other guidebook. They personally visit thousands of hotels, restaurants, palaces, trails, galleries, temples and more. They speak with dozens of locals every day to make sure you get the kind of insider knowledge only a local could tell you. They take pride in getting all the details right, and in telling it how it is. Think you can do it? Find out how at **lonelyplanet.com**.

PHILIPS
SAMS
ING

THIS IS HONG KONG

A city that forces you to make some rapid adjustments. From the calm and cool of a Kowloon hotel lobby, the heat and hustle of teeming streets engulf you. You fight your way through multitudes only to stumble into sudden shade, greenery and space.

Hong Kong is a place that provokes questions, some without answers. Those five-star hotels and soaring skyscrapers are first world, but those crumbling tenements look third world, don't they? Where has all the oil-slick slow traffic come from and where on earth is it going? How do seven million people fit on this tiny speck of land? And how do they decide where to eat in the City of 10,000 Restaurants? How can a simmering tureen of tripe stock look so evil yet smell so good? And what, exactly, is in the food product you saw in the supermarket labelled 'vegetarian gizzard'?

Pondering, you reach the water and stare across to Hong Kong Island. Nothing has quite prepared you for the spectacle up close: freighters and motor junks forever plying their harbour trade and, beyond them, a *Futurama* cityscape rising from near-vertical jungle slopes.

After this sensory wave has rolled over you, there's no option but to start swimming with the tide in this energetic city of merchants, chancers and grifters. You soon learn that Hong Kong rewards those who grab experience by the scruff of the neck, who try that bowl of shredded jellyfish, who consume conspicuously, who roar with the Happy Valley punters as the winner thunders home. It rewards, too, those with the yen to explore centuries-old temples in half-deserted walled villages or to stroll surf-beaten beaches far from all the neon and steel and people.

It's an intoxicating place – spectacular, exotic and accessible. If you're visiting for business, you'll find pleasure sneaks up on you. If you're visiting for pleasure, there's no shortage of locals who make it their business to please.

Top Stroll through the serene Hong Kong Zoological & Botanical Gardens (p43) **Bottom** Jump aboard a traditional Chinese-style boat to get an excellent vantage point from which to take in the spectacle of the city

>HIGHLIGHTS

Burning incense to bring good fortune in the streets above Soho

>1 STAR FERRY

JUMP ABOARD FLOATING HISTORY IN VICTORIA HARBOUR

You can't say you've 'done' Hong Kong until you've taken a ride on the implausibly inexpensive Star Ferry (p189). For a mere $2 you can board the upper deck of one of this small fleet of diesel-electric boats first launched in 1888. With names like *Morning Star, Celestial Star* and *Twinkling Star*, the ferries are most romantic at night. The boats are festively strung with lights, the city buildings beam onto the rippling water, the frenzy of Hong Kong by day has eased (somewhat) and Hong Kong Island bathes the harbour in its neon glow. If possible, try to take the trip on a clear night from Kowloon side to Central; it's not half as dramatic in the other direction. The trip takes about nine minutes (as long as it used to take to read the now-defunct *Hong Kong Star*, a lowbrow tabloid newspaper, it was said), and departures are very frequent. Indeed, morning and evening, the Star Ferry is a genuinely useful and commonly used way for local people to hop from island to mainland and back again.

>2 HONG KONG VIEWS

OPEN YOUR EYES TO AMAZING VISTAS

It's hard not to revert to cliché, purple prose and overblown superlatives when attempting to describe the Hong Kong skyline and harbour. But words, and photographs, really do fail to convey the rush of energy you get from taking in this futuristic megacity's outline and the amazing natural topography on which it's built. You need distance and perspective to do this properly and getting as high as you can (we mean physically) is one good way to enjoy this simple thrill. Head for the Bank of China Tower (p42) designed by China-born American architect IM Pei in 1990. Take the express lift to the 43rd floor from where you'll be rewarded with a panoramic view over Hong Kong. From here you are about the same height as the Hongkong & Shanghai Bank (p44) to the northwest. It's a pity that you aren't allowed to go any higher, as it's exciting swaying with the wind at the top. Even higher (though arguably not as dramatic) is the view from the windows of the Hong Kong Monetary Authority Information Centre on the 55th floor of the Two International Finance Centre (p46). For perhaps the ultimate show-stopping view, stand at the harbour edge in Tsim Sha Tsui (p112) and take in Hong Kong Island's skyscrapers' gradient-defying march up steep jungle slopes by day, and by night marvel at its captivating neon lightshow.

>3 WET MARKET

REACH SENSORY OVERLOAD IN THE WET MARKET'S COLOUR, AROMA AND GORE

Prepare to have your senses (and maybe sensibilities) assailed if you tour a wet market, places that feed Hong Kong's appetite for fresh (and, in many cases, live) food. Stalls of exotic fresh produce – star fruit, custard apples and dragon fruit – are piled high next to ones selling other local delicacies and staples, such as preserved eggs (the ready-to-eat greenish-black ones packed in a mixture of ash, lime and salt and buried for 100 days) or fresh white bean curd scooped still steaming from wooden pails. Be warned, though: those of a squeamish disposition might find wet markets unnerving. All manner of live crustaceans and reptiles lie blinking and squirming in baskets while live fish are sliced lengthways, their exposed hearts left beating on the slab. Our favourite is the outdoor Graham St Market (p56). Walk up from Queen's Rd Central (or down from Hollywood Rd) and prepare yourself for the cacophony and bustle, and the press of people lingering over, discussing and bargaining for food.

>4 TRAMS

ROCK & ROLL ALONG HONG KONG ISLAND'S NORTHERN COAST

It doesn't matter how many times we visit Hong Kong Island, a ride on a tram (p188) still offers a thrill right up there with the Star Ferry. Yes, it's slow, not air-conditioned and fully exposed to the noise and bustle, but that's part of the appeal. For a couple of dollars, you'll make stately progress through a sliver of Hong Kong Island, your journey along the tram tracks offering a mesmeric and slowly scrolling urban panorama. These 164 tall, narrow streetcars comprise the world's only fully double-decker tramcar fleet, and they roll (and rock) along 13km of track from Kennedy Town in the west to Shau Kei Wan in the east, carrying almost a quarter of a million passengers a day. Try to get a seat at the front window on the upper deck for a first-class view while rattling through the crowded streets. Tall passengers will find it uncomfortable standing up as the ceiling is low, but there is more space at the rear of the tram on both decks. And be prepared to elbow your way through the crowd to alight, particularly on the lower deck.

>5 SHEUNG WAN

SHUFFLE THROUGH SHEUNG WAN'S HISTORIC ALLEYS

A short distance from Central's sharp, shiny edges but seemingly a world away, the streets of Sheung Wan (p40) form Hong Kong Island's old Chinese heart. It's a vibrant, colourful area that's best explored on foot. Although high-rise development is creeping west from Central, there's still a much more Chinese and old-fashioned character to the area and nary a shopping mall in sight. Follow your nose along Queens Rd West to the area around Wing Lok St and you've found the source of the area's pervasive fishy smell: the profusion of dried seafood and Chinese medicine wholesalers. Towering above the bins of dried bivalves and small fry, the piles of dried shark fins are a stark sign of their popularity in Hong Kong as a high-status delicacy, particularly at wedding receptions and other banquets. Several shops in the area also seem to base their business entirely on the sale of ginseng roots or swallow's nests, gathered at great risk high up in Malay sea caves. The latter are constructed entirely of swallow's spittle, and are used in a number of Chinese

dishes but most commonly for bird's nest soup, also commonly served as an entrée at formal dinners. Slightly uphill from here, the further western reaches of Hollywood Rd are also worth exploring for more interesting nooks and shops, including ones selling paper votives (such as Hell banknotes) burned to keep the dead in pocket money. The incense-filled Man Mo Temple (p44) is a nearby sight and opposite this you'll find Upper Lascar Row, also known as Cat St (p42), another traditional hunting ground for antiques, bric-a-brac and junk.

HK SEAFOOD: THE CATCH

When you see the piles of shark fins on sale in Sheung Wan, you won't be surprised to learn that half the world's shark species are now endangered. While scientists and conservation groups push for global limits on numbers caught, diners wishing to eat sustainably should avoid the soup the fins are commonly used to make. Regrettably many other fish served in Hong Kong are also on the endangered list. To find out which are threatened and how to best avoid them, consult the website of the **World-wide Fund for Nature** (wwf.org.hk) for a guide to eating sustainable seafood.

>6 WALLED VILLAGES

SEE HOW THE 'FOREIGN' NATIVES LIVED AND ATE

The Punti (pronounced 'boon-day') were among the earliest clans to settle in Hong Kong. Punti means indigenous, yet these Cantonese-speaking newcomers from the mainland were anything but.

The famous Five Clans began setting up house in the New Territories around the 11th century. The first and most powerful were the Tang, who founded the walled villages now showcased on the impressive Ping Shan Heritage Trail. The clan's best known descendant today is the flamboyant William Tang, a fashion designer who has created uniforms for the MTR corporation and Dragon Air and staged fashion shows in the ancestral hall in Ping Shan. The Tang were followed by the Hau and the Pang – who spread around Sheung Shui and Fan Ling – and, later, the Liu and the Man.

The 1km Ping Shan Heritage Trail, with its magnificent historic buildings, will give you an idea of how these clans lived. To get a taste of what they ate, head to Dah Wing Wah (p139). Its head chef, Hugo Leung Man-to, is celebrated for enhancing and preserving traditional dishes; he sources local ingredients from small farms whenever possible and applies contemporary innovations in cooking to their preparation.

>7 PENINSULA HOTEL

TAKE A SIP OF LUXURY AT HONG KONG'S LEGENDARY HOTEL

For service as smooth as it comes, a regal atmosphere and a string quartet discreetly sawing away upstairs, afternoon tea at the Peninsula offers an affordable taste of the luxury Hong Kong. Undeniably one of the world's great hotels, the Peninsula (p110) is both a landmark and a Hong Kong icon. Though it was being called 'the finest hotel east of Suez' a few years after opening in 1928, the Peninsula was in fact one of several prestigious hostelries across Asia where everybody who was anybody stayed, up there with the likes of Raffles in Singapore, the Peace (then the Cathay) in Shanghai and the Strand in Rangoon (now Yangon). If you plan to take tea, dress neatly (no jacket required, though) and be prepared to queue for a table. While you're waiting, salivate at the sight of everyone else's cucumber sandwiches, scones and dainty cakes. The price of afternoon tea, served from 2pm to 7pm daily, for one is $268 and it's $398 per couple. It attracts a mixed clientele – from Japanese tourists to *tai tais* (any married women but especially the leisured wives of wealthy businessmen), who grab the most prominent tables, sip and gossip with their friends (mostly via mobile phones). When you're through (and to bring yourself back to earth) cross Nathan Rd and have a look round the shopping arcade of the rabbit warren called Chungking Mansions (p108).

>8 THE PEAK

A BREATH OF FRESH AIR AT THE TOP OF HONG KONG ISLAND

The Peak (p74), Hong Kong Island's highest point, has been *the* place to live ever since the British arrived in the 19th century. The taipans built summer houses here to escape the heat and humidity (it's usually about 5°C cooler than down below). The Peak remains the most fashionable – and expensive – area to live in Hong Kong and is the territory's foremost tourist destination. Not only is the view from the summit one of the world's most spectacular cityscapes, it's also a good way to get Hong Kong into perspective. And the only way up, as far as we are concerned, is via the Peak Tram (see pp188-9 and boxed text, p77).

Rising above the Peak Tram terminus is the seven-storey Peak Tower, an anvil-shaped building containing shops, restaurants, tourist tat and a viewing terrace. Opposite is the Peak Galleria, a three-storey mall of shops and restaurants. Like the tower, it's designed to withstand winds of up to 270km/h, theoretically more than the maximum velocity of a No 10 typhoon.

When people in Hong Kong refer to the Peak, they usually mean the plateau and surrounding residential area at about 400m. The summit, Victoria Peak (552m), is about 500m northwest of the Peak

Tram terminus up steep Mt Austin Rd. The governor's mountain lodge near the summit was burned to the ground by the Japanese during WWII, but the gardens remain and are open to the public.

You can walk around Victoria Peak without exhausting yourself. Harlech Rd and Lugard Rd slope together form a 3.5km loop that takes about an hour. If you feel like a longer stroll (and want to avoid the Peak Tram and its crowds on the way down), you can continue for a further 2km along Peak Rd to Pok Fu Lam Reservoir Rd, which leaves Peak Rd near the car park exit. This goes past the reservoir to the main Pok Fu Lam Rd, where you can get bus 7 back to Central. Another good walk leads down to Hong Kong University. First walk to the west side of Victoria Peak by taking either Lugard or Harlech Rds. After reaching Hatton Rd, follow it down. The descent is steep, but the path is clear.

PRICES AT A PEAK

If you're in the market for one of the world's priciest homes, head to the Peak's Severn Rd, the second-most expensive street on earth (beaten to top spot only by Monaco's Ave Princess Grace). The best properties, those commanding the heights and so the most spectacular city views, cost around $120,000 per sq metre. Can we interest you in the four-bedroom place (plus maid's room) at No 23, which was valued a while back at $500m? Or perhaps you'd prefer to rent it, a snip at $380,000 per month (maid not included).

>9 SIK SIK YUEN WONG TAI SIN TEMPLE

PRAY FOR GOOD FORTUNE IN NEW KOWLOON

Sik Sik Yuen Wong Tai Sin Temple (p133) is an explosion of colour with red pillars, bright-yellow roofs and green-and-blue latticework. What's particularly striking is its popularity with locals. If you visit in the late afternoon or early evening, you can watch the hordes praying and divining the future with *chim*, bamboo 'prediction sticks' that must be shaken out of a box on to the ground and then read (they're available free to the left of the main temple). Behind the main temple and to the right are the Good Wish Gardens, replete with colourful pavilions (the hexagonal Unicorn Hall with carved doors and windows is the most beautiful), zigzag bridges and artificial ponds. Just below the main temple and to the left as you enter the complex is an arcade filled with dozens of booths operated by fortune-tellers. Some speak decent English (and advertise the fact on signs above their counters), so if you really want to know what fate has in store for you, this is your chance. The busiest times at the temple are around the Chinese New Year, Wong Tai Sin's birthday (23rd day of the eighth month – usually in September) and on weekends, especially Friday evening.

>10 HONG KONG MUSEUM OF HISTORY

TAKE A TRIP BACK THROUGH TIME

Hong Kong, in case you hadn't noticed, is a city whose commercially minded movers and shakers have their eyes firmly on the future, never much minding if the past gets torn up. This makes the few remnants of the past – be they listed buildings and monuments or old-fashioned observances (such as a computer-shop owner tending a shrine to the Earth God Tou Tei in his shop) – precious indeed. 'The Hong Kong Story' at the Hong Kong Museum of History (p109) takes visitors on a fascinating walk through the territory's past via eight galleries, starting with the natural environment and prehistoric Hong Kong on the ground floor – about 6000 years ago, give or take a lunar year – and ending with the territory's return to China in 1997 and a moving video collage of Hong Kong through the ages on the 2nd. Along the way you'll encounter replicas of village dwellings; traditional Chinese costumes and beds; a re-creation of an entire arcaded street in Central from 1881, including an old Chinese medicine shop; a tram from 1913; and film footage of WWII, including recent interviews with Chinese and foreigners taken prisoner by the Japanese. A favourite exhibit remains the jumble of toys and collectables from the 1960s and '70s when 'Made in Hong Kong' meant 'Christmas stocking trash'.

>11 DIM SUM

INDULGE IN SOME YUM-YUM YUM CHA

Yum cha (literally 'drink tea') is the usual way to refer to dim sum, the uniquely Cantonese 'meal' eaten as breakfast, brunch or lunch between about 7am and 3pm. Eating dim sum is a social occasion, consisting of many separate dishes that are meant to be shared. The bigger your group, the better. Dim sum delicacies are normally steamed in small bamboo baskets. The baskets are stacked up on trolleys and rolled around the dining room. You don't need a menu (though these exist, too, but are almost always in Chinese); just stop the waiter and choose something from the trolley. It will be marked down on a bill left on the table. Don't try to order everything at once. Each trolley has a different selection, so take your time and order as they come. It's said that there are about a thousand dim sum dishes, but you'd be doing well to sample 10 in one sitting.

cha siu baau – steamed buns stuffed with barbecued pork
cheun gyun – spring rolls
cheung fan – steamed rice-flour rolls with shrimp, beef or pork
ching chaau si choi – stir-fried seasonal greens
fu pei gyun – fried bean-curd rolls
fung jaau – chickens' feet in black bean sauce
har gaau – steamed shrimp dumplings

TEA TOO

Choosing the tea is as important to Chinese people as selecting the dishes at yum cha. Basically there are three main types: green (or unfermented) tea *(luk cha);* black tea (*hung cha* in Chinese, which translates as 'red tea'), which is fermented and includes the ever-popular *bole;* and oolong *(wu lung cha)* tea, which is semifermented. In between are countless scented variations, such as *heung ping* (jasmine), which is a blend of black tea and flower petals. When your teapot is empty and you want a refill, signal the waiter by taking the lid off the pot and resting it on the handle.

no mai gai – glutinous rice wrapped in lotus leaf
paai gwat – spareribs in black-bean sauce
saan juk ngau yuk – steamed balls of minced beef
siu maai – steamed pork and shrimp dumplings

Dim sum restaurants are normally brightly lit and very large and noisy – it's rather like eating in an aircraft hangar. See boxed text, p163, for a list of the best.

>12 HONG KONG PARK

ESCAPE TO THE CITY'S RAINFOREST AVIARY

Deliberately designed to look anything but natural, Hong Kong Park (p80) is one of the most unusual parks in the world, emphasising artificial creations, such as its fountain plaza, conservatory, artificial waterfall, indoor games hall, playground, t'ai chi garden, viewing tower, museums and an arts centre. For all its artifice, the eight-hectare park is beautiful in its own weird way and, with a wall of skyscrapers on one side and mountains on the other, makes for dramatic photographs. Its best feature by far is the Edward Youde Aviary, named after a much-loved former governor (1982–87) and China scholar who died suddenly while in office. Home to hundreds of birds representing some 150 different species, the aviary is a huge and convincing re-creation of tropical forest habitat. Visitors walk along a wooden bridge suspended 10m above ground, at eye level with tree branches where most of the birds are; there are about a dozen viewing platforms. Schedule your visit for the morning, when the birds are most active. Volunteers from the Hong Kong Bird Watching Society lead visitors through the park and aviary, identifying various exotic species, including sulphur-coloured cockatoos, Chinese bulbuls and blue magpies.

>13 TEMPLE STREET NIGHT MARKET

DINNER AND A SHOW FOR A SONG

Temple St, named after the temple dedicated to Tin Hau at its centre, hosts the liveliest night market (p124) in Hong Kong. It used to be known as 'Men's St' because the market sold only men's clothing and to distinguish it from the 'Ladies' Market' on Tung Choi St (p125) to the northeast. Though there are still a lot of items on sale for men, vendors don't discriminate – anyone's money will do. But don't come here just to shop; this is also a place for eating and entertainment. For street food, head for Woo Sung St, running parallel to the east, or to the section of Temple St north of the temple towards Man Ming Lane. You can get anything from a fried snack to go or a simple bowl of noodles to a full meal served at your very own kerbside table. There are a few seafood and hotpot restaurants as well, or you might pop into Mido (p128), Hong Kong's best known *cha chaan tang* (café with local dishes). You'll also find a surfeit of fortune-tellers and herbalists and some free, open-air Cantonese opera performances here. The market officially opens in the afternoon and closes at midnight, but it is at its best from about 7pm to 10pm, when it's clogged with stalls and people. If you want to carry on, visit the colourful wholesale fruit market (corner Shek Lung and Reclamation Sts), which is always a hive of activity from midnight to dawn.

>14 ABERDEEN TYPHOON SHELTER

HOME OF FISHERMEN AND DRAGON-BOAT RACING

You know the small, smelly looking harbour bobbing with sampans and junks housing entire families seen in such movies as *Tomb Raider 2* and *The World of Suzie Wong*? That's the Aberdeen typhoon shelter, and is where the homes of the boat-dwelling Tanka, a group that arrived in Hong Kong before the 10th century, were once moored. In the 1960s the fishing population here was 30,000; now just a few hundred remain. Yet the majority of Aberdeenians today are descendants of fishermen and still see themselves as 'people of the water' (sui seung yan).

Each year this identity is celebrated with flags and fanfare at the many dragon-boat races throughout the territory (see p102). On weekday evenings you'll see teams practising under the moon in the typhoon shelter or chilling out in the Ap Lei Chau Market Cooked Food Centre (p104), just across the water, where some of the territory's best and cheapest seafood is to be enjoyed. Sightseeing sampans depart from various points along Aberdeen Promenade and will take you past fishing boats docked next to luxury yachts, and skyscrapers towering over rusty shipyards – a setting not exactly idyllic but charming nonetheless.

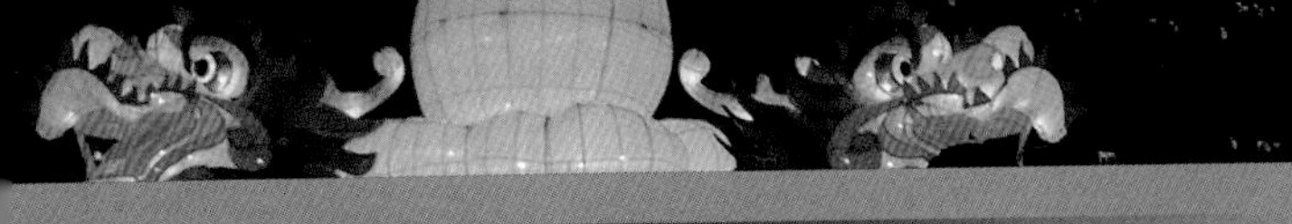

>HONG KONG DIARY

No matter what the time of year, you're almost certain to find some colourful festival or event occurring in Hong Kong. The choices seem endless – from long-established cultural events, like the Hong Kong Arts Festival, to traditional celebrations, such as the Dragon Boat Festival. Major sporting events such as the Hong Kong Rugby World Cup Sevens bring excitement and hordes of revellers, but nothing is quite as colourful as Hong Kong's traditional Chinese holidays, especially the Mid-Autumn Festival.

Giant lanterns light up the night for the Mid-Autumn Festival (p30)

JANUARY

Chinese New Year

www.discoverhongkong.com

China's most important public holiday (23 January 2012) is welcomed in by flower markets, fireworks and a huge international parade.

Hong Kong City Festival

www.hkfringe.com.hk

Get a taste of the city's culture during these three weeks of eclectic performances both local and from overseas.

FEBRUARY

Hong Kong Arts Festival

www.hk.artsfestival.org

A month-long extravaganza of music, performing arts and exhibitions by hundreds of local and international artists.

Spring Lantern Festival

www.discoverhongkong.com

This colourful lantern festival on the 15th day of the first moon (6 February 2012) marks the end of the lunar new year period and is a day for lovers.

Local children play an important part in the parade for the Cheung Chau Bun Festival

MOVABLE FEASTS

Many Chinese red-letter days, both public holidays and privately observed affairs, go back hundreds, even thousands, of years, and the true origins of some are often lost in the mists of time. Dates vary from year to year, so if you want to time your visit to coincide with a particular event, check the website of the **Hong Kong Tourism Board** (www.discoverhongkong.com). In modern-day Hong Kong there's a festival for everything: film and the arts, salsa, winter, all things French, Italian, Spanish and Mexican – even shopping gets its own spot on the calendar.

MARCH

Hong Kong Art Walk

www.hongkongartwalk.com

More than 60 galleries throw open their doors.

Hong Kong Rugby World Cup Sevens

www.hksevens.com.hk

This seven-a-side tournament attracts teams and spectators from all over the world.

Man Hong Kong International Literary Festival

www.festival.org.hk

Features novelists, short-story writers and poets from around the region and world.

Hong Kong International Film Festival

www.hkiff.org.hk

Screenings of over 300 films from 50 countries worldwide.

APRIL

Le French May

www.frenchmay.com

A celebration of French literary, visual, performance and culinary arts (runs for one month from late April).

Birthday of Tin Hau

www.discoverhongkong.com

This festival honours the patroness of sailors and fisherfolk – one of the territory's most popular goddesses.

MAY

Birthday of Lord Buddha

www.discoverhongkong.com

On this public holiday (28 April 2012) Buddha's statue is taken from the various monasteries and temples around Hong Kong and ceremonially bathed in scented water.

Cheung Chau Bun Festival

www.cheungchau.org

This unusual Taoist festival involving buns is observed uniquely on the island of Cheung Chau (p142).

Hong Kong International Art Fair

www.hongkongartfair.com

Over 150 art galleries from 30 countries in Asia and the West display their wares at the Convention and Exhibition Centre.

JUNE

Dragon Boat Festival

www.discoverhongkong.com

This festival (23 June 2012) evolved from rituals to appease spirits, but is more popularly known as a commemoration the death of a 3rd-century-BC poet-statesman who hurled himself into a river to protest against a corrupt government. Dragon-boat races are held throughout the territory but the most famous are at Stanley.

JULY

Hong Kong Book Fair

www.hkbookfair.com

This fair (20 to 26 July 2011) has printed and multimedia publications for all ages, and also features seminars and forums. It gets packed!

AUGUST

Hungry Ghost Festival

www.discoverhongkong.com

Marks the day when the gates of hell are opened and restless spirits are freed for two weeks to walk the earth. Paper 'hell' money and votives in the shape of cars, houses and clothing are burned on the last day.

SEPTEMBER

Mid-Autumn Festival

www.discoverhongkong.com

Held on the 15th night of the eighth moon (12 September 2011), this colourful festival involves eating little round 'moon' cakes while gazing at the full moon.

OCTOBER

Cheung Yeung

www.discoverhongkong.com

This festival is based on a Han dynasty story, where an oracle advised a man to take his family to a high place to escape a plague. Many people still head for the hills on this day and also visit the graves of ancestors.

NOVEMBER

Hong Kong International Cricket Sixes

www.hksixes.com

This two-day tournament pits Hong Kong's top cricketers against select teams from the eight Test-playing nations.

Hong Kong International Jazz Festival

www.hkja.org

A week of concerts and jam sessions by international and local talent at locations all over town.

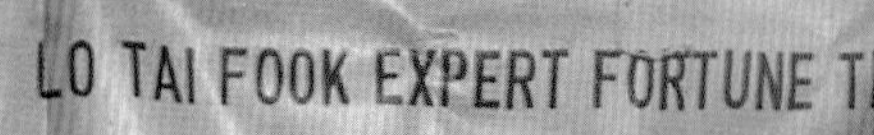

>ITINERARIES

Find out what fate has in store – meet with a fortune teller at the Temple St Night Market (p124)

ITINERARIES

Whether you have a few hours to kill between flights or several days to enjoy, Hong Kong's super-efficient transport system and the city's compact nature means you can be sure to spend your leisure time profitably in the city and the wild areas on its fringes.

ONE DAY

Catch the Peak Tram up to the Peak (p74) for fine views of the city and a morning constitutional along the summit's circular path. Back down the hill take a stroll through Hong Kong Park (p80) before taking a tea break at the Lock Cha Tea Shop (p49) in the KS Lo Gallery. A lift in the Island Shangri-La Hong Kong Hotel will take you down to Pacific Place (p78) for some shopping. Take the westernmost exit from Pacific Place to emerge close to Wing Fung St for lunch at Xi Yan Sweets (p86) or a light lunch at Naturo+ (p84). Before you've finished nosing around this corner of Wan Chai relax over a drink at the Pawn (p88) before taking the Mass Transit Railway (MTR) to Central and weighing up the many options for dinner in Lan Kwai Fong and Soho (p61).

TWO DAYS

If your stay in Hong Kong amounts to a weekend, on day two take the Star Ferry (p189) to Tsim Sha Tsui to the Hong Kong Museum of History (p109). Meander over Nathan Rd for a stroll in Kowloon Park, then head south for lunch and views at Hutong (p117). Nip across to Harbour City for shopping at Lane Crawford (p113) or into Star House for Chinese crafts (p112) and computer bargains (p115) until you're ready for afternoon tea at the Peninsula Hotel (p110). Wander up to Yau Ma Tei (p122) and the Jade Market (p124). A mere hop, skip and slip northeast is Temple St Night Market (p124), where you can sample street food, have your fortune told and, if you're lucky, catch some open-air Cantonese opera.

THREE DAYS

On the third day, wander around Central and Sheung Wan (p40), poking your head into traditional shops (p14). The Macau Ferry Terminal is just

Top The Peak tram (p18) traverses the steep incline from Central to the Peak **Bottom** Old religious sculptures for sale in an antique shop in Sheung Wan (p40)

across the road – why not hop aboard? Have lunch at the Clube Militar de Macau (p151) before visiting the Ox Warehouse (p148) for the latest in local art or trying your luck at the Wynn Macau Casino (p154). Finish with a meal at Restaurante Litoral (p151). Back in Hong Kong spend the evening carousing in Lan Kwai Fong (p65).

ISLAND ESCAPADE

Hong Kong's crowds – everywhere at all times and always directly in your path – can become wearing. Escape them by fleeing to Lantau: take the MTR to Tung Chung and board the Ngong Ping Skyrail (p143) to Ngong Ping and the Tian Tan Buddha (p143). After a vegetarian lunch at the canteen of Po Lin Monastery (p144) board bus 21 for the traditional village of Tai O (p143). Bus 1 will return you to Mui Wo (Silvermine Bay) and the ferry to Central. Along the way, get off at Upper Cheung Sha beach (p143) for a swim or stroll.

RAINY DAY

If the rain has set in determinedly, trying to take in the sights is no fun as you weave and dodge through a thousand low-flying umbrella spikes. Take your pick from the museums of Tsim Sha Tsui (p108) to while away the best part of a day, string out a luxurious afternoon tea at the Peninsula Hotel (p110), take shelter deep in the gilded heart of Central's shopping malls (p47), many of them connected by walkways, or simply make a dash for one of the bars of Lan Kwai Fong and Soho (p65) in time for the lengthy happy hour.

FOR FREE

When the only thing in your pocket is 'shrapnel' (the little brown coins that make up $1), don't despair. Admission to places like the Flagstaff House Museum of Tea Ware (p80) in Hong Kong Park and the Hong Kong Heritage Discovery Centre in Kowloon Park (p110) is always gratis, but Wednesday is 'admission free' day at seven museums: Hong Kong Heritage Museum (p138), Hong Kong Museum of Art (p108), Hong Kong Museum of Coastal Defence (see boxed text, p96), Hong Kong Museum of History (p108), Dr Sun Yat-sen Museum (p76), Hong Kong Science Museum and Hong Kong Space Museum (p109), excluding the Space Theatre. For something more spectacularly dramatic, head for the public viewing deck at the Bank of China (p42).

FORWARD PLANNING

Three weeks before you go Bag the best hotel rooms early. Hong Kong can fill up, especially during the conference and exhibition seasons in spring and autumn. See hotels .lonelyplanet.com for hotel bookings; get to know what's going on – both in the headlines and after hours – online by reading the local media, such as *South China Morning Post* at www.scmp.com.hk, *Hong Kong Standard* at www.thestandard.com.hk and *Time Out* at www.timeout.com.hk for its weekly listings; check to see if your visit coincides with any major holidays or festivals (p27); make sure your passport and other documents are in order.

One week before you go Book tickets for any major concerts or shows that might interest you at places like Hong Kong City Hall (p53), the Hong Kong Cultural Centre (p121) or the Fringe Club (p69); book that table at Caprice (p49) or Spring Deer (p117).

The day before you go Reconfirm your flight; check the Hong Kong websites for any last-minute changes or cancellations at entertainment venues; buy some Hong Kong dollars; cancel the milk.

OPEN ALL HOURS

So, jetlag is playing havoc with your body clock. If it's very early in the morning, why not walk in a daze through Graham St Market (p56) and see the stallholders setting up before the 6am opening? At all hours the Hong Kong Island skyline from Tsim Sha Tsui (p112) is a marvel to sit and gape at, although if you're on the Hong Kong Island side after midnight, a taxi will be your only option to get here. Or perhaps you're desperate for a quick nap but don't want to pay for a hotel room. Never fear. Head to any *cha chaan teng*, make a beeline for a booth seat and pretend to meditate, eyes closed, over your iced lemon tea. After a late bite? Try Tsui Wah Restaurant (p64), which serves up yummy Chinese fast food around the clock.

>NEIGHBOURHOODS

Lan Kwai Fong (p54) is a great place to experience the city's hustle and bustle

NEIGHBOURHOODS

Think of Hong Kong as being divided into four main areas: Hong Kong Island, Kowloon, the New Territories and the Outlying Islands. The beating commercial and social heart of Hong Kong lies in the first two of these areas – the skyscraper-clad northern edge of Hong Kong Island and the busy district of Kowloon.

Central, on the northern side of Hong Kong Island, is where much of what happens (or is decided) in Hong Kong takes place; come here for business, sightseeing, and entertainment in Lan Kwai Fong and Soho.

Just to the west, Sheung Wan manages to retain the feel of pre-war Hong Kong in parts, and rising above Central are the Mid-Levels residential area and the Peak, home to the rich, the famous and the Peak Tram.

East of Central lies Admiralty, really just a cluster of office towers, hotels and shopping centres, and Wan Chai, a seedy red-light district during the Vietnam War but now a popular entertainment area. Beyond that lies Causeway Bay, the most popular shopping district on Hong Kong Island.

On the southern edge of the island are small popular seaside towns, including Stanley, with its fashionable restaurants, cafés and famous market.

North of Hong Kong Island is Kowloon, its epicentre the shopping, cultural and entertainment district of Tsim Sha Tsui. North of Tsim Sha Tsui are the working-class areas of Yau Ma Tei and Mong Kok, where you'll stumble upon outdoor markets, Chinese pharmacies and mahjong parlours.

The New Territories, once Hong Kong's country playground, is today a mixed bag of housing estates and some surprisingly unspoiled rural areas and country parks containing temples, monasteries, old walled villages, wetlands, forested nature reserves and the idyllic Sai Kung Peninsula.

Among the so-called Outlying Islands accessible on a day trip from Hong Kong Island are: Cheung Chau, with its traditional village and fishing fleet; Lamma, celebrated for its restaurants and easy country walks; and Lantau, the largest island of all, with excellent beaches and country trails.

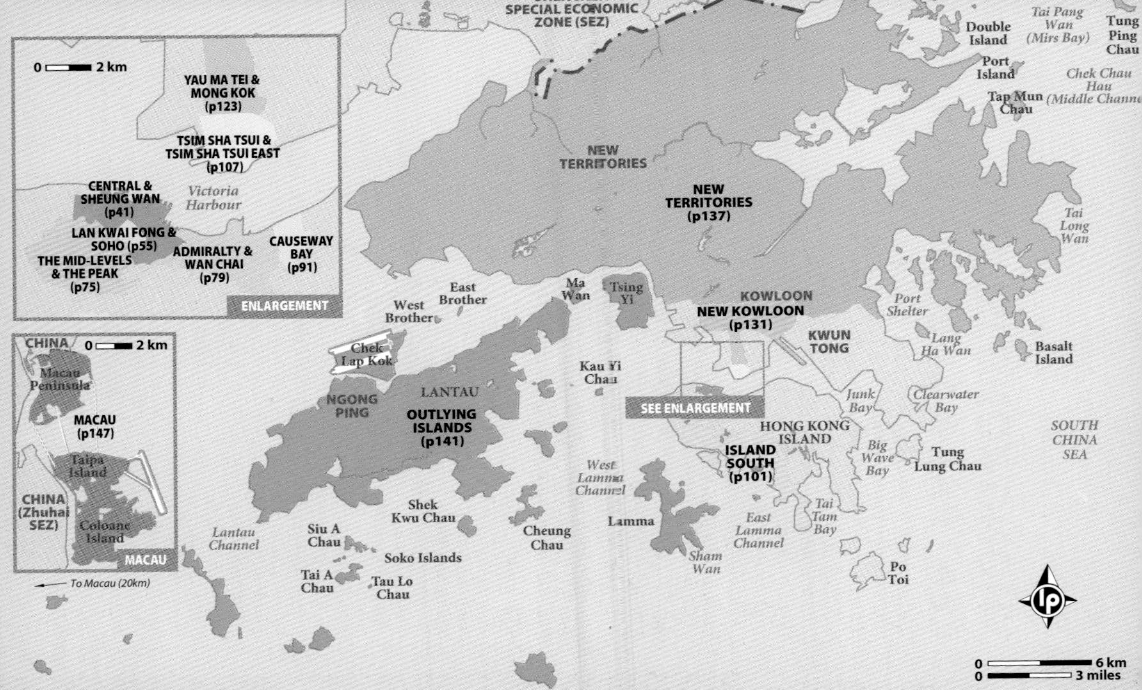
SPECIAL ECONOMIC ZONE (SEZ)
0 2 km
YAU MA TEI & MONG KOK (p123)
TSIM SHA TSUI & TSIM SHA TSUI EAST (p107)
CENTRAL & SHEUNG WAN (p41)
Victoria Harbour
LAN KWAI FONG & SOHO (p55)
THE MID-LEVELS & THE PEAK (p75)
ADMIRALTY & WAN CHAI (p79)
CAUSEWAY BAY (p91)
ENLARGEMENT
CHINA
0 2 km
Macau Peninsula
MACAU (p147)
Taipa Island
CHINA (Zhuhai SEZ)
Coloane Island
MACAU
To Macau (20km)
NEW TERRITORIES
NEW TERRITORIES (p137)
Double Island
Port Island
Tap Mun Chau
Tai Pang Wan (Mirs Bay)
Tung Ping Chau
Chek Chau Hau
Tai Long Wan
West Brother
East Brother
Ma Wan
Tsing Yi
KOWLOON
NEW KOWLOON (p131)
KWUN TONG
Port Shelter
Lang Ha Wan
Basalt Island
Chek Lap Kok
NGONG PING
LANTAU
OUTLYING ISLANDS (p141)
Kau Yi Chau
SEE ENLARGEMENT
Junk Bay
Clearwater Bay
HONG KONG ISLAND
ISLAND SOUTH (p101)
Big Wave Bay
Tung Lung Chau
SOUTH CHINA SEA
West Lamma Channel
Shek Kwu Chau
Cheung Chau
Lamma
East Lamma Channel
Tai Tam Bay
Lantau Channel
Siu A Chau
Soko Islands
Tai A Chau
Tau Lo Chau
Sham Wan
Po Toi
0 6 km
0 3 miles

>HONG KONG ISLAND: CENTRAL & SHEUNG WAN

The pulsating financial, political and retail heart of Hong Kong, sharp-suited Central is a heady mix of exclusive boutiques, peaceful parks, fine dining, modern corporate cathedrals and even a few historic colonial buildings (including a real cathedral marooned among the high-rises). Central is very much a 24-hour part of town. You can shop until late in a trio of huge, high-end, air-conditioned shopping malls and then stroll to nearby Lan Kwai Fong and Soho for a tempting variety and profusion of eating and drinking options. Arguably even more rewarding to explore, Sheung Wan still carries the echo of 'Old Hong Kong' in places, with its traditional shops and old 'ladder streets' (steep inclined streets with steps). Stroll the length of Hollywood Rd from east to west and you'll experience a good cross-section of both of these enticing neighbourhoods.

CENTRAL & SHEUNG WAN

SEE

Bank of China Tower 1 F3
Cat St Market 2 B2
Central Police Station Compound 3 D3
Exchange Square 4 E2
Former French Mission Building 5 E3
Government House 6 E4
Hong Kong Monetary Authority Information Centre ....(see 17)
Hong Kong Zoological & Botanical Gardens 7 D4
Hongkong & Shanghai Bank 8 E3
Kwun Yam Temple 9 B2
Legislative Council Building 10 E3
Man Mo Temple 11 C2
Pak Sing Ancestral Hall 12 B2
Para/Site Art Space 13 B2
St John's Cathedral 14 E4
Statue Square 15 E3
Tai Sui Temple 16 B2
Two International Finance Centre 17 E1
Western Market 18 C1

SHOP

Blanc de Chine 19 D3
Dymocks Booksellers ..20 E2
Hanart TZ Gallery 21 E3
HMV 22 E3
Hong Kong Book Centre 23 E2
Joyce 24 D3
Lock Cha Tea Shop 25 C2
Shanghai Tang 26 D3

EAT

ABC Kitchen 27 B1
Caprice 28 D1
City Hall Maxim's Palace 29 F3
Honeymoon Dessert ..(see 18)
Island Tang 30 E3
Lung King Heen 31 E1
Tim's Kitchen 32 C1

DRINK

Captain's Bar 33 E3
Red Bar 34 E1
Sevva 35 E3

PLAY

Grappa's Cellar 36 E2
Hong Kong City Hall 37 F3
Spa at the Four Seasons 38 E1

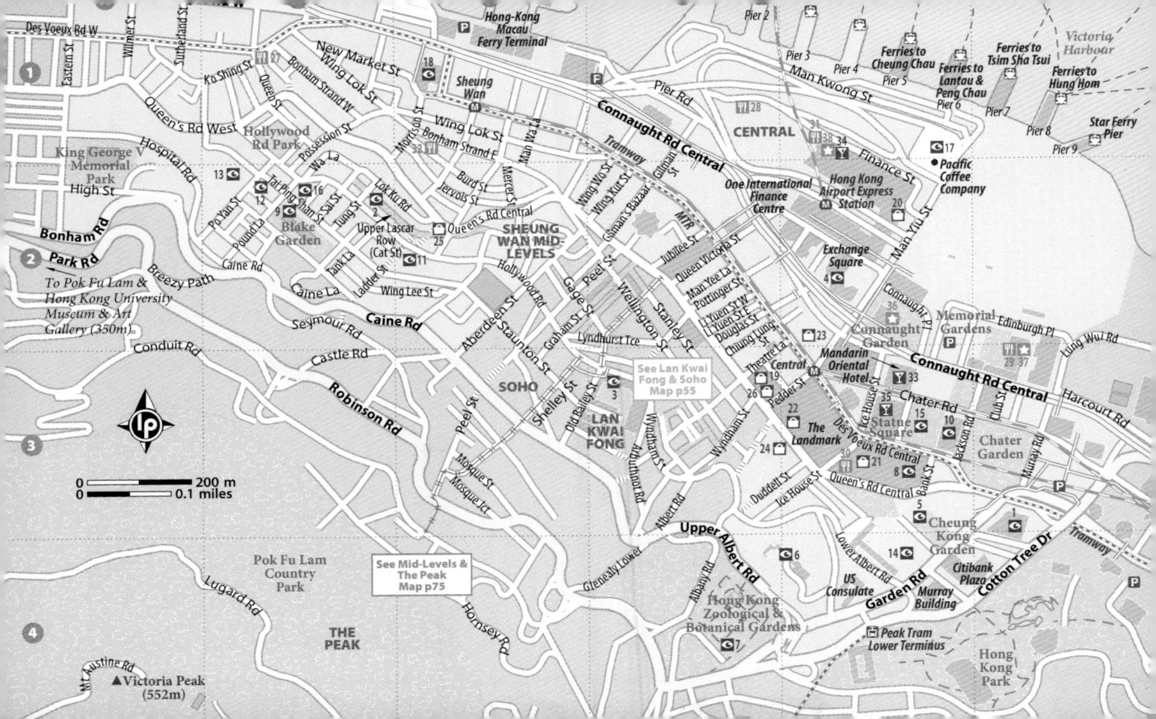

Hong-Kong Macau Ferry Terminal
Pier 2
Pier 3
Pier 4
Pier 5
Pier 6
Pier 7
Pier 8
Pier 9
Ferries to Cheung Chau
Ferries to Lantau & Peng Chau
Ferries to Tsim Sha Tsui
Ferries to Hung Hom
Victoria Harbour
Star Ferry Pier
Des Voeux Rd W
Eastern St
Wilmer St
Sutherland St
Ko Shing St
Queen St
Bonham Strand W
New Market St
Wing Lok St
Sheung Wan
Man Kwong St
Pier Rd
Connaught Rd Central
CENTRAL
Finance St
Pacific Coffee Company
Queen's Rd West
Hollywood Rd Park
Possession St
Morrison St
Wing Lok St
Bonham Strand E
Man Wa La
Tramway
Gilman St
King George V Memorial Park
High St
Hospital Rd
Wa La
Burd St
Jervois St
Mercer St
Wing Wo St
Wing Kut St
Gilman's Bazaar
MTR
One International Finance Centre
Hong Kong Airport Express Station
Man Yiu St
Po Yan St
Pound La
Tai Ping Shan St
Sai St
Tung St
Lok Ku Rd
Blake Garden
Upper Lascar Row (Cat St)
Queen's Rd Central
SHEUNG WAN MID-LEVELS
Jubilee St
Queen Victoria St
Exchange Square
Bonham Rd
Park Rd
To Pok Fu Lam & Hong Kong University Museum & Art Gallery (350m)
Breezy Path
Caine Rd
Caine La
Tank La
Ladder St
Wing Lee St
Hollywood Rd
Aberdeen St
Peel St
Gage St
Wellington St
Stanley St
Man Yee La
Pottinger St
Li Yuen St W
Li Yuen St E
Douglas St
Chiung Lung St
Connaught Pl
Memorial Gardens
Edinburgh Pl
Connaught Garden
Lung Wui Rd
Seymour Rd
Caine Rd
Conduit Rd
Castle Rd
Staunton St
Graham St
Lyndhurst Tce
Theatre La
Central
Mandarin Oriental Hotel
Connaught Rd Central
Harcourt Rd
SOHO
Shelley St
Old Bailey St
See Lan Kwai Fong & Soho Map p55
Pedder St
Ice House St
Chater Rd
Club St
Robinson Rd
Peel St
LAN KWAI FONG
Wyndham St
The Landmark
Statue Square
Jackson Rd
Chater Garden
Murray Rd
Des Voeux Rd Central
0
200 m
0.1 miles
Mosque St
Mosque Jct
Arbuthnot Rd
Albert Rd
Duddell St
Ice House St
Queen's Rd Central
Bank St
Upper Albert Rd
Cheung Kong Garden
Pok Fu Lam Country Park
See Mid-Levels & The Peak Map p75
Glenealy Lower
Albany Rd
Lower Albert Rd
US Consulate
Garden Rd
Murray Building
Citibank Plaza
Cotton Tree Dr
Tramway
Lugard Rd
Hornsey Rd
Hong Kong Zoological & Botanical Gardens
Peak Tram Lower Terminus
THE PEAK
Hong Kong Park
Mt Austine Rd
Victoria Peak (552m)

SEE

BANK OF CHINA TOWER 中國銀行大廈

1 Garden Rd, Central; admission free; 8am-6pm Mon-Fri; M Central (exit J2)

This stunning, 70-storey structure is one Hong Kong's tallest and certainly most striking buildings. The angular design gives the building an aggressive stance that is said to cast bad energies on nearby buildings. The views from the 43rd floor are terrific (p11).

CAT ST MARKET 摩囉街

Upper Lascar Row, Sheung Wan; 10am-6pm; 26 M Sheung Wan

Head to Upper Lascar Row (the official name of what has become known as Cat St and a pedestrian-only laneway) for dozens of stalls offering antiques, curios, cheap jewellery, ornaments, carvings and newly minted 'antique' coins. It's a fun place to trawl through for a trinket or two, but expect a lot of rough, and few (if any), diamonds.

BRUTAL BUILDING

Elegant it may be to some, but geomancers (practitioners of the art of feng shui) see the Bank of China Tower as a huge violation of its principles. The bank's four triangular prisms are negative symbols in the geomancer's rule book; being the opposite to circles, these contradict what circles suggest – perfection and (importantly in Hong Kong) prosperity. Furthermore, the huge crosses on the sides of the building suggest negativity and its shape has been likened to a praying mantis (a threatening symbol), complete with radio masts as antennae.

CENTRAL POLICE STATION COMPOUND 中區警署

http://amo.gov.hk/en/oe_central_police_station.php; 10 Hollywood Rd; M Central (exit D1)

This disused police–magistracy–prison complex comprises 27 buildings in Victorian and Edwardian styles modeled after London's Old Bailey. It offered one-stop, handcuff-to-leg-iron service before the word 'streamlining' existed. The complex, flanked by Hollywood Rd to the north and Chancery Lane to the south, is closed except when hired for events.

EXCHANGE SQUARE 交易廣場

8 Connaught Place, Central; admission free; M Central (exit A)

A good place to sit and relax beside the fountain and several sculptures, including one by Henry Moore. This complex of three elevated office towers above Central bus station is home to the Hong Kong Stock Exchange and many businesses.

FORMER FRENCH MISSION BUILDING 前法國外方傳道會大樓

1 Battery Path, Central; admission free; M Central (exit K)

Buddhas, beads and baubles – plenty to buy at the Cat St Market

Just behind pretty Cheung Kong Garden abutting St John's Cathedral is this charming structure built by an American trading firm in 1868. It served as the Russian consulate in Hong Kong until 1915 when the French Overseas Mission bought it and added a chapel and a dome. Today it houses the Court of Final Appeal, the highest judicial body in Hong Kong.

GOVERNMENT HOUSE
香港禮賓府

www.ceo.gov.hk/gh; ☎ 2530 2003; Upper Albert Rd, Central; admission free; 1st Sun in Mar & Nov; 3B, 12, 23, 103

Parts of this one-time residence of Hong Kong's governors date back to 1853, though the commanding tower was added by the Japanese during WWII. Both the current chief executive, Donald Tsang, and his predecessor, Tung Chee Hwa, refused to take up residence here, ostensibly because the feng shui isn't quite right.

HONG KONG ZOOLOGICAL & BOTANICAL GARDENS
香港動植物公園

☎ 2530 0154; www.lcsd.gov.hk/parks/hkzbg; Albany Rd, Central; admission free; terrace gardens 6am-10pm, zoo & aviaries 6am-7pm, greenhouses 9am-4.30pm; 3B, 12, 40, 40M

These 5.6-hectare gardens, which first welcomed visitors in

GREEN ENGINEERING

On Hong Kong Island only, and especially in Central and Sheung Wan, you'll see what are called 'wall trees', ancient banyan trees (mostly) sprouting from openings in stone retaining walls. To prevent landslides on steep Hong Kong Island, masonry workers from the late 19th century until well after WWII shored up many slopes adjacent to main roads with retaining walls. Open joints between the stones allowed strong species such as Chinese banyans to sprout, further strengthening the walls. Today slopes are, sadly but more reliably, stabilised by cement.

1864, are a pleasant assembly of fountains, sculptures, greenhouses, a playground, a zoo and some fabulous aviaries. There are hundreds of species of birds in residence as well as exotic trees, plants and shrubs. The zoo is surprisingly comprehensive and one of the world's leading centres for the captive breeding of endangered species. Albany Rd divides the gardens, with the plants and aviaries to the east off Garden Rd and most of the animals to the west.

HONGKONG & SHANGHAI BANK 香港上海匯豐銀行

HSBC; 1 Queen's Rd Central, Central; admission free; 9am-4.30pm Mon-Fri, 9am-12.30pm Sat; M Central (exit K)

This 179m-tall glass-and-aluminium building is an innovative masterpiece. Locals call it the 'Robot Building' because you can see the chains and motors of the escalators and other moving parts whirring away inside. Structurally, the building is equally radical, built on a 'coat-hanger' frame and boasting some wonderful feng shui, according to master geomancers. See also p11 and the boxed text, opposite.

LEGISLATIVE COUNCIL BUILDING 立法會大樓

8 Jackson Rd, Central; admission free; M Central (exit J1)

This colonnaded, domed neoclassical building is the former Supreme Court, built in 1912 of granite quarried on Stonecutter Island. Standing atop the pediment is a blindfolded statue of Themis, the Greek goddess of justice.

MAN MO TEMPLE 文武廟

☎ 2540 0350; 124-126 Hollywood Rd, Sheung Wan; admission free; 8am-6pm; 26

Follow the smell of incense to this atmospheric, low-lit 'Civil and Martial' temple, one of the oldest in Hong Kong, and dedicated to a statesman of the 3rd century BC called Man Cheung, who is worshipped as the god of literature, and a military deity called Kwan Yu, a soldier born in the 2nd century AD and now venerated as the red-cheeked god of war.

PARA/SITE ART SPACE
藝術空間

☎ 2517 4620; www.para-site.org.hk; 4 Po Yan St, Sheung Wan; admission free; noon-7pm Wed-Sun; M Sheung Wan 26

This adventurous, artist-run space knows no boundaries when it comes to mixing media. Most art on display is local but there are occasional exhibitions by international artists as well.

ST JOHN'S CATHEDRAL
約翰座堂

☎ 2523 4157; www.stjohnscathedral.org.hk; 4-8 Garden Rd, Central; admission free; 7am-6pm; M Central (exit J2)

One of the few colonial structures still standing in Central and lost in a forest of skyscrapers, this Anglican cathedral, built in the shape of a cross, is a relic of Hong Kong's colonial past. It suffered heavy damage during WWII; after the war the front doors were remade using timber salvaged from the British warship HMS *Tamar,* and the beautiful stained glass was replaced. A peaceful, cool and contemplative space. Enter from Battery Path.

STATUE SQUARE
皇后像廣場

Edinburgh Pl, Central; M Central (exit K)

A chinless banker (and no, that's not rhyming slang) is the only statue you'll find here. The rest of the carvings that once stood in the square (British royals in the main) were carted off by the Japanese in WWII. In a city with Hong Kong's commercial drive and institutional indifference to culture, the slightly bathetic statue of Sir Thomas Jackson (a particularly successful Victorian-era manager of the Hongkong & Shanghai

JUST LION THERE

Say hello to Stephen and Stitt, the pair of handsome bronze lions guarding the southern side of the Hongkong & Shanghai Bank (HSBC; opposite) headquarters. Named after the general managers of the two main branches in Hong Kong and Shanghai when they were cast in the 1930s, they have been through the wars (well, one actually). Bullet scars from WWII still pepper their noble rumps and for years a piece of unexploded ordnance was lodged inside one of them until removed by a bomb disposal team. Rub their mighty paws for luck.

Bank) somehow fits right in. On the northern side of Chater Rd is the Cenotaph (1923) dedicated to Hong Kong residents killed during the two world wars.

TAI PING SHAN TEMPLES 太平山街廟宇

42, 34 & 9 Tai Ping Shan St; 8am-6pm; 26

Tai Ping Shan St has three atmospheric temples. **Pak Sing Ancestral Hall** 百姓廟 (c 1851), the 'people's temple', was a clinic for Chinese patients refusing treatment by Western medicine, and a storeroom for bodies awaiting burial in China. **Kwun Yam Temple** 觀音堂 worships the Goddess of Mercy. You can burn sticks of incense for your Chinese zodiac animal at **Tai Sui Temple** 太歲廟.

WORTH THE TRIP

East of Sheung Wan in Pok Fu Lam district is the **Hong Kong University Museum & Art Gallery** (2241 5500; www.hku.hk/hkumag; Fung Ping Shan Bldg, 94 Bonham Rd; admission free; 9.30am-6pm Mon-Sat, 1.30-5.30pm Sun; 23, 40, 40M) containing important collections of ceramics and bronzes, plus a lesser number of paintings and carvings. There's an intriguing display of almost a thousand crosses made by Nestorians, a Christian sect that arose in Syria and moved into China during the 13th and 14th centuries.

TWO INTERNATIONAL FINANCE CENTRE 國際金融中心二期

2878 1111; www.hkma.gov.hk; 8 Finance St, Central; admission free; 10am-6pm Mon-Fri, 10am-1pm Sat; M Hong Kong (exit F)

At 88 storeys, Two IFC, soaring above the terminus of the Airport Express and Tung Chung MTR lines, is Hong Kong's tallest building and has been christened 'Sir Y K Pao's Erection', a reference to the owner of the development company that built the tower. You can get as far as the 55th floor by visiting the **Hong Kong Monetary Authority Information Centre**, which contains exhibition areas related to the Hong Kong currency, fiscal policy and banking history, and a research library. There are guided tours at 2.30pm Monday to Friday and at 10.30am on Saturday. See also p11.

WESTERN MARKET 西港城

323 Des Voeux Rd Central, Sheung Wan; 9am-7pm; M Sheung Wan (exit C)

This three-storey Edwardian market (1906) reopened in 1991 as a shopping centre to house textile vendors driven out of the lanes linking Queen's Rd and Des Voeux Rd Central. The ground floor has modern shops selling curios, jewellery and toys; the 1st

You'll find no shortage of shopping options at the Two International Finance Centre Mall

floor is given over mostly to bolts of cloth, including some decent silks. On the top floor there's a picturesque restaurant and ballroom dancing space.

SHOP

Sumptuous temples to couture and conspicuous consumption prosper inside Central's swish shopping malls (take your pick from the Princes Building, the Landmark or the IFC Malls), although you'll also find midrange clothing brands here. Hollywood Rd, which links Central and Sheung Wan, is particularly good for antiques, fine art and curios, while Stanley St in Central is the spot for quality film cameras. For an 'only-in-Hong-Kong' experience, visit Li Yuen St East and West, two narrow alleyways that link Des Voeux Rd Central with Queen's Rd Central, for a jumble of inexpensive clothing, handbags and jewellery.

BLANC DE CHINE 源

Clothing & Accessories

www.blancdechine.com; ☎ 2524 7875; Shop 201-203A, 2nd fl, Pedder Bldg, 12 Pedder St, Central; 10am-7pm Mon-Sat, noon-5pm Sun; M Central

Men's traditional Chinese jackets,

off the rack or made to measure, silk dresses for her, and an exquisite collection of satin bed linens are the specialities here.

DYMOCKS BOOKSELLERS
恬墨書舍 *Books*

☎ 2117 0360; www.dymocks.com.hk; Shop 2007-2011, 2nd fl, IFC Mall, 1 Harbour View St, Central; 9am-9.30pm Sun-Thu, from 9.30am Fri & Sat; M Central, Hong Kong

The large Australian chain offers a solid mainstream selection of page turners, travel books, magazines and, in particular, books of local interest. This is one of its seven Hong Kong branches.

HANART TZ GALLERY
漢雅軒 *Fine Art*

☎ 2526 9019; www.hanart.com; Room 202, 2nd fl, Henley Bldg, 5 Queen's Rd Central, Central; 10am-6.30pm Mon-Fri, 10am-6pm Sat; M Central (exit K)

One of the most influential and innovative galleries in Hong Kong, Hanart shows contemporary Chinese art with a thoroughbred stable of figurative and conceptual painters, sculptors and video artists, many of them based in Hong Kong.

HMV *Music*

☎ 2739 0268; www.hmv.com.hk; 1st fl, Central Bldg, 1-3 Pedder St, Central; 9am-10pm Mon-Sun; M Central (exit D1)

This Aladdin's cave of music has the city's largest selection of CDs and DVDs, including those of music and film (mostly mainstream) from Hong Kong, Taiwan and mainland China. There is also a great range of music-related literature.

HONG KONG BOOK CENTRE
Books

☎ 2522 7064; www.swindonbooks.com; Basement, On Lok Yuen Bldg, 25 Des Voeux Rd Central, Central; 9am-6.30pm Mon-Fri, 9am-5.30pm Sat, 1-5pm public holiday, closed Sun; M Central (exit B)

This basement shop has a vast selection of books and magazines, including a mammoth number of business titles.

STUBBED OUT
Smoking is banned in all restaurants, bars, shopping malls and museums, even at beaches and parks, in Hong Kong; but you can light up in 'alfresco' areas. Some bars, however, will risk getting fined in order to attract more customers – you know which ones they are by the ashtray they nonchalantly leave on your table. An exception to the ban is on cross-border trains to mainland China. On these trains you can smoke in the restaurant car and the vestibules at either end of the cars, but not in the main seating area.

TRADITIONAL MEDICINE
Chinese herbalists are popular in Hong Kong, selling general health tonics or, after a diagnosis, tailored brews for specific ailments. Why not try one? Ingredients might include deer's horn, tail and penis; snake skin; monkey's visceral organs; and ground dinosaur teeth. Drink up now.

JOYCE
Clothing & Accessories
☎ 2810 1120; www.joyce.com; Ground fl, New World Tower, 16 Queen's Rd Central, Central; 10.30am-7.30pm; M Central
This multidesigner store is a good choice if you're short of time rather than money: Issey Miyake, Alexander McQueen, Marc Jacobs, Comme des Garçons, Chloé, Pucci, Yohji Yamamoto and several Hong Kong fashion names are just some of the designers whose wearable wares are on display.

LOCK CHA TEA SHOP
樂茶軒 *Food & Drink*
www.lockcha.com; ☎ 2805 1360; Upper ground fl, 290b Queen's Rd Central (enter from Ladder St), Sheung Wan; 11am-7pm; M Sheung Wan (exit A2)
This favourite shop sells Chinese teas, tea sets, wooden tea boxes and well-presented gift packs of various cuppas. You can try before you buy.

SHANGHAI TANG 上海灘
Clothing & Accessories
☎ 2525 7333; www.shanghaitang.com; basement & ground fl, Pedder Bldg, 12 Pedder St, Central; 10.30am-8pm Mon-Sat, 11am-7pm Sun; M Central
This stylish shop has sparked something of a fashion wave with its updated versions of traditional yet neon-coloured Chinese garments. It also sells accessories and delightful gift items.

EAT

ABC KITCHEN *European* $
☎ 9278 8227; Shop 7, Queen's St Cooked Food Market, 1 Queen St, Sheung Wan; noon-2.30pm & 6.30-10pm Mon-Sat, dinner only Sun; M Sheung Wan (Exit C)
Enjoy authentic bouillabaisse, cochinillo asado and fluffy souffle at this hawker-style food market, all for the price of an entree and served under crystal chandeliers. Booking advised for dinner.

CAPRICE
Modern French $$$
☎ 3196 8888; www.fourseasons.com/hongkong; Four Seasons Hotel, 8 Finance St, Central; noon-2.30pm & 6-10.30pm; M Hong Kong (exit E1)
At Michelin-starred Caprice, diners get to savour French dishes exquisitely prepared in an open kitchen. An illuminated catwalk, harbour

New and old combine to stylish effect at the exclusive Shanghai Tang

views and impeccable service complete the celebrity experience. Booking a must (see also p72).

CITY HALL MAXIM'S PALACE
大會堂美心皇宮
Dim Sum $$

☎ 2521 1303; 3rd fl, Low Block, Hong Kong City Hall, 1 Edinburgh Pl, Central; ☎ 11am-4.30pm & 5.30-10.45pm Mon-Sat, 9am-4.30pm & 5.30-10.45pm Sun; Ⓜ Central (exit K)

You'll find the real Hong Kong dim sum deal, with all its clatter and clutter, in Hong Kong City Hall on Saturday or Sunday morning. Cacophonous but delectable.

HONEYMOON DESSERT
滿記甜品 *Chinese Desserts* $

☎ 2851 2606; www.honeymoon-dessert.com; Shop 4-8. Western Market, 323 Des Voeux Rd Central, Sheung Wan; noon-midnight; Ⓜ Sheung Wan (exit C); Ⓥ

Branches in 20 locations, including **Sai Kung** (9-10A, B&C Po Tung Rd, Sai Kung; 1pm-2.45am), attest to Honeymoon's uncontested appeal. The sweet soups, crêpes, puddings and fruit-based concoctions are indeed impressive.

ISLAND TANG 海島廳

Cantonese $$$

☎ 2526 8798; www.islandtang.com; Shop 222, the Galleria, 9 Queen's Rd Central, Central; ⏲ noon-10pm; Ⓜ Central (exit D1)

The art deco interior may evoke Shanghai c 1930s, but the menu is defiantly Cantonese, complete with all-day dim sum. Selections range from homely to exotic, as do the prices.

LUNG KING HEEN 龍景軒

Chinese $$$

www.fourseasons.com/hongkong; ☎ 3196 8888; Four Seasons Hotel, 8 Finance St, Central; ⏲ noon-2.30pm & 6-10.30pm Mon-Sat, 11.30am-3pm & 6-10.30pm Sun ; Ⓜ Central

It's not just the view that you should come here for, it's also the plump and fresh crustaceans and the divine roast duck ($560 each, good for six people to share).

TIM'S KITCHEN 桃花源小廚

Cantonese $$

☎ 2543 5919; www.timskitchen.com.hk; Shop A, ground fl & 1st fl, 84-90 Bonham Strand, Sheung Wan; ⏲ noon-3pm & 6.30-10.30pm Mon-Sat; Ⓜ Sheung Wan (exit A1)

One of Hong Kong's top eateries according to gourmands, this understated place serves masterfully executed Cantonese fare. Signature dishes like crab claw poached with wintermelon require preordering. Reservations essential.

DRINK

CAPTAIN'S BAR *Bar*

www.mandarinoriental.com/hongkong/; ☎ 2825 4006; ground fl, Mandarin Oriental, 5 Connaught Rd Central, Central; ⏲ 11am-2am Mon-Sat, 11am-1am Sun; Ⓜ Central

This clubby, suited place remains just as comfortable and familiar as ever. It serves ice-cold draught beer in chilled silver mugs and some of the best martinis in town. A good place to linger and witness Hong Kong movers and shakers talking shop.

RED BAR *Bar*

www.pure-red.com; ☎ 8129 8882; L4, Two IFC, 8 Finance St, Central; ⏲ noon-midnight Mon-Thu, noon-3am Fri & Sat, noon-10pm Sun; Ⓜ Central

A fantastic combination of al fresco drinking and harbour views is hard to beat on Hong Kong Island. DJs playing funk and jazz turn up the volume as the weekend approaches.

Gloria Chang 張韻琪

Seasoned environmentalist with Greenpeace, dubbed 'Petite Pepper' by the media for her feisty style; new mum

Being an environmentalist in Hong Kong It's love and hate. The people are doing their bit to reduce carbon, while many shopping malls, hotels and office buildings are hardly contributing. The main environmental problem here is air pollution. **Tips for green travel** Take the tram and the ferries as much as you can. They're clean, green and full of history. The scenery that unfolds as the tram makes its way from west to east on the island is quite amazing; kids are thrilled by the different boats in the harbour. Go hiking in Hong Kong's lovely countryside. Stay at two- or three-star hotels or hostels; many can be far more environmentally friendly than luxury hotels. Avoid eating deepwater fish and shark's fin. Some of the mid-to-low-budget Chinese eateries serve hefty portions, so don't over order.

SEVVA *Bar*

☎ 2537 1388; www.sevva.hk; 25th fl Prince's Bldg, 10 Chater Rd; noon-midnight Mon-Thu, to 2am Fri & Sat; M Central (exit H)

With skyscrapers dizzingly close, the view from Sevva's balcony is almost second to none – when seen at night it leaves you breathless. And Sevva's fancy cocktails and ultra-chic decor are great reasons to let it.

PLAY

GRAPPA'S CELLAR

Live Music

☎ 2521 2322; www.elgrande.com.hk/outlets/HongKong/GrappasCellar; 1 Connaught Place, Central; M Central (Exit A)

For at least two weekends a month this restaurant morphs into an indie-music venue. Call or visit their website for event details.

HONG KONG CITY HALL

香港大會堂

Performing Arts Venue

www.lcsd.gov.hk/hkch/; ☎ 2921 2840, bookings 2734 9009; www.cityhall.gov.hk; Low Block, 1 Edinburgh Pl, Central; M Central

Built in 1962, Hong Kong City Hall is still a major cultural venue in Hong Kong, with concert and recital halls, a theatre and exhibition galleries.

SPA AT THE FOUR SEASONS *Health & Fitness*

☎ 3196 8888; www.fourseasons.com; Four Seasons Hotel, 8 Finance St, Central; M Central

This vast (20,000 sq ft) and ultra high-end spa pretty much offers it all. As well as a comprehensive range of beauty, massage and health treatments, there's an ice fountain, hot cups, moxibustion and something called a herbal cocoon room.

>HONG KONG ISLAND: LAN KWAI FONG & SOHO

Lan Kwai Fong and Soho, actually parts of Central, form the partying epicentre of Hong Kong Island. Much of Central's nightlife revolves around Lan Kwai Fong, a narrow alleyway doglegging south and then west from D'Aguilar St. In the not-so-distant past it was an area of squalid tenements, rubbish and rats, but it has since been scrubbed, face-lifted and

LAN KWAI FONG & SOHO

SEE

Graham St Market 1 B2
Midlevels Escalator 2 B3

SHOP

Amours Antiques 3 A2
Arch Angel Antiques 4 B2
Arch Angel Contemporary Art 5 B2
Chine Gallery 6 B3
Eu Yan Sang 7 B1
Flow Bookshop 8 C3
Giordano Ladies 9 D2
Grotto Fine Art 10 C4
Homeless 11 A1
Honeychurch Antiques 12 B3
Jilian, Lingerie on Wyndham 13 C4
Joint Publishing 14 D2
Karin Weber Antiques ... 15 A2
Kowloon Soy Company 16 C2
Linva Tailor 17 C2
Lulu Cheung 18 C3
Mountain Folkcraft 19 D3
Photo Scientific 20 D3
Plum Blossoms 21 C3
Ranee K 22 B1
Tai Yip Art Book Company 23 C2
Vintage HK 24 B2
Wah Tung Ceramic Arts 25 B2
Wattis Fine Art 26 B3

EAT

Dumpling Yuan 27 C2
Kau Kee 28 B1
Lan Fong Yuen 29 B3
Life 30 B3
Lin Heung Tea House ... 31 B1
Luk Yu Tea House 32 D3
Magushi 33 A3
Mak's Noodle 34 C2
Nha Trang 35 C2
Sargrantino 36 C3
Ser Wong Fun 37 C2
Tai Cheong Bakery 38 B3
Tsui Wah Restaurant ... 39 D3
Vbest Tea House 40 A2
Yun Fu 41 C4
Yung Kee 42 D3

DRINK

Barco 43 A2
Bit Point 44 C4
Club 71 .... 45 B2
Club Feather Boa 46 A3
Dragon-I 47 C4
Gecko Lounge 48 C3
Peak Cafe Bar 49 B3
Solas .... (see 47)
Staunton's Wine Bar & Cafe 50 B3
T:ME .... (see 45)
Tastings Wine Bar 51 D3
Tivo 52 C4

PLAY

Backstage Live Restaurant 53 C3
Drop 54 B3
Elemis Day Spa 55 D3
Fringe Club, Theatre & Studio 56 D4
Happy Foot Reflexology 57 C2
Joyce is Not Here 58 B2
Makumba 59 B3
Peel Fresco 60 B2
Propaganda 61 C3
Pure Fitness 62 B3
Sense of Touch 63 C4
Skylark Lounge 64 C4
Tazmania Ballroom 65 C4
Works 66 C4
Yumla 67 C3

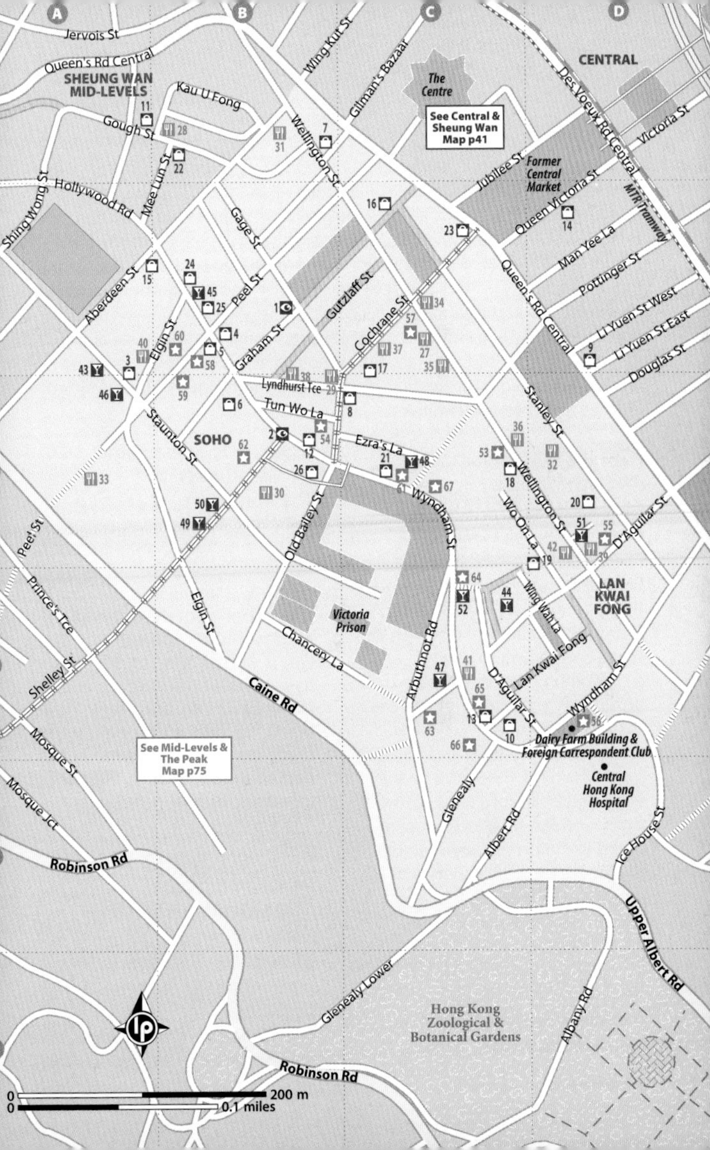
A
B
C
D
Jervois St
Queen's Rd Central
SHEUNG WAN MID-LEVELS
Kau U Fong
Gough St
Mee Lun St
Hollywood Rd
Shing Wong St
Wing Kut St
Gilman's Bazaar
The Centre
See Central & Sheung Wan Map p41
CENTRAL
Des Voeux Rd Central
Victoria St
Wellington St
Jubilee St
Former Central Market
Queen Victoria St
MTR Tramway
Man Yee La
Pottinger St
Li Yuen St West
Li Yuen St East
Douglas St
Gage St
Aberdeen St
Peel St
Gutzlaff St
Cochrane St
Graham St
Elgin St
Lyndhurst Tce
Tun Wo La
Ezra's La
SOHO
Staunton St
Wyndham St
Old Bailey St
Stanley St
Wo On La
D'Aguilar St
Victoria Prison
Chancery La
Arbuthnot Rd
Wing Wah La
Lan Kwai Fong
LAN KWAI FONG
Caine Rd
Peel St
Prince's Tce
Shelley St
Mosque St
Mosque Jct
See Mid-Levels & The Peak Map p75
Dairy Farm Building & Foreign Correspondent Club
Central Hong Kong Hospital
Glenealy
Albert Rd
Ice House St
Upper Albert Rd
Robinson Rd
Glenealy Lower
Hong Kong Zoological & Botanical Gardens
Albany Rd
Robinson Rd
0
200 m
0
0.1 miles

closed to traffic. Lan Kwai Fong's clientele tends to be relatively young and upwardly mobile, and expats mix easily with local business types and trendies. The action has spilled further up the hill all the way along Wyndham St, where you'll find a dozen or so smarter bars and restaurants, all of them abuzz almost every night of the week. Nearby Soho (short for 'south of Hollywood Rd') is more geared to dining than drinking. The area also offers shoppers a welcome and atmospheric contrast to the enclosed megamalls in nearby Central. Along Hollywood Rd you'll find fierce tomb guards and other ancient Chinese antiquities alongside classic and contemporary art. Soho meanwhile is becoming, almost by the day, a more interesting hunting ground for quirky independent clothes and interiors retailers.

SEE

GRAHAM ST MARKET

Graham St, Central; admission free; M Central

On the lower reaches west of the 800m-long Midlevels Escalator, the market stalls and open-air canteens centred on Graham St are a compelling destination to stroll around to get a close look at the exotic produce that Hong Kong prides itself in selling and consuming. Preserved 'thousand year' eggs and fresh tofu curd scooped from wooden tubs are just some of the items on display. It's not for the squeamish; fish are cut lengthwise, hearts still beating, for display on the slab. See also p12.

MIDLEVELS ESCALATOR

中環至半山自動扶梯

Cochrane St, cnr Shelley & Peel Sts, Central; admission free; down 6-10am, up 10.30am-midnight; M Central (exit C)

The world's longest covered outdoor people mover zigzags from Central's offices to homes near Conduit Rd. Embark and let the streets unveil – Stanley and Wellington with their glamour and tradition; Gage and Lyndhurst where florists and prostitutes once hawked their wares; Hollywood, Hong Kong's second oldest street; Staunton, whose porcelain shops made way for Soho; then Shelley, named unromantically after an infamous auditor-general.

SHOP

AMOURS ANTIQUES

Antiques, Clothing

2803 7877; 45 Staunton St, Soho; noon-9pm Mon-Sat, noon-7pm Sun; 26

This wonderful shop stocks rhinestone jewellery, frocks, and

Exquisite wares create a sublime aesthetic – and tempting purchase potential – at Arch Angel Antiques

a darling clutch of beaded and tapestry bags dating back to the early 20th century.

ARCH ANGEL ANTIQUES

Antiques, Fine Art

☎ 2851 6848; www.archangelgalleries.com; 53-55 Hollywood Rd, Central; 9.30am-6.30pm; 26

Though its specialities are ancient porcelain and tomb ware, Arch Angel packs a lot more into its three floors: everything from mahjong sets and terracotta horses to palatial furniture. It also runs an art gallery, **Arch Angel Contemporary Art** (☎ 2851 6882; 58 Hollywood Rd, Central; 10am-6.30pm), which is across the road and deals in fine art.

CHINE GALLERY 華苑

Antiques

☎ 2543 0023; www.chinegallery.com; 42A Hollywood Rd, Soho; 10am-6pm Mon-Sat; 13, 26, 40M

This delightful shop sells carefully restored furniture (we love the lacquered cabinets) from all over China and hand-knotted rugs from remote regions, such as Xinjiang, Ningxia, Gansu, Inner Mongolia and Tibet.

EU YAN SANG 余仁生

Medicine

☎ 2544 3870; 152-156 Queen's Rd Central, Soho; ⏲ 9am-7.30pm; Ⓜ Central
Eu Yan Sang, with branches throughout Hong Kong, is the town's most famous dispenser of traditional Chinese medicines, and the staff speak good English. It's also an interesting place to browse as many of the healing ingredients are displayed and explained.

FLOW BOOKSHOP

Used Books

☎ 2964 9483; 1st fl, 40 Lyndhurst Terrace, Central; ⏲ noon-7:30pm; 🚌 40M
You could spend a whole day browsing at this speciality store for second-hand CDs, vinyl albums and videos. You can also sell your used items here.

GIORDANO LADIES

Clothing

☎ 2921 2955; www.giordanoladies.com; ground fl & 1st fl, Lansing Hse, 43-45 Queen's Rd Central, Central; Ⓜ Central (Exit D1)
Giordano Ladies offers elegant clothing for women, signified by soft, flowing lines and a conservative colour palette. There is feminine office attire, leisurewear that toes the smart-casual line, and basic items meant to mix and match well with most wardrobes.

GROTTO FINE ART
嘉圖現代藝術有限公司

Fine Art

☎ 2121 2270; www.grottofineart.com; 2nd fl, 31C-D Wyndham St, Central; ⏲ 11am-7pm Mon-Sat
This small but exquisite gallery represents predominantly Hong Kong artists whose work covers everything from painting and sculpture to mixed media.

HOMELESS

Furniture, Clothing & Accessories

☎ 2581 1160, 2581 1880; www.homelessconcept.com; 28 & 29 Gough St, Sheung Wan; ⏲ 11.30am-9.30pm Mon-Sat, noon-6pm Sun; Ⓜ Sheung Wan (exit E2)
At these two lifestyle stores, furniture, clothing, and a range of retro and idiosyncratic accessories are tossed together attractively in an industrial setting. Watch out in particular for products decorated with the fantastical drawings of Carrie Chau, a local designer.

HONEYCHURCH ANTIQUES

Antiques

☎ 2543 2433; 29 Hollywood Rd, Central; ⏲ 10am-6pm Mon-Sat; 🚌 26
This fine shop specialises in antique Chinese furniture, jewellery and antique English silver. There's a wide range of stock, with items from the early Chinese dynasties right up to the 20th century.

JILIAN, LINGERIE ON WYNDHAM

Clothing & Accessories

☎ 2826 9295; www.jilian.com.hk; Ground fl, 31 Wyndham St, Central;

Swimwear and lingerie from gossamer delicates small enough to swallow with a glass of water to rather outré corsetry with strings and stays and such. There's even a select range of men's smalls if you just can't put up with your man's industrial-sized underpants any more.

JOINT PUBLISHING *Books*

☎ 2868 6844; www.jointpublishing.com; 9 Queen Victoria St, Central; 10am-8pm; M Central (exit A)

This primarily Chinese-language bookshop has a good range of English titles about China, CDs and DVDs for studying Chinese, and a strong collection of maps of Hong Kong and China. English titles are found on the mezzanine floor.

KARIN WEBER ANTIQUES

Antiques, Fine Art

☎ 2544 5004; www.karinwebergallery.com; 20 Aberdeen St, Soho; 11am-7pm Mon-Sat, 2-6pm Sun; 26

Karin Weber has a good mix of Chinese country antiques and contemporary Asian artworks. She gives short and useful lectures on antiques and the scene in Hong Kong.

KOWLOON SOY COMPANY

九龍醬園 *Chinese Condiments*

☎ 2544 3695; www.kowloonsoy.com; 9 Graham Street, Soho, Central; 8am-6.15pm Mon-Fri, to 6pm Sat; M Central (Exit D1); V

The shop (c 1917) for artisanal soy sauce and Chinese condiments; also sells preserved eggs (*pei darn*, 皮蛋) and pickled ginger (*suen geung*, 酸姜). Did you know that young red wines consumed with preserved eggs taste fuller-bodied? Just try it.

LINVA TAILOR

年華時裝公司

Clothing & Accessories

☎ 2544 2456; 38 Cochrane St, Central; 9.30am-6.30pm Mon-Sat; 13, 40M

This is the place to come to buy or have your own cheongsam stitched up. Bring your own silk or choose from Mr Leung's selection.

LULU CHEUNG *Clothing*

☎ 2537 7515; www.lulucheung.com.hk; Shop B, 50 Wellington St, Central; 10am-8pm Sun-Thu, to 9pm Fri & Sat; M Central

Local designer Lulu Cheung makes sophisticated casualwear, work clothes and evening gowns for the urban woman, using natural fabrics, such as wool, cotton, silk and linen, in whites and earth tones. The look is subtle and feminine without being prudish.

MOUNTAIN FOLKCRAFT
高山民藝 *Gifts & Souvenirs*

☎ 2523 2817; 12 Wo On Lane, Central; 9.30am-6.30pm Mon-Sat; M Central

One of the nicest shops in town for folk crafts. There's batik, clothing, woodcarvings and lacquerware made by Chinese and other Asian ethnic minorities. Shop attendants are friendly, and prices reasonable.

PHOTO SCIENTIFIC
攝影科學
Photographic Equipment

☎ 2525 0550; ground fl, Eurasia Bldg, 6 Stanley St, Central; 9am-7pm Mon-Sat; M Central

This shop is the favourite of Hong Kong's professional photographers. You may find cheaper equipment elsewhere, but Photo Scientific has a rock-solid reputation, with labelled prices and no bargaining.

PLUM BLOSSOMS 萬玉堂
Fine Art

☎ 2521 2189; www.plumblossoms.com; ground fl, Chinachem Hollywood Centre, 1 Hollywood Rd, Central; 10am-9pm Mon-Sat; M Central (exit D2) 26

The gallery where the late Rudolf Nureyev used to buy his baubles (and other celebrities continue to do so) is one of the most interesting and well established in Hong Kong.

RANEE K 郭翠華 *Clothing*

☎ 2108 4068; www.raneek.com; 16K Gough St, Central; 10am-6.30pm; M Central

US-trained local designer Ranee Kok is known for her combinations of dramatic prints and textures, and deft adoption of the cuts, patterns and styles from both the East and West in her evening and ready-to-wear lines.

TAI YIP ART BOOK COMPANY 大業 *Books*

☎ 2524 5963; www.taiyipart.com.hk; 4th fl, 9 Cochrane St, Central; 10am-7pm Mon-Fri, 10am-6.30pm Sat & Sun; M Central

Tai Yip has a terrific selection of books about anything that is Chinese and arty: calligraphy, jade, bronze, costumes, architecture, symbolism. There are outlets in several of Hong Kong's museums, including the Hong Kong Museum of Art (p108).

VINTAGE HK *Clothing*

☎ 2545 9932; 57-59 Hollywood Rd, Central; 11am-8pm; M Central

Definitely worth a look for a small, select range of vintage wear that does not need much of a rummage.

WAH TUNG CERAMIC ARTS
華通陶瓷 *Gifts & Souvenirs*

☎ 2543 2823; www.wahtungchina.com; 7th fl, Lee Roy Commercial Bldg, 57-59

Hollywood Rd, Central; 9am-6pm Mon to Fri, to 5pm Sat; 26
The world's largest supplier of hand-decorated ceramics, Wah Tung has everything from brightly painted vases and ginger jars to reproduction Tang dynasty figurines. And what you don't see, staff will source for you.

WATTIS FINE ART *Antiques*

2524 5302; www.wattis.com.hk; 2nd fl, 20 Hollywood Rd, Soho; 10.30am-6pm Mon-Sat; 26
No place in Hong Kong has a better collection of antique maps for sale than this place; the selection of old photographs of Hong Kong and Macau is also very impressive. Enter from Old Bailey St.

EAT

DUMPLING YUAN 餃子園

Northern Chinese $

2541 9737; 98 Wellington St, Central; 11am-10.30pm Mon-Sat; 40M; V
Locals and visitors from the north flock to this little shop for its nine varieties of juicy bundles of heaven more commonly known as lamb and cumin, pork and chives, egg and tomato or vegetarian dumplings.

KAU KEE 九記 *Noodles* $

2850 5967; 21 Gough St; 12.30-7.15pm & 8.30-11.30pm Mon-Sat; M Sheung Wan (exit E2)
The discerning regulars of this famous beef brisket (牛腩, *ngau laam*) shop order their favourite cuts (see p72), but even the ordinary stuff is excellent with noodles.

LAN FONG YUEN 蘭芳園

Local Café $

2544 3895, 2854 0731; 2 Gage St, Soho, Central; 7am-6pm Mon-Sat; cover charge $20; 5B
Lan Fong Yuen (1952) is a *cha chaan tang*, one of the many local neighbourhood eateries that appeared in the 1950s, serving pseudo-Western snacks and drinks to those who couldn't afford the real deal. Lan is believed to have invented the strong and silky 'pantyhose milk tea' ($13). Watch them work their magic while you wait for a seat.

LIFE *Vegetarian* $

2810 9777; www.lifecafe.com.hk; 10 Shelley St, Soho; 9am-10pm; 26; V
Life is a vegetarian's dream come true, serving vegan food and dishes free of gluten, wheat, onion and garlic. Nonvegetarians note – this is tasty stuff. There's a **delicatessen** and **shop** (8am-10.30pm Mon-Fri, from 9am Sat & Sun) on the ground floor, a café on the 1st floor and seating up in the rooftop garden.

MIND YOUR TABLE MANNERS

Dining in Hong Kong is an all-in affair: everyone shares dishes, chats loudly and sometimes makes a mess. Food is to be enjoyed whole-heartedly, not picked at discreetly. There are, however, a few points of etiquette it doesn't hurt to know about.

> Wait for others to start before digging in (though as a guest you may be encouraged to start).
> Say thank you if someone puts food into your bowl – this is a courteous gesture.
> Cover your mouth with your hand when using a toothpick.
> Don't try to clean up dishes and detritus – a stained tablecloth is a sign of a good meal.
> Don't be afraid to ask for a fork if you can't manage chopsticks (most Chinese restaurants have them).
> Don't stick chopsticks upright into rice as they can look like incense sticks in a bowl of ashes – a sign of death.
> Don't flip a fish over to reach the flesh on the bottom as the next boat you ride on will capsize.

LIN HEUNG TEA HOUSE

蓮香樓 *Cantonese* $

☎ 2544 4556; 160-164 Wellington St, Central; 6am-11pm, dim sum to 3.30pm; M Sheung Wan (exit E2)

This older-style Cantonese restaurant is worth a visit for the tableau: old men reading the newspaper, extended families chatting and large office groups noshing. There's decent dim sum served from trolleys, so it's good for a late bite or those eating alone.

LUK YU TEA HOUSE

陸羽茶室 *Dim Sum* $$

☎ 2523 5464; 24-26 Stanley St, Central; 7am-10pm; M Central; V

This old-style teahouse is a museum piece in more ways than one. Most of the staff have been here since the early Ming dynasty and are as grumpy as an emperor deposed. Still, it's *the* place for tasty **dim sum** (7am-5pm) in atmospheric surrounds.

MAGUSHI 真串

Japanese $$

☎ 2868 1428; www.magushi.com; 74 Peel St, Soho, Central; noon-2.30pm & 6-11.30pm Mon-Fri, 6-11.30pm Sat & Sun; Midlevels escalator

The yakitori (Japanese skewers) and sushi at this friendly place are well worth the climb up Peel St, but the dizzying sake collection could make your descent a perilous journey. Smoking is allowed in the backroom.

MAK'S NOODLE
麥奀雲吞麵世家

Cantonese $

☎ 2854 3810; 77 Wellington St, Central; dishes $25-50; 🕑 11am-8pm; Ⓜ Central, then bus 40M westbound from Wan Chai Ferry or Pacific Place, Admiralty

This noodle shop sells excellent wonton soup, and the beef brisket noodles, more of a Western taste than a Chinese one, are highly recommended. Go for lunch or eat early; it's shut tight by 8pm.

NHA TRANG 芽莊

Vietnamese $

☎ 2581 9992; 88 Wellington St, Central; 🕑 noon-11pm; Ⓜ Central; Ⓥ

The regular Vietnamese clientele at this simple but stylish restaurant is testament to the quality and authenticity of the food.

SAGRANTINO

Japanese, Italian $$

www.sagrantino.com.hk; ☎ 2521 5188; 5th fl, The Loop, 33 Wellington St, Central; 🕑 11.30am-3pm & 6-11pm Mon-Sat, dinner only Sun; Ⓜ Central (Exit D1)

The Japanese chef of this classy 'Italian' restaurant combines yellow tail, salmon roe, oysters and other Japanese seafood with European-style sauces and pasta, to create flavours far richer than the sum of the ingredients. For purists and conservatives, there are tasty strictly Italian offerings.

A vegetarian's paradise – tasty, healthy, meat-free treats are the catch of the day at Life

BUDGET BITES

Familiar Western fast-food chains are everywhere, but if you want a quick fix of something slightly more exotic, try the following local fast-food chains. They are all pretty cheap – about $30 to $65 a meal – and branches are everywhere, but especially in large shopping malls and near MTR stations.

Genki Sushi (www.genkisushi.com.sg) Cheap but tasty sushi, carousel-style.
Maxim's (www.maxims.com.hk) Canto dishes with a focus on Chinese barbecued meat.
Mix (www.mix-world.com) Excellent smoothies, wraps and salads, and free internet.
Oliver's (www.olivers-supersandwiches.com) Sandwiches and salads.
Café de Coral (www.cafedecoral.com) A huge range of Chinese dishes.
Fairwood (www.fairwood.com.hk) Similar to Café de Coral

SER WONG FUN 蛇王芬

Cantonese $

☎ 2543 1032; 30 Cochrane St, Central; 11am-10.30pm; Ⓜ Central (exit D1)

While this place is known for its snake soup ($65), which is consumed in winter with dried lemon leaves, the more faint-hearted will be relieved to know its old-school Cantonese dishes, such as liver sausage, claypot rice and scrambled eggs with shrimp, are just as good.

TAI CHEONG BAKERY

泰昌餅家 *Bakery* $

☎ 2544 3475; www.taicheongbakery.com; 35 Lyndhurst Tce, Central; 7.30am-9pm Mon-Sat, from 8.30am Sun; 40M

Photos of a former governor inhaling its egg custard tarts line this bakery's walls, though we believe the *beignets* (*sa yung*) give 'Fat Patten egg tarts' a run for their money.

TSUI WAH RESTAURANT

翠華餐廳 *Local Café* $

☎ 2525 6338; www.tsuiwahrestaurant.com; ground fl & 1st fl, 15-19 Wellington St, Central; Ⓜ Central (exit D2)

This modern 24-hour local café is where clubbing models and bankers go when stricken with the munchies. Its menu, comprising health-conscious, vegetarian and traditional options, reads like a glossary of Hong Kong-style fast food.

VBEST TEA HOUSE

緻好茶館 *Cantonese* $

☎ 3104 0890; www.vbest.com.hk; 17 Elgin St, Soho, Central; noon-3pm & 6-11pm Mon-Sat; Midlevels escalator

This subdued but cozy family affair serves delicious Chinese comfort food free of MSG, just like the owners cooked for their children growing up. We recommend the pork-and-chive wontons and prawns with rice vermicelli. It's also a good place to try Cantonese soup.

YUN FU 雲府
Northern Chinese $$$

☎ 2116 8855; basement, Yu Yuet Lai Bldg, 43-45 Wyndham St, Central; 6-11pm; M Central

There's a *Crouching Tiger, Hidden Dragon* feel to this fantastical place. After an exotic cocktail garnished with dry seahorses or lizards, try the goose liver soaked in dark soy sauce, the sliced duck fillet wrapped in tofu paper or the whole roasted bamboo shoot served in its bark.

YUNG KEE 鏞記酒家
Cantonese $$$

☎ 2522 1624; www.yungkee.com.hk; 32-40 Wellington St, Central; 11am-11.30pm; M Central (exit D2)

This long-standing institution is one of the best-known Cantonese restaurants in town. Its roast goose has been the talk of the town since 1942, and its **dim sum** (2-5.30pm Mon-Sat, 11am-5.30pm Sun) is excellent.

BOOKING & TIPPING

It's advisable to book ahead in all but the cheapest restaurants, especially on Friday and Saturday nights. Most restaurants add a 10% service charge to the bill. If the service at a top-end restaurant was outstanding, you might consider adding another 5% or 10% on top of the service charge. At cheap or midrange places, a couple of coins is sufficient.

DRINK

BARCO *Wine Bar*

☎ 2857 4478; 42 Staunton St, Soho; 4pm-1am Sun-Thu, 4pm-late Fri & Sat, happy hr 4-8pm; M Central

One of our favourite Soho bars, Barco has great staff, is small enough to never feel empty, and attracts a cool mix of locals and expats.

BIT POINT *German Bar*

☎ 2523 7436; 31 D'Aguilar St, Lan Kwai Fong, Central; noon-3am Mon-Sat, 4pm-3am Sun; M Central (Exit D1)

Smack in the thick of the LKF action, German-style Bit Point has a good selection of German beers on tap and a sausage platter to stoke your thirst. Take a table by the entrance if you want to smoke.

CLUB 71 *Bar*

☎ 2858 7071; Basement, 67 Hollywood Rd, Central; 3pm-2am Mon-Sat, 6pm-1am Sun, happy hr 3-9pm; 26

When Club 64, the counter-culture nerve centre of Lan Kwai Fong (a name recalling the 4 June 1989 Tiananmen Square massacre in Beijing), was forced to close, some of the owners relocated to this alley north of Hollywood Rd. Named after the huge protest march held on 1 July 2003, Club 71 is again one of the best drinking spots for nonposeurs. Get to

Dine beneath red phoenix-print lanterns in Dragon-I's plush restaurant

it via a small footpath running west off Peel St.

CLUB FEATHER BOA *Bar*

☎ 2857 2586; 38 Staunton St, Soho; 8pm-late Tue-Sat; Ⓜ Central

Feather Boa is a plush lounge hidden behind gold drapes. Part camp lounge, part bordello – part those curtains and get stuck into one of its infamous mango daiquiris.

DRAGON-I *Bar*

☎ 3110 1222; Upper ground fl, The Centrium, 60 Wyndham St, Central; noon-midnight Mon-Sat, happy hr 5-9pm; Ⓜ Central

This delightful venue on the edge of Soho has both an indoor bar and restaurant and a huge terrace overlooking Wyndham St filled with caged songbirds. You'd *almost* think you were in the country.

GECKO LOUNGE *Bar, Live Music*

☎ 2537 4680; Lower ground fl, 15-19 Hollywood Rd, Central; 4pm-2am Mon-Thu, 4pm-6am Fri & Sat, happy hr 6-9pm; Ⓜ Central

Gecko is a relaxed hideout that attracts a fun crowd, especially to its live jazz sessions on Tuesday and Wednesday. The well-hidden

DJ mixes good grooves with kooky Parisian tunes at weekends. There's a great wine list. Enter from Ezra's Lane off Cochrane or Pottinger Sts.

PEAK CAFE BAR 山頂餐廳 *Bar, Café*

☎ 2140 6877; 9-13 Shelley St, Soho; 11am-2am Mon-Sat, 11am-midnight Sun, happy hr 5-8pm; 13, 26, 40M

The fixtures and fittings of the much-missed Peak Cafe, from 1947, have moved down the hill to this comfy bar with super cocktails and excellent nosh. The only thing missing is the view.

SOLAS *Bar*

☎ 3162 3710; www.solas.com.hk; 60 Wyndham St, Central; noon-2am Mon-Sat; M Central

If the nasty man wouldn't let you into Dragon-I upstairs, never mind.

HAPPY HOUR

During certain hours of the day, most pubs, bars and even some clubs in Hong Kong give discounts on drinks (usually a third to half off) or offer a two-for-one deal. Happy hour is usually in the late afternoon or early evening (eg 4pm to 8pm) but the times vary widely from place to place. Depending on the season, the day of the week and the location, some pub happy hours run from midday till as late as 10pm, and some resume after midnight for an hour or so.

This relaxed, friendly place, where a DJ spins chilled lounge sounds and the cocktails pack a punch, isn't a bad consolation prize.

STAUNTON'S WINE BAR & CAFE *Bar, Café*

☎ 2973 6611; 10-12 Staunton St, Soho; 8.30am-2am midnight, happy hr 5-9pm; 13, 12, 26

Staunton's is swish, cool and on the ball, with decent wine and a lovely terrace. For eats, there's light fare downstairs and a modern international restaurant called Scirocco above.

T:ME *Gay Bar*

☎ 2332 6565; www.time-bar.com; basement, 65 Hollywood Rd, Central; 6.30pm-2am Mon-Wed, Fri & Sat, from 6pm Thu

Friendly gay-owned bar next to Club 71, with a young crowd made up of Asian and Western clientele.

TASTINGS WINE BAR *Wine Bar*

☎ 2523 6282; www.tastings.hk; basement, Yuen Yick Bldg, 27 & 29 Wellington St; 5pm-2am Mon-Sat; M Central (exit D2)

Awash with blue light, this cool basement bar has five Enomatic wine dispensing machines from Italy, which allows you to get inebriated – by sips, half-glasses or

Soaking up the Soho atmosphere at Staunton's Wine Bar & Cafe (p67)

full glasses – on 40 vintages out of 160 on the bar's list.

TIVO *Bar*

☎ 2116 8055; www.aqua.com.hk; 43-55 Wyndham St, Central; noon-2am Mon-Sat; M Central

One of the best of a lively little string of bars that have sprung up here, sophisticated Tivo is a cut above the nuts and beer standard of the 'Fong, just around the corner. Italian aperitivo-type snacks are available to eat with the wine or cocktails.

PLAY

BACKSTAGE LIVE RESTAURANT *Live Music*

2167 8985; www.backstagelive.hk; 1st fl, Somptueux Central, 52-54 Wellington St, Central; 11.30am-late Mon-Fri, 6.30pm-late Sat; M Central (exit D1)

Gigs of new indie, alternative and post punk from Hong Kong and overseas are played four or more nights a week at Backstage Live, a name synonymous with independent music. Check website for the latest.

DROP *Club*

☎ 2543 8856, 2543 9230; basement, On Lok Mansion, 39-43 Hollywood Rd, Central; 7pm-2am Tue, to 3am Wed, to 4am Thu, to 5am Fri, 10pm-5am Sat, 9pm-2am Sun, happy hr 7-10pm Tue-Fri; 13, 26, 40M

Deluxe lounge decor, excellent bleep bleep music, potent cocktails and an up-for-it crowd keep Drop strong on the scene. The members-only policy after 11pm from Thursday to Saturday is enforced to keep the dance-floor capacity at a manageable 'in like sardines' level. Enter from Cochrane St.

ELEMIS DAY SPA *Health & Fitness*

☎ 2521 6660; www.elemisdayspa.com.hk; 9 fl, Century Sq, 1 D'Aguilar St, Central; M Central

The Elemis provides luxurious surroundings and utterly soothing treatments without absolutely breaking the bank. Pampering and treatments range from basic facials to deep tissue massage. There are separate sections (and treatment menus) for men and women. Its very central location is another plus.

FRINGE CLUB, THEATRE & STUDIO 藝穗會 *Live Music, Theatre*

☎ 2521 7251, theatre bookings 2521 9126; www.hkfringeclub.com; ground & 1st fl, Dairy Farm Bldg, 2 Lower Albert Rd, Central; noon-midnight Mon-Thu, noon-3am Fri & Sat; M Central (exit G)

The Fringe, a friendly and eclectic venue on the border of the Lan Kwai Fong quadrant, has original music in its gallery-bar from 10.30pm on Friday and Saturday, with jazz, rock and world music

Pumping music, killer cocktails and wall-to-wall revellers – just another night out on the tiles at Drop (p69)

getting the most airplay. There's a pleasant rooftop bar open in the warmer months. The intimate theatres, each seating up to a hundred, host eclectic local and international performances in English and Cantonese.

HAPPY FOOT REFLEXOLOGY
知足樂 *Health & Fitness*

☎ 2544 1010; 11th & 13th fl, Jade Centre, 98-102 Wellington St, Central; 10am-midnight; Ⓜ Central

Give your walk-weary tootsies (or other bits and pieces) a pampering at the aptly named Happy Foot. Foot/body massages start at $220 for 50 minutes. A pedicure costs $175.

JOYCE IS NOT HERE
Live Music

☎ 2851 2999; www.joycebakerdesign.com; 38-44 Peel St, Soho; 4.30pm-late Tue-Fri, 1.30pm-late Sat & Sun; 13, 26, 40M

This super-chilled café-bar in reds, whites and blacks has something for everyone – from poetry readings and live music to Sunday brunch – attracting a good mix of expats and locals. Love the place.

MAKUMBA *Bar*

☎ 2522 0544; www.makumba.hk; 48 Peel St, Central; 6pm-late; Midlevels escalator

A cavern saturated with earthy vibes and pulsating rhythms, Makumba has a spacious dance floor where a predominantly African crowd moves to music performed by a Senegalese band or visiting artists. The atmosphere will seduce even the coolest hipster into dancing.

PEEL FRESCO *Live Jazz*

☎ 2540 2064; www.peelfresco.com; 49 Peel St, Central; 5pm-late Mon-Sat; Midlevels escalator

Charming Peel Fresco has live jazz six nights a week, with local and overseas acts performing on a small but spectacular stage next to teetering Renaissance-style paintings. The action starts around 9.30pm, but go at 9pm to secure a seat.

PROPAGANDA *Club*

☎ 2868 1316; Lower ground fl, 1 Hollywood Rd, Central; weekend cover $100; 9pm-late Tue-Sat; Midlevels escalator

Hong Kong's premier gay dance club has a sister club down Wyndham St – **Works** (1st fl, 30-32 Wyndham St). Enter from Ezra's Lane.

PURE FITNESS *Heath & Fitness*

☎ 2970 3366; www.pure-fit.com; 1st, 2nd & 3rd fl, Kinwick Centre, 32 Hollywood Rd, Soho; 6am-midnight Mon-Sat, 8am-10pm Sun; M Central

Enter this favourite of the Soho set from Shelley St.

SENSE OF TOUCH *Health & Fitness*

☎ 2526 6918; www.senseoftouch.com.hk; 1st-5th fl, 52 D'Aguilar St, Lan Kwai Fong; 11am-midnight Mon-Fri, 10.30am-7pm Sat, 10.30am-7pm Sun; M Central

This award-winning spa offers every conceivable form of treatment (cappuccino wrap, anyone?) but most are Asian in origin, including ayurvedic massage ($600 per hour)

WHAT'S ON WHERE & WHEN

Artslink (www.hkac.org.hk) A monthly with listings of performances, exhibitions and art-house film screenings. Published by the Hong Kong Arts Centre.

bc magazine (www.bcmagazine.net) A free biweekly guide to Hong Kong's entertainment and partying scene.

Cityline (☎ 2314 4228; www.cityline.com.hk) Affiliate of Urbtix; also good for bookings.

hkclubbing.com (www.hkclubbing.com) Especially useful for clubbing and parties.

HK Magazine (www.asia-city.com) A very comprehensive entertainment listings magazine. It's free, appears on Friday, and can be found at restaurants, bars, shops and hotels.

Time Out (www.timeout.com.hk) An authoritative fortnightly guide and listings of what's on.

Urbtix (☎ 2111 5999; www.urbtix.gov.hk) Bookings for most cultural events can be made online or by phone.

Sherman Chan 陳卓敏

Cook at Caprice, previously at L'Atelier de Joel de Robuchon; staged at Alinea (Chicago), Per Se (New York) and The French Laundry (California); so passionate about food she quit university in order to work in the kitchen

Food recommendations For dim sum: Lin Heung (p62), Luk Yu (p62) and Tim Ho Wan (p129). Feel the culture at ghetto places like Lan Fong Yuen (p61). Kowloon Soy Company (p59) sells 'premier cru' Chinese miso (古勞豉; *gu lo see*), the first layer upon drying – the caramel of Chinese miso. If you go to Caprice (p49), order the specials, the langoustine ravioli and the cheese. My favourite cut at Kau Kee (p61) is butterfly brisket (爽腩; *song laam*), which is chewier than regular brisket. **Authentic versus Chinatown** Chinatown Chinese tends to be strongly flavoured and heavy on MSG; it's what you drown your sorrows in, not comfort food. Authentic Chinese has more depth and culture.

and Thai hot-poultice therapy. If you're trying to shift that jetlag at a weird hour, there are 'night spa' treatments until midnight.

SKYLARK LOUNGE *Live Jazz*

☎ 2801 6018; www.skylarklounge.hk; 1st fl, Parekh Hse, 63 Wyndham St, Central; 8.30pm-late; M Central (Exit D1)

There's live jazz every night of the week (and the odd comedy gig) at this bar above a 7-Eleven store. Performances begin at 9.30pm and happy hour at 8.30pm. Check website for band list.

TAZMANIA BALLROOM *Club*

☎ 2801 5009; www.tazmaniaballroom.com; 1st fl, LKF Tower, 33 Wyndham St, Central; 5am-late; M Central (exit D2)

At this dark, stylish lair, models dressed to the hilt smoke on the balcony, while investment bankers play pool on one of the gold-plated tables. When night falls, the tables are lifted away to make space for a dance-floor.

YUMLA *Club*

☎ 2147 2383; www.yumla.com; Lower basement, 79 Wyndham St, Central; 5pm-2am Mon-Thu, 5pm-4am Fri & Sat, 7pm-2am Sun, happy hr 5-9pm Mon-Sat, 7-9pm Sun; 13, 26, 40M

This place known for its cool crowd and excellent non-mainstream dance music is arguably the least pretentious club in Hong Kong. Watch out for the murals. The entrance is on Pottinger St.

>HONG KONG ISLAND: THE MID-LEVELS & THE PEAK

Not taking the trip up Hong Kong's Peak (the highest point on the island) is like visiting Paris without ascending the Eiffel Tower. It's on every visitor's list and rightly so. On a clear day (sadly an increasingly rare thing) the views are spectacular but at any time, day or night, the cool breezes and the views down onto the concrete canyons are wonderful. The 3km walk around the base of the Peak's summit presents a shaded panoramic view of harbour, city and sea. The Peak is also one of the best places to dine with a view, and it's a jumping-off point for the Hong Kong Trail. To get there board the hair-raisingly steep Peak Tram and perhaps on the way back down take a taxi or bus to do some billionaires' mansion spotting. The Mid-Levels, halfway up the Peak, is solidly residential and has relatively little to offer tourists in the way of sights, though there are a few gems.

THE MID-LEVELS & THE PEAK

SEE

Dr Sun Yat Sen Museum ..1 C2
Hong Kong Museum of Medical Sciences 2 B1
Ohel Leah Synagogue 3 B2
Roman Catholic Cathedral of the Immaculate Conception 4 D3

EAT

Cafe Deco 5 C6
Peak Lookout 6 B6
Pearl on the Peak 7 C6

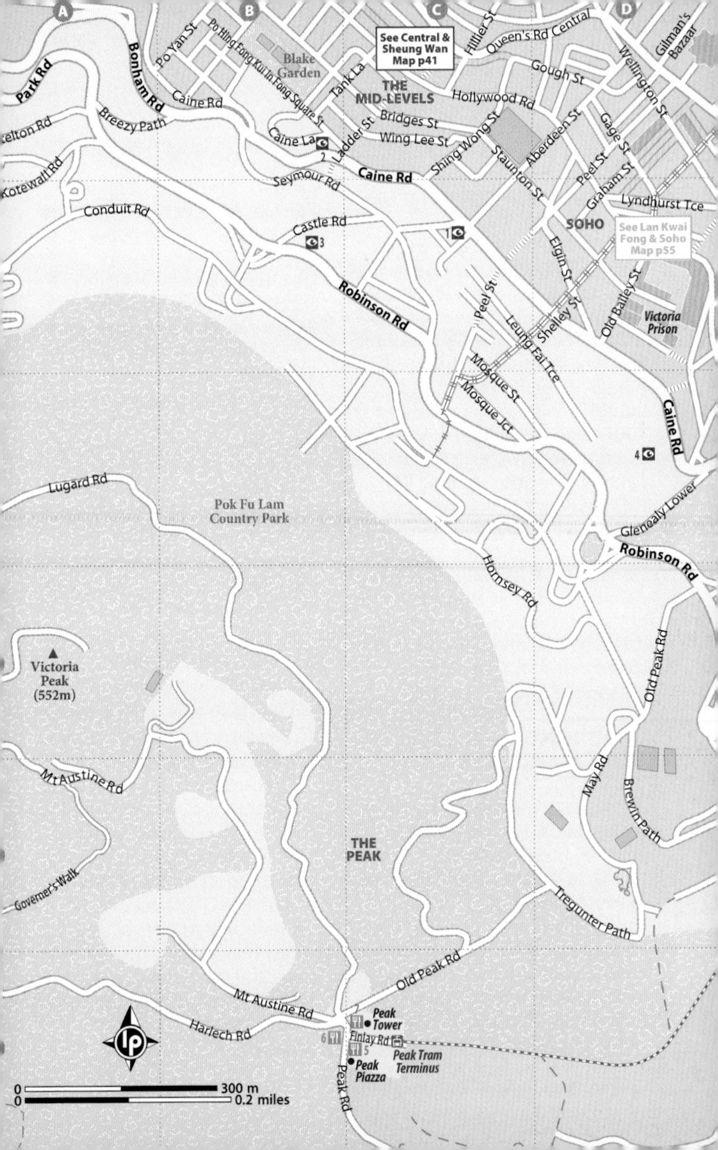

A
B
C
D
See Central & Sheung Wan Map p41
Park Rd
Bonham Rd
Po Yan St
Po Hing Fong
Kui In Fong
Square St
Blake Garden
Tank La
Hillier St
Queen's Rd Central
Gilman's Bazaar
Wellington St
Gough St
THE MID-LEVELS
Hollywood Rd
Caine Rd
Breezy Path
Kotewall Rd
Bridges St
Wing Lee St
Caine La
Ladder St
Shing Wong St
Staunton St
Aberdeen St
Gage St
Peel St
Graham St
Seymour Rd
Caine Rd
Lyndhurst Tce
Conduit Rd
Castle Rd
SOHO
See Lan Kwai Fong & Soho Map p55
Elgin St
Old Bailey St
Victoria Prison
Robinson Rd
Peel St
Shelley St
Leung Fai Tce
Mosque St
Mosque Jct
Caine Rd
Lugard Rd
Pok Fu Lam Country Park
Glenealy Lower
Robinson Rd
Hornsey Rd
Victoria Peak (552m)
Old Peak Rd
May Rd
Mt Austine Rd
Brewin Path
THE PEAK
Governer's Walk
Tregunter Path
Old Peak Rd
Mt Austine Rd
Harlech Rd
Peak Tower
Finlay Rd
Peak Tram Terminus
Peak Piazza
Peak Rd
0
300 m
0
0.2 miles
1
2
3
4
5
6

SEE

DR SUN YAT SEN MUSEUM
孫中山紀念館

☎ 2367 6373; www.lcsd.gov.hk/CE/Museum/sysm; 7 Castle Rd, Mid-Levels; adult/child, student or senior over 60 $10/5, free after 2pm Tue; 10am-6pm Mon-Wed & Fri & Sat, 10am-7pm Sun; 3B, alight at Hong Kong Baptist Church on Caine Rd

A hugely significant historical figure, Dr Sun Yat Sen was an early 20th-century revolutionary dedicated to overthrowing the Qing dynasty. Educated in Hong Kong, his experience of the colony and the efficient manner in which it was run was one of the formative experiences that put him on the path to revolution. His story is one of the more interesting chapters in Hong Kong and China's history, so the museum's certainly worth a visit. Audioguides cost $10.

HONG KONG MUSEUM OF MEDICAL SCIENCES
香港醫學博物館

☎ 2549 5123; www.hkmms.org.hk; 2 Caine Lane, Mid-Levels; adult/child $10/5; 10am-5pm Tue-Sat, 1-5pm Sun; 3B, 23, 23B, 40, 40M, 103, green minibus 8 (from GPO)

This small museum of medical implements and accoutrements is less interesting for its exhibits than for its architecture and attached herb garden. It occupies what was once the Old Pathological Institute, an Edwardian brick-and-tile structure built in 1905. The exhibits comparing Chinese and Western approaches to medicine are unusual and instructive.

OHEL LEAH SYNAGOGUE

☎ 2589 2621; www.ohelleah.org; 70 Robinson Rd, Mid-Levels; admission free; 10.30am-7pm Mon-Thu; 3B, 13, 23, 23B, 40

This 'Moorish Romantic' temple, completed in 1902, is named after Leah Gubbay Sassoon, matriarch of a wealthy (and philanthropic) Sephardic Jewish family that can trace its roots back to the beginning of the colony. Bring your passport and expect a thorough security check if you plan to visit the sumptuous interior.

POLICE MUSEUM

☎ 2849 7019; www.police.gov.hk/ppp_en/01_about_us/pm.html; 27 Coombe Rd, the Peak; admission free; 9am-5pm Wed-Sun, 2-5pm Tue; 15 or 15B

This museum occupying a former police station deals with the Hong Kong Police Force. Its location in an affluent neighbourhood is interesting, given that triads and drug dealers (both featured inside the museum) don't live here, unless they're really good at what they do. If you're taking the bus, alight at the stop between Stubbs Rd and Peak Rd.

TRAM BEATS SEDAN

Until 1940, Peak Tram compartments were divided into three classes: first class for Western passengers; second class for soldiers and policemen; and third class for servants of the wealthy colonials residing on the Peak. The Chinese population was barred from the tram and the Peak itself. Unthinkable today, but back then it was already an improvement, of sorts: in pre-Tram days, Peakies' only mode of transport were sedan chairs carried by Chinese 'chairmen'.

ROMAN CATHOLIC CATHEDRAL OF THE IMMACULATE CONCEPTION

☎ 2522 8212; http://cathedral.catholic.org.hk; 16 Caine Road, Midlevels; 7am-7pm; Midlevels escalator

Hong Kong's most representative Catholic building was constructed in 1888 in Gothic Revival style, and financed by money from Macau's Portuguese faithful. It's one of the city's two cathedrals (the other being St John's Cathedral; p45).

EAT

CAFE DECO

International $$$

☎ 2849 5111; Levels 1 & 2, Peak Galleria, 118 Peak Rd, the Peak; 11.30am-midnight Mon-Thu, 11.30am-1am Fri & Sat, 9.30am-midnight Sun; Peak Tram 15;

Most punters would be content with the views, live **jazz** (7-11pm Thu-Sat) and stylish art-deco furnishings. But the eclectic menu – offering everything from the simple but fresh (oysters, sushi) to more complex bistro and Indian dishes – is way above average. There's also an excellent weekend **brunch** (11.30am-2.30pm).

PEAK LOOKOUT

International, Asian $$$

☎ 2849 1000; 121 Peak Rd, the Peak; 10.30am-midnight Mon-Fri, 8.30am-1am Sat, 8.30am-midnight Sun; Peak Tram 15

East meets West at this colonial-style restaurant, serving everything from Indian and French to Thai and Italian in the handsome dark-wood interior and the leafy terrace. Food-wise, this is easily the Peak's best, but the views, though nice, are to the south of the island, not over the harbour.

PEARL ON THE PEAK

International, Fusion $$$

☎ 2849 5123; Level 1, Peak Tower, 128 Peak Rd, the Peak; noon-2.30pm & 6-10.30pm; Peak Tram 15

This is a tourist restaurant, so the food is merely good and the prices are high, but the views are great. It's just a shame it doesn't aim higher than the pasta to curry, with twists of Oz, menu. The signature pearl meat (air-freighted) flash-fried with shiitake, chives, ginger and soy is an un-ecofriendly exception.

>HONG KONG ISLAND: ADMIRALTY & WAN CHAI

Things are changing for the better in Wan Chai. The cheap canteen-style eating places, a dozen or so seedy hostess bars and a clutch of expat watering holes between Gloucester and Hennessy Rds are all much the same as ever. But head inland and you'll find a new side to Wan Chai. Just east of the Pacific Place mall and south of the tram tracks, you'll find great little restaurants, bars and boutiques sharing space with traditional shops, markets and temples. On the other side of Pacific Place in Admiralty there are a few buildings of note amid a slightly confusing and disjointed tangle of bridges and underpasses. They include the blindingly gold **Far East Finance Centre**, known locally as 'Amah's Tooth', a reference to the traditional Chinese maids' preference for gold fillings and caps; and the modernist **Lippo Centre**, twin office towers reminiscent of koalas hugging a tree, which was built by American 'brutalist master' Paul Rudolph.

ADMIRALTY & WAN CHAI

SEE

- Far East Finance Centre ... **1** B2
- Flagstaff House Museum of Tea Ware .. **2** B2
- Happy Valley Racecourse ... **3** F4
- Hong Kong Park ... **4** A3
- Hong Kong Racing Museum ... **5** F4
- Hung Shing Temple ... **6** D3
- KS Lo Gallery ... **7** B2
- Lippo Centre ... **8** B2
- Pak Tai Temple ... **9** D4

SHOP

- Anteprima ... (see 12)
- Daydream Nation ... **10** C3
- Design Gallery ... **11** D1
- Kelly & Walsh ... (see 12)
- Kent & Curwen ... (see 12)
- Pacific Custom Tailors ... (see 12)
- Pacific Place ... **12** B2
- Vivienne Tam ... (see 12)
- Wan Chai Computer Centre ... **13** D3
- Wise Kids ... (see 12)

EAT

- American Restaurant .. **14** C2
- Bo Innovation ... **15** D3
- Café Too ... **16** B3
- Carriana Chiu Chow Restaurant ... **17** E2
- Hang Zhou Restaurant .. **18** E3
- Naturo+ ... **19** C3
- Olala ... **20** C3
- Pawn ... **21** D3
- Xi Yan Sweets ... **22** C3
- Yin Yang ... **23** D3

DRINK

- 1/5 ... **24** C3
- Champagne Bar ... **25** D2
- Classified Mozzarella Bar ... **26** C3
- Delaney's ... **27** D2
- Devil's Advocate ... **28** D2
- Maya ... **29** D2
- Mes Amis ... **30** D2
- Pawn ... (see 21)

PLAY

- Agnès B Cinema ... **31** D2
- Dusk till Dawn ... **32** D2
- Hong Kong Academy for Performing Arts .. **33** C2
- Hong Kong Arts Centre .. **34** D2
- Hong Kong Visual Arts Centre ... **35** A3
- Lock Cha Tea Shop ... (see 7)
- Wanch ... **36** C2

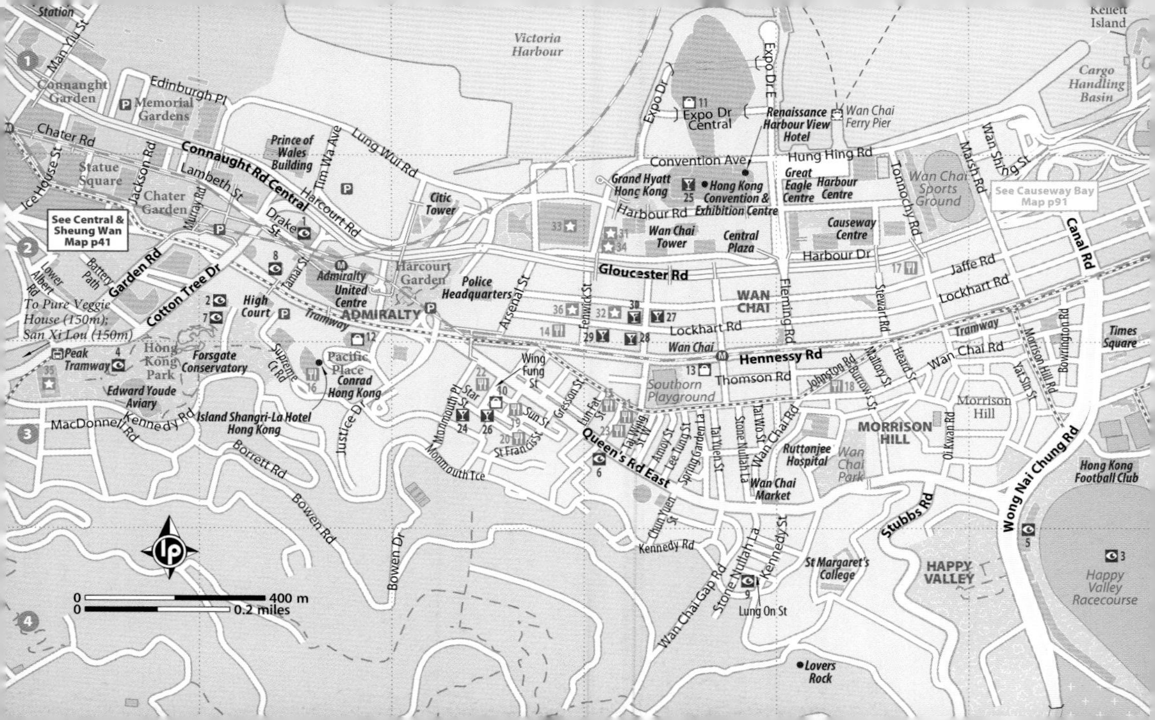

Station
Man Yiu St
Victoria Harbour
Kellett Island
Cargo Handling Basin
Connaught Garden
Edinburgh Pl
Memorial Gardens
Expo Dr
Expo Dr E
Expo Dr Central
Renaissance Harbour View Hotel
Wan Chai Ferry Pier
Chater Rd
Prince of Wales Building
Tim Wa Ave
Lung Wui Rd
Connaught Rd Central
Convention Ave
Hung Hing Rd
Wan Shing St
Marsh Rd
Ice House St
Statue Square
Jackson Rd
Chater Garden
Lambeth St
Murray Rd
Grand Hyatt Hong Kong
Hong Kong Convention & Exhibition Centre
Great Eagle Centre
Harbour Centre
Tonnochy Rd
Wan Chai Sports Ground
See Causeway Bay Map p91
See Central & Sheung Wan Map p41
Drake St
Harcourt Rd
Citic Tower
Harbour Rd
Canal Rd
Wan Chai Tower
Central Plaza
Causeway Centre
Harbour Dr
Lower Albert Rd
Battery Path
Garden Rd
Cotton Tree Dr
Tamar St
Admiralty
United Centre
Harcourt Garden
Police Headquarters
Arsenal St
Gloucester Rd
Fenwick St
Jaffe Rd
Lockhart Rd
To Pure Veggie House (150m); San Xi Lou (150m)
High Court
ADMIRALTY
Tramway
WAN CHAI
Fleming Rd
Stewart Rd
Lockhart Rd
Tramway
Morrison Hill Rd
Bowrington Rd
Times Square
Peak Tramway
Hong Kong Park
Forsgate Conservatory
Supreme Ct Rd
Pacific Place
Conrad Hong Kong
Wing Fung St
Wan Chai
Hennessy Rd
Johnston Rd
Mallory St
Heard St
Wan Chai Rd
Yat Sin St
Edward Youde Aviary
Star St
Southorn Playground
Thomson Rd
Burrows St
Morrison Hill
MacDonnell Rd
Kennedy Rd
Island Shangri-La Hotel Hong Kong
Justice Dr
Monmouth Pl
Sun St
Gresson St
Lun Fat St
Tai Wong St W
Amoy St
Lee Tung St
Spring Garden La
Tai Yuen St
Stone Nullah La
Tai Wo St
Wan Chai Rd
MORRISON HILL
Oi Kwan Rd
Wong Nai Chung Rd
St Francis St
Queen's Rd East
Ruttonjee Hospital
Wan Chai Park
Hong Kong Football Club
Borrett Rd
Monmouth Tce
Wan Chai Market
Bowen Rd
Chun Yuen St
Stubbs Rd
Bowen Dr
Kennedy Rd
Kennedy St
St Margaret's College
HAPPY VALLEY
Happy Valley Racecourse
Wan Chai Gap Rd
Stone Nullah La
Lung On St
0
400 m
0
0.2 miles
Lovers Rock

SEE

HONG KONG PARK 香港公園

☎ 2521 5041; www.lcsd.gov.hk/parks/hkp/en/index.php; 19 Cotton Tree Dr, Admiralty; admission free; park 6am-11pm, conservatory & aviary 9am-5pm, tours 8-10am Wed; 12A M Admiralty (exit C1)

We like to visit the park primarily to walk among our fine-feathered friends at their level (p24), but there are a couple of other draw-cards here, including the **Flagstaff House Museum of Tea Ware** (☎ 2869 0690; www.lcsd.gov.hk/CE/Museum/Arts/english/tea/intro/eintro.html; 10 Cotton Tree Dr, Admiralty; admission free; 10am-5pm Wed-Mon) housed in the oldest colonial building (1846) extant in Hong Kong. It contains a collection of antique Chinese tea ware. Next door the **KS Lo Gallery** (10am-5pm Wed-Mon) contains rare Chinese ceramics and stone seals collected by the gallery's eponymous benefactor. There is also a squash and sports centre for those so inclined.

HUNG SHING TEMPLE 洪聖廟

☎ 2527 0804; www.ctc.org.hk/en/indirectcontrol/temple1.asp; 129-131 Queen's Rd E, Wan Chai; 8am-5.30pm; M Wan Chai (exit A3)

Originally a shrine overlooking the sea when the shoreline ran close to its gates, tiny Hung Shing Temple (c 1847) still sits on a boulder, now staring at buildings and traffic. A red wooden staircase connects to the upper floor where a fortune-teller runs his business.

PAK TAI TEMPLE 北帝廟

www.ctc.org.hk/en/directcontrol/temple10.asp; 2 Lung On St, Wan Chai; 8am-5pm; M Wan Chai (exit A3)

This majestic Taoist temple was constructed 140 years ago by residents of Wan Chai, then a fishing village, to honour Pak Tai (North God) because life-sustaining rivers flowed from the north. A 3m-tall statue of the deity (1604) sits in the main hall – long-haired, barefooted and with a creaseless face not the least perturbed by the ever-present threat of gentrification.

BEWARE: FAKE MONKS

Real monks never solicit money. During your stay, however, you may be approached in temples, even in bars and shops at any time of the day, by con artists in monks' habits who will try to make you part with your money. The more aggressive ones may offer fake Buddhist amulets for sale, or force 'blessings' on you then pester you for a donation. Many speak putonghua and a few words of English. When accosted, just tell them 'no' and ignore them.

SHOP

ANTEPRIMA *Clothing*

☎ 2918 0886; www.anteprima.com; Shop 223, 2nd fl, Pacific Place, 88 Queensway, Admiralty; 🕒 11am-8pm Sun-Thu, 11.30am-8.30pm Fri & Sat; Ⓜ Admiralty (exit F)

This subtle and sophisticated womenswear by a Milan-based Japanese designer, in silk, wool and fine cotton, comes with hefty price tags that belie the ethereality of the designs. That said, most of the pieces are made to outlast fashion fads. Best sellers include the knitwear and signature 'wire bag'.

DAYDREAM NATION *Clothing*

☎ 2817 6313; www.daydream-nation.com; 21 Wing Fung St, Wan Chai; 🕒 noon-8.30pm; Ⓜ Admiralty (exit F)

A winner of the 'Vogue Talent 2010' contest, Daydream Nation is a wonderful brand created by local fashion designer Kay Wong and her musician brother Jing. The clothes and accessories are edgy with a touch of theatricality, yet highly wearable. The second floor is a workshop and party venue.

DESIGN GALLERY
Gifts & Souvenirs

☎ 2584 4146; www.hkdesigngallery.com; Level 1, Hong Kong Convention & Exhibition Centre, 1 Harbour Rd, Wan Chai; 🕒 10am-7.30pm Mon-Fri, 10am-7pm Sat, noon-7.30pm Sun; 🚌 18 Ⓜ Wan Chai

Hung Shing Temple

Supported by the Hong Kong Trade Development Council, this shop showcases Hong Kong design in the form of jewellery, toys, ornaments and gadgets. It's a somewhat chaotic – but often rewarding – gaggle of goodies.

KELLY & WALSH *Books*

☎ 2522 5743; www.swindonbooks.com; Shop 236, 2nd fl, Pacific Place, 88 Queensway, Admiralty; 🕒 10.30am-8pm Sun-Thu, 10.30am-8.30pm Fri & Sat; Ⓜ Admiralty 🚊

This smart shop has a great choice of art, design and culinary books, and the staff know the stock well. The children's books are shelved in a handy kids' reading lounge.

KENT & CURWEN

Clothing & Accessories

☎ 2840 0023; Shop 224, 2nd fl, Pacific Place, 88 Queensway, Admiralty; 10am-8pm Sun-Thu, 10am-9pm Fri & Sat; M Admiralty

Distinguished suits, dress shirts, ties, cufflinks and casual tops for the gentleman who'd rather look to the manor born than arriviste broke.

PACIFIC CUSTOM TAILORS

Clothing & Accessories

☎ 2845 5377; www.pacifictailor.com.hk; Shop 113, 1st fl, Pacific Place, 88 Queensway, Admiralty; 9.30am-7.30pm Mon-Sat; M Admiralty

This is our favourite bespoke tailor in Hong Kong, wrapping us in new duds many times. Staff will make or copy anything; turnaround on most items is two or three days, including two fittings. Excellent, personable service.

SALE ON

Winter sales are held during the first three weeks of January and summer sales in late June and early July. Hong Kong pretties itself up for **Fashion Week** (www.hktdc.com/fair/hkfashionweeks s-en), the industry's most important annual event, in mid-January (autumn and winter) and mid-July (spring and summer). The main parades and events take place at the **Hong Kong Convention & Exhibition Centre** in Wan Chai, but keep an eye out for shows and shindigs in shopping malls around the territory.

VIVIENNE TAM

Clothing & Accessories

☎ 2918 0238; www.viviennetam.com; Shop 209, 2nd fl, Pacific Place, 88 Queensway, Admiralty; 11am-8.30pm Sun-Thu, 11am-9pm Fri & Sat; M Admiralty

Sophisticated yet adventurous womenswear from New York–based designer Vivienne Tam, who was trained in Hong Kong.

WAN CHAI COMPUTER CENTRE 灣仔電腦城

Computers

1st fl, Southorn Centre, 130-138 Hennessy Rd, Wan Chai; 10am-8pm Mon-Sat; M Wan Chai

A busy warren of dozens of shops just above Wan Chai MTR station selling portable media players, smart phones, digital electronics, computer-related gadgets, and accessories for all of the above.

WISE KIDS *Toys*

☎ 2868 0133; www.wisekidstoys.com; Shop 134, 1st fl, Pacific Place, 88 Queensway, Admiralty; 10am-8pm Sun-Wed, 10am-9pm Thu-Sat; M Admiralty

Nothing to plug in and nothing with batteries: Wise Kids concentrates on kids generating energy with what's upstairs. Along with stuffed toys, card games and things to build, there are practical items such as toilet-lid locks and carryalls.

EAT

The Wan Chai dining scene is changing fast and much for the better. The area around Johnston Rd and Ship St is especially promising with new places popping up all the time.

AMERICAN RESTAURANT
美利堅京菜

Northern Chinese $$

☎ 2527 7277; ground fl, Golden Star Bldg, 20 Lockhart Rd, Wan Chai; 🕑 11.30am-11pm; Ⓜ Wan Chai

This place, which chose its name to lure American sailors on R&R through its doors during the Vietnam War, has been serving earthy Northern Chinese cuisine for over half a century. As you'd expect, the Peking duck ($275) and the beggar's chicken ($385) are tops.

BO INNOVATION 廚魔

Molecular Cuisine $$$

☎ 2850 8371; www.boinnovation.com; 2nd fl, 60 Johnston Rd; 🕑 noon-2pm & 7-10pm Mon-Fri, dinner only Sat; Ⓜ Wan Chai (Exit A3)

Bo deconstructs well-known Chinese dishes and reassembles them in visually and gastronomically surprising ways, by means of processes known as molecular gastronomy. *Xiao long bao* (pork dumpling) is a spherical blob of ginger-infused pork soup encased in a transparent wrapper that explodes in the mouth when consumed.

CAFÉ TOO

International $$

☎ 2820 8571; 7th fl, Island Shangri-La Hong Kong, Pacific Place, Supreme Court Rd, Admiralty; 🕑 6.30am-1am; Ⓜ Admiralty

This immensely popular, beautifully designed food hall has half a dozen stations preparing dishes from around the world and one of the best buffets in town. There are à la carte options and lighter fare, such as sandwiches.

CARRIANNA CHIU CHOW RESTAURANT
佳寧娜潮州菜

Chiu Chow $$$

☎ 2511 1282; 1st fl, AXA Centre, 151 Gloucester Rd, Wan Chai; 🕑 11am-11.30pm; Ⓜ Wan Chai

For Chiu Chow food, the Carrianna still rates very high after all these years. Try the cold dishes (sliced goose with vinegar, crab claws), pork with tofu or Chiu Chow–style chicken. Enter from Tonnochy Rd.

HANG ZHOU RESTAURANT 杭州酒家

Hangzhou, Shanghainese $$

☎ 2591 1898; 1st fl, Chinachem Johnston Plaza, 178-188 Johnston Rd, Wan Chai; 11.30am-2.30pm & 5.30-10.30pm; M Wan Chai (exit A5)

This food critics' darling specialises in Hangzhou cooking, the delicate sister of Shanghainese cuisine. Its succulent trademark dish, braised 'Dongpo' pork belly served with steamed buns (aka cholesterol sandwich), is named after the Song Dynasty poet Su Dongpo.

NATURO+ 天廷食品

Café $$

☎ 2865 0388; 6 Sun St, Wan Chai; 11am-10pm; M Wan Chai

Peaceful outdoor seating and a small range of snacks and sandwiches, plus wonderful cheesecake made from Tibetan yak's milk, make this leafy, secluded Wan Chai wholefood store and café a great spot for lunch. See also opposite.

OLALA 一碗麵

Noodles, Shanghainese $

☎ 2294 0426; 33 St Francis St, Wan Chai; 11.30am-10.30pm; M Admiralty (exit Γ)

Extravagant Shanghainese-style noodles in a delicious broth simmered with handpicked Iberico ham, French rose shrimp and other culinary treasures.

PAWN *Gastropub* $$$

☎ 2866 3444; 62 Johnston Rd, Wan Chai; 11am-late; M Wan Chai

Occupying an old colonial-era building with some great terrace dining overlooking the trams, the Pawn serves accomplished modern British pub grub (fish and chips, ham hock and prune salad) and roast pork belly, plus a great list of wines by the glass, carafe or bottle. It's popular, so book ahead.

PURE VEGGIE HOUSE 心齋

Vegetarian, Chinese $$

☎ 2525 0556; www.topstandard.com.hk/pureveggiehouse; 3rd fl, Coda Plaza, 51 Garden Rd, Admiralty; 11am-10pm; 12A from M Admiralty; V

This excellent vegetarian restaurant shows how, in the right hands, a Chinese vegetarian menu doesn't have to read like the rundown of a meat lookalike contest. All dishes and dim sum, some created in the kitchen here, are delicious and MSG-free. The service is impeccable.

SAN XI LOU 三希樓

Sichuanese $$

☎ 2838 8811; www.topstandard.com.hk/sanxilou; 7th fl, Coda Plaza, 51 Garden Rd, Admiralty; 11am-10.30pm; 12A from M Admiralty

Ellen Leung

Founder of wholefood store Naturo+, Wan Chai

What's new in old Wan Chai? Our corner of Wan Chai is developing a personality of its own. There are galleries, tiny boutiques, great little bars, restaurants and, of course, our store and café. There's more on the way. The developers are trying to turn it into an arty area. **How come you ended up here?** I started Naturo+ (opposite) because I got tired of working for a big food group and I wanted to help peasants in China improve their income. We find trusted suppliers and connect them with the consumer. **What's inside the deli counter?** We've got Tibetan yak's cheese, wild honey collected from tree trunks in Yunan, rice from the Yixiang highlands, and Tongan coffee and spices. The quality is superb. We've even got some organic veg from Yuen Long in Hong Kong. **And on the café menu?** Come over for a wine or coffee tasting, or drop in for our special cheesecake, made from yak's milk. It's fantastic.

Sichuan's contribution to the world's vocabulary of hot-and-spiciness is *maa* (tongue-numbing spicy). Here it's mixed with a perfect dose of *laat* (hotness) and skilfully combined with fresh ingredients to create Hong Kong's most authentic Sichuanese dishes.

XI YAN SWEETS 囍宴甜藝

Cantonese, Fusion *$$*

2833 6299, 8 Wing Fung St, Wan Chai; 11.30am-10.30pm; Admiralty (exit F)

The new joint from a local TV chef who runs private dining club Xi Yan serves an oddly successful fusion of Asian savoury dishes (shrimp and pomelo salad, osmanthus smoked duck eggs, Sichuan hot and spicy beef) and otherworldly puddings (ice cream with durian fruit, or glutinous rice and banana).

YIN YANG 鴛鴦飯店

Cantonese *$$$*

2866 0868; 18 Ship St, Wan Chai; noon-2.30pm & 7-10.30pm Mon-Sat; Wan Chai

Inspiration from the chef's Hakka roots, freshly made sauces, home-grown organic veg and old-style cooking techniques (including an old clay oven) combine to create some wonderfully flavoursome home-style cooking here, from the exotic (steamed sea urchin custard) to the everyday (lemon chicken). Book ahead.

DRINK

Wan Chai used to be all about avoiding the awful hostess bars along Lockhart Rd, while heading for the busy bar, club and live music action at the western ends of Jaffe and Lockhart Rds. This is the part of town that kicks on latest, but several worthwhile alternatives await south of the tram tracks in the resurgent little areas between Monmouth Place and St Francis St near Admiralty and around Ship St in Wan Chai.

1/5

Bar, Club

2520 2515; 1st fl, Starcrest Bldg, 9 Star St, Wan Chai; 6pm-3am Mon-Thu, 6pm-4am Fri, 9pm-5am Sat, happy hr 6-9pm Mon-Fri; Admiralty

Pronounced 'one-fifth', this lounge bar–club has a broad bar backed by a two-storey drinks selection from which bar staff concoct some of Hong Kong's best cocktails. Thursday is salsa night.

CHAMPAGNE BAR

Bar, Live Music

2588 1234 ext 7321; ground fl, Grand Hyatt Hong Kong, 1 Harbour Rd, Wan Chai; 5pm-1am; Wan Chai

Take your fizz in the sumptuous surrounds of the Grand Hyatt's Champagne Bar, kitted out in art-deco furnishings realistic enough to evoke the Paris of the 1920s. Live blues or jazz rings through the bar most evenings, and the circular main bar is always busy.

CLASSIFIED MOZZARELLA BAR *Wine Bar*

2528 3454; 31 Wing Fung St, Wan Chai; 11am-midnight; M Admiralty (exit F)

A relaxing and stylish bar opening onto a quiet neighbourhood. Take a seat near the pavement and people-watch as you enjoy your pick among 150 bottles and some tapas.

DELANEY'S *Bar*

2804 2880; ground & 1st fl, One Capital Place, 18 Luard Rd, Wan Chai; noon-3am, happy hr noon-9pm; M Wan Chai

At this immensely popular Irish watering hole you can choose between the ground-floor pub, or the sports bar and restaurant on the 1st floor. There's also a branch in Tsim Sha Tsui.

DEVIL'S ADVOCATE *Bar*

2865 7271; 48-50 Lockhart Rd, Wan Chai; noon-late Mon-Sat, 1pm-late Sun, happy hr noon-9pm daily, midnight-1am Fri & Sat; M Wan Chai

This pleasant pub is as relaxed as they come. The bar spills out on to the pavement, and the staff are charming.

MAYA *Bar*

2866 6200; 68-70 Lockhart Rd, Wan Chai; 11am-2am Sun-Thu, 11am-3am Fri & Sat, happy hr noon-9pm; M Wan Chai

This lovely new bar has a name that apparently means 'illusion' in Sanskrit. It's a design-minded oasis in Wan Chai. We love the bold black-and-white patterns on the wall, the bright-red bar and, of course, the (almost) never-ending happy/relaxing/two-for-one hour(s).

MES AMIS

Bar, Wine Bar

2527 6680; 83 Lockhart Rd, Wan Chai; noon-2.30am Sun-Tue & Thu, noon-5am Wed, noon-6am Fri & Sat, happy hr 4-9pm Mon-Thu, noon-9pm Sat & Sun; M Wan Chai

This easygoing bar may be in the lap – so to speak – of girly club land but it's poles (again, as it

AMAH HOLIDAY

Explore central Hong Kong on a Sunday and you may notice a lot more people out and about, many of them young women gathered in groups, sitting, chatting, cooking and singing. These are Hong Kong's maids, the majority of them from the Philippines and Indonesia, grabbing what free space they can in parks and on pavements and enjoying their only day off.

were) apart. It has a good range of wine and a Mediterranean-style snack list. There's a DJ from 11pm on Wednesday, Friday and Saturday nights.

PAWN *Pub*

2866 3444; 62 Johnston Rd, Wan Chai; 11am-late; M Wan Chai
Downstairs from the Pawn's gastropub, the beaten-up sofas with space to sprawl make the ideal location to sample a great selection of lagers, bitters and wine at this excellent Wan Chai newcomer.

PLAY

AGNÈS B CINEMA *Cinema*

2582 0200; www.hkac.org.hk; Upper basement, Hong Kong Arts Centre, 2 Harbour Rd, Wan Chai; 18 M Wan Chai
Despite its branded name, this very uncommercial cinema is *the* place for classics, revivals, alternative screenings and travelling film festivals.

DUSK TILL DAWN *Live Music*

2528 4689; 76-84 Jaffe Rd, Wan Chai; noon-7am Mon-Fri, 3pm-7am Sat & Sun, happy hr 5-9pm; M Wan Chai
Live music from 10.30pm, with an emphasis on beats and vibes that will get your booty shaking. The dance floor can be packed, but the atmosphere is more friendly than sleazy. The food sticks to easy fillers such as meat pies and burgers.

HONG KONG ACADEMY FOR PERFORMING ARTS
香港演藝學院
Theatre, Music

2584 8500, bookings 3128 8288; www.hkapa.edu; 1 Gloucester Rd, Wan Chai; performances $80-750; M Wan Chai
Stages local and overseas performances of dance, drama and music. The building (1985), with its striking triangular atrium and exterior Meccano-like frame, was designed by local architect Simon Kwan.

HONG KONG ARTS CENTRE
香港藝術中心 *Theatre*

2582 0200; www.hkac.org.hk; 2 Harbour Rd, Wan Chai; performances $80-400; 18 M Wan Chai

The local live music scene is rockin' at Wanch

WORTH THE TRIP

Just south of Wan Chai and accessible by tram from Hennessy Rd is the famous **Happy Valley Racecourse** (☎ 2895 1523, 2966 8111; http://racecourses.hkjc.com; 2 Sports Rd, Happy Valley; admission $10; ⌚ from 7pm Wed Sep–early Jul; 🚌 75, 90, 97), a hugely atmospheric venue that buzzes on race nights when tens of thousands of punters come to wager millions of dollars. If the races aren't on, or your visit is during the day, there's also the esoteric but complete **Hong Kong Racing Museum** (☎ 2966 8065; www.hkjc.com; 2nd fl, Happy Valley Stand, Wong Nai Chung Rd; admission free; ⌚ 10am-5pm Tue-Sun & most public holidays). If a day race meeting is being held, it's open from 10am to 12.30pm.

This independent contemporary arts centre showcases home-grown talent and its Shouson Theatre hosts drama (often in English). The centre also publishes a monthly listings magazine called *Artslink*. It's home to Agnès B Cinema (opposite).

HONG KONG VISUAL ARTS CENTRE *Arts Centre*

7A Kennedy Road, Central; 10am-9pm, closed Tue; Ⓜ Admiralty (Exit C1), 🚌 3B, 12

This place, barely inside Hong Kong Park, features exhibitions, workshops and lectures in the visual arts.

LOCK CHA TEA SHOP 樂茶軒 *Chinese Music, Tea Appreciation $*

☎ 2801 7177; www.lockcha.com, KS Lo Gallery, Hong Kong Park, Admiralty; ⌚ 10am-10pm, Chinese music 7-9pm Sat & 4-6pm Sun, tea appreciation class 4-5pm Mon; Ⓜ Admiralty (exit C1); V

A gem housed in a lovely historic building inside Hong Kong Park offering weekend Chinese music performances, tea appreciation classes conducted in English (hugely popular - register as early as possible), a fine selection of Chinese teas, and great vegan dim sum.

WANCH *Live Music*

☎ 2861 1621; 54 Jaffe Rd, Wan Chai; ⌚ 11am-3am Mon-Fri, 2pm-3am Sat & Sun, happy hr 11am-10pm Mon-Fri, 2-10pm Sat & Sun; Ⓜ Wan Chai

The Wanch has live music (mostly rock and folk) happening nightly from 9pm or 10pm, with the occasional solo guitarist thrown into the mix. Jam night is Wednesday at 9pm. If you're not here for the music, well, the Wanch also has a reputation for being a serious pulling place.

>HONG KONG ISLAND: CAUSEWAY BAY

Shopping is not the only reason to come to Causeway Bay, but it is the main one. Shoppers come for the massive Japanese department stores and the clusters of smaller outlets selling eclectic fashion in the neighbourhood's streets and mini-malls. Victoria Park at the eastern edge of the area is an ideal spot for some recreation, including a dip in the large outdoor pool or just for some respite from teeming crowds. The historic significance of the area to Hong Kong is, sadly, hardly visible today except in a few street names. Called Tung Lo Wan (Copper Gong Bay) in Cantonese, Causeway Bay was the site of a British settlement in the 1840s. It was also once an area of godowns (a Hong Kong business or pidgin English word for warehouses), and a well-protected harbour for fisherfolk and boatpeople. The new Causeway Bay, one of Hong Kong's top shopping areas, was built up from swampland and sand from the bottom of the harbour. Jardine Matheson, one of Hong Kong's largest *hongs* (major trading houses or companies), set up shop here, which explains why many of the streets in the district bear its name: Jardine's Bazaar, Jardine's Crescent and Yee Wo St (Cantonese for 'Jardine Matheson').

CAUSEWAY BAY

SEE

Noonday Gun **1** B2
Tin Hau Temple **2** D2
Victoria Park **3** C2

SHOP

Camper .... (see 7)
DMop **4** C2
G.O.D. **5** B3
Island Beverley **6** B3
LCX **7** B2
Shine **8** B2
Spy Henry Lau .... (see 8)
Yiu Fung Store **9** B3

EAT

Arirang **10** A3
Da Domenico **11** B4
Golden Bull .... (see 10)
Kung Tak Lam **12** B2
Le Pain Grillé **13** B4
Loshan Snow Garden ... **14** B3
Sushi Hiro **15** B3
Tai Ping Koon **16** B3
Wasabisabi **17** A3
West Villa **18** B3

DRINK

Brecht's Circle **19** B3
Dickens Bar **20** B2
Executive B.A.R. **21** A4

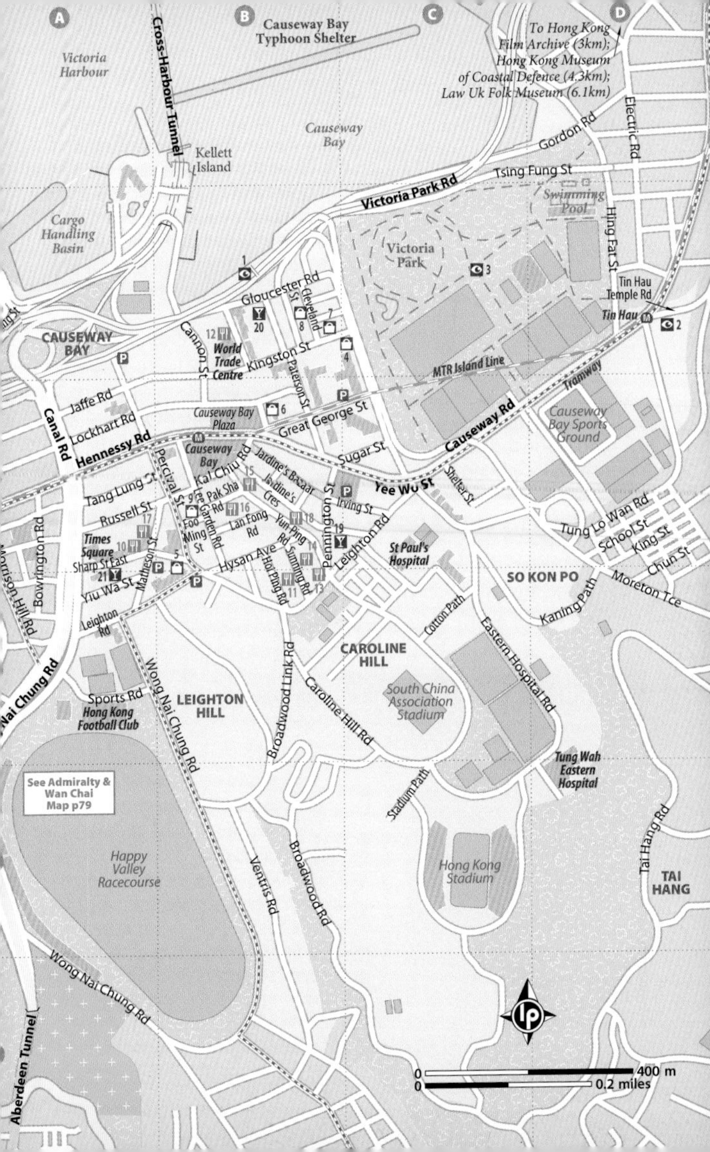

A
B
C
D
Causeway Bay Typhoon Shelter
Victoria Harbour
Cross-Harbour Tunnel
To Hong Kong Film Archive (3km); Hong Kong Museum of Coastal Defence (4.3km); Law Uk Folk Museum (6.1km)
Causeway Bay
Kellett Island
Cargo Handling Basin
Gordon Rd
Electric Rd
Tsing Fung St
Victoria Park Rd
Swimming Pool
Victoria Park
Hing Fat St
Tin Hau Temple Rd
Tin Hau
Gloucester Rd
Cleveland St
CAUSEWAY BAY
Cannon St
World Trade Centre
Kingston St
Paterson St
MTR Island Line
Tramway
Jaffe Rd
Lockhart Rd
Canal Rd
Causeway Bay Plaza
Great George St
Causeway Rd
Causeway Bay Sports Ground
Hennessy Rd
Causeway Bay
Percival St
Kai Chiu Rd
Jardine's Bazaar
Sugar St
Jardine's Cres
Yee Wo St
Shelter St
Tang Lung St
Pak Sha Rd
Pennington St
Irving St
Russell St
Lee Garden Rd
Foo Ming St
Lan Fong Rd
Yun Ping Rd
Leighton Rd
Tung Lo Wan Rd
School St
King St
Chun St
Times Square
Matheson St
St Paul's Hospital
Sharp St East
Hysan Ave
Sunning Rd
Hoi Ping Rd
Bowrington Rd
Morrison Hill Rd
Yiu Wa St
SO KON PO
Moreton Tce
Kaning Path
Leighton Rd
Cotton Path
Eastern Hospital Rd
CAROLINE HILL
Wong Nai Chung Rd
Broadwood Link Rd
Caroline Hill Rd
South China Association Stadium
Sports Rd
Hong Kong Football Club
LEIGHTON HILL
Tung Wah Eastern Hospital
Stadium Path
Tai Hang Rd
See Admiralty & Wan Chai Map p79
Happy Valley Racecourse
Ventris Rd
Broadwood Rd
Hong Kong Stadium
TAI HANG
Wong Nai Chung Rd
Aberdeen Tunnel
0
400 m
0
0.2 miles

 SEE

NOONDAY GUN 午炮

221 Gloucester Rd, Causeway Bay; admission free; subway access 7am-midnight; M Causeway Bay (exit D1)

One of the few remnants of Causeway Bay's colonial past is this 3lb quick-firing cannon built by Hotchkiss of Portsmouth in 1901. It is fired daily at noon by a uniformed Jardine employee. Noel Coward made the gun famous with his satirical song 'Mad Dogs and Englishmen' (1924) about colonists who braved the heat of midday while local people stayed indoors: 'In Hong Kong/they strike a gong/and fire off a noonday gun/to reprimand each inmate/who's in late.' The gun stands opposite the Excelsior Hong Kong hotel and is accessible via a tunnel under the road from the World Trade Centre basement, through a door marked 'Car Park Shroff, Marina Club & Noon Gun'.

SHOCK OF THE NEW

When Hong Kong's electric trams first started running more than a century ago, they caused a sensation. Stops were packed with people, but not many of them actually wanted to go anywhere; a great number just jumped on, walked through having a gawp and treading on toes, then got off again, not quite ready to ride. The trams were also delayed by hawkers who took advantage of the tramway by dragging their heavy carts along the well-made tracks. In 1911 a law was passed banning carts with the same wheel gauge as the trams. The law is still in effect today.

TIN HAU TEMPLE 天后廟

☎ 2721 2326; 10 Tin Hau Temple Rd, Causeway Bay; admission free; 7am-6pm; M Tin Hau (exit B)

Southeast of Victoria Park, Hong Kong Island's most famous Tin Hau temple is small; before reclamation in the last century this temple, dedicated to the patroness of seafarers, stood on the waterfront. It has been a place of worship for three centuries, though the current structure is only about 200 years old.

VICTORIA PARK 維多利亞公園

☎ 2890 5824; www.lcsd.gov.hk/parks/vp/en/index.php; Causeway Rd, Causeway Bay; admission free; 24hr; M Causeway Bay (exit E), Tin Hau (exit A2)

At 17 hectares, Victoria Park is one of the biggest patches of public greenery in urban Hong Kong, and a popular city escape. The best time to take take a stroll around is during weekday mornings when it becomes a forest of people practising the slow-motion martial

Causeway Bay's colonial past is still very much in daily action with the Noonday Gun

art of t'ai chi. The park becomes a vibrant flower market a few days before the Chinese New Year.

SHOP

Causeway Bay is a crush of department stores and smaller outlets selling eclectic fashion. Jardine's Bazaar has low-cost garments, and there are several sample shops for cheap jeans on Lee Garden Rd. There's a cluster of cool brands and independent clothing boutiques on the streets between Cleveland St and Victoria Park. The shops in the area open till late – 10pm.

CAMPER

Clothing & Accessories

☎ 2882 7810; 9 Kingston St, Causeway Bay; noon-10pm; M Causeway Bay

Camper, emblazoned with thought-provoking slogans and aphorisms out the front, is one of the most popular outlets in Hong Kong for locally designed fashion.

DMOP *Clothing*

☎ 2203 4130; www.d-mop.com.hk; 8 Kingston St, Causeway Bay; M Causeway Bay (Exit E)

Decked out stylishly in wood and steel, DMop has a diverse selection ranging from edgy dressy to chic street, and brands from all over the world. It's one of the sole retailers of Y-3 and Nike White Label.

G.O.D. *Lifestyle, Gifts*

☎ 2890 5555; www.god.com.hk; Leighton Ctr, Sharp St E, Causeway Bay; noon-10pm; M Causeway Bay (Exit A)

If you have time for only one souvenir place, make it G.O.D. This cheeky lifestyle store named with an acronym that, according to them, means 'goods of desire' and nothing else, gives a witty take on objects belonging to an older and less affluent Hong Kong. If you're into retro with a twist (think mousepads printed with images of Chinese tenement blocks or butcher's lamps in whacky colours), you'll dig it here. G.O.D. has five branches, including one at JCCAC (p133).

ISLAND BEVERLEY 金百利商場 *Clothing & Accessories*

1 Great George St, Causeway Bay; M Causeway Bay

Crammed into buildings, up escalators and in back lanes are Hong Kong's malls of micro-shops selling designer threads, a kaleidoscope of kooky accessories and an Imelda Marcos of funky footwear. Island Beverley is where Hong Kong's youngest mall trawlers shop for clothes and trinkets.

BAMBOO VS STEEL (& PLASTIC & WOOL...)

The bamboo scaffolding used to build even the tallest skyscrapers and lashed in place with plastic ties might look alarmingly low tech, but it works. Bamboo is lighter, cheaper and more flexible than bolted steel tubing and copes brilliantly with tensile stress, as you'll see if you watch builders scuttle around in their thin-soled slippers, barely causing a ripple. Product and industrial designers are now waking up to the potential of this green material, used in products as diverse as laptop casings, bicycle frames and even its softened fibres for clothing.

LCX *Clothing & Accessories*

☎ 2890 5200; www.lcx-group.com; 9 Kingston St, Fashion Walk, Causeway Bay; noon-10pm Mon-Fri, noon-10.30pm Sat & Sun; M Causeway Bay

Inside the lit plate glass of this fashion outlet you will find clothes and accessories from urban labels, including Marc by Marc Jacobs, TOUGH Jeansmith and Dr. Martens, plus toys, lifestyle gadgets and cosmetics that are similarly geared towards the young, moneyed and trendy.

SHINE *Clothing*

☎ 2890 8261; Cleveland Mansion, 5-7 Cleveland Street, Causeway Bay; M Causeway Bay (Exit E)

One of *the* places in town for unique pieces from emerging designers around the world. Don't miss local representative Johanna Ho's beautiful women's wear.

SPY HENRY LAU *Clothing*

☎ 2317 0806; www.spyhenrylau.com; Suite B, 1st fl, Cleveland Mansion, 7 Cleveland St, Causeway Bay; 1-11pm; M Causeway Bay (Exit E)
A wearable interpretation of local designer Henry Lau's edgy and at times over-the-top fashion sense.

YIU FUNG STORE 么鳳 *Chinese Snacks*

☎ 2576 2528; 3 Foo Ming St, Causeway Bay; 11am-10pm; M Causeway Bay (Exit A); V
Hong Kong's most famous store (c 1960s) for Chinese pickles and preserved fruit features sour plum, liquorice-flavoured lemon, tangerine peel, pickled papaya and dried longnan.

EAT

ARIRANG 阿里朗 *Korean* $$

☎ 2506 3298; Shop 1205, 12th fl, Food Forum, Times Sq, 1 Matheson St, Causeway Bay; noon-3pm & 6-11pm; M Causeway Bay
A branch of the upmarket restaurant chain, with the usual barbecues along with excellent hotpot dishes. It's great for a bargain set lunch.

DA DOMENICO *Italian* $$$

☎ 2882 8013; 8 Hoi Ping Rd, Causeway Bay; 12.15-1.30pm & 7-9.30pm Mon-Sat; M Causeway Bay (exit A)
This airy restaurant is well worth a visit if money is not an issue and you're prepared to take your chances with a moody Roman. That said, volatility applies strictly to the people skills of the chef-owner – his culinary creations are always impeccable. Dinner reservations essential.

GOLDEN BULL 金牛苑 *Vietnamese* $$

☎ 2506 1028; 1103 Food Forum, 11th fl, Times Square, 1 Matheson St, Causeway Bay; noon-3pm & 6-11pm; M Causeway Bay (exit A); V
The descending crowds don't come for the portions (small) and the prices (high) but for the pleasant décor and the tasty Vietnamese food. The beef pho ($98) is excellently made, if not 100% authentic.

KUNG TAK LAM 功德林 *Vegetarian, Chinese* $$

☎ 2881 9966; 10th fl, World Trade Centre, 280 Gloucester Rd, Causeway Bay; 11am-11pm; M Causeway Bay; V
This long-established place, which serves Shanghai-style meatless

dishes, has a more modern feel than most vegetarian eateries in Hong Kong. All vegies served are 100% organic and dishes are MSG free.

LE PAIN GRILLÉ

Café $$$

☎ 2577 2718; Shop 1, ground fl, 111 Leighton Rd, Causeway Bay; ⏲ noon-10.30pm Sun-Thu, noon-11pm Fri & Sat; Ⓜ Causeway Bay

Ideal for a light lunch and afternoon tea, this calm little spot with dark wood tables and tiled floors makes for an ideal pre- or post-shopping pit stop. The menu is stuffed with French classics, including onion soup, snails, *confit de canard* (preserved duck) and slow-cooked spring chicken.

LOSHAN SNOW GARDEN

雪園飯店 *Shanghainese* $$

☎ 2881 6837; www.snow-garden.com; 2nd fl, Ming An Plaza, 8 Sunning

WORTH THE TRIP

A handful of top-class museums make a trip along the island's northern coast more worthwhile.

The history of Hong Kong's once booming and hard-boiled film industry is interesting and the **Hong Kong Film Archive** (☎ 2739 2139; www.filmarchive.gov.hk; 50 Lei King Rd, Sai Wan Ho; admission free; ⏲ 10am-8pm, resource centre 10am-7pm Mon-Wed & Fri, 10am-5pm Sat, 1-5pm Sun; Ⓜ Sai Wan Ho, exit A) is the place to hear (and watch) it. The archive houses some 5600 films, runs a rich calendar of local and foreign movie screenings in its 127-seat **cinema** (☎ 2734 9009; tickets $30-50; ⏲ box office noon-8pm Mon-Wed & Fri-Sun), and exhibits wonderful posters and other fine film paraphernalia. Check the website for screenings and times.

The history of Hong Kong's coastal defences and battles is well presented at **Hong Kong Museum of Coastal Defence** (☎ 2569 1500; www.lcsd.gov.hk/ce/museum/coastal; 175 Tung Hei Rd, Shau Kei Wan; adult/child $10/5, free Wed; ⏲ 10am-5pm Fri-Wed; 🚌 84, 85 Ⓜ Shau Kei Wan, exit B2, then 15min walk north along Tung Hei Rd) in restored Lei Yue Mun Fort (1887), which took quite a beating during WWII. Exhibits in the old redoubt cover the Ming and Qing dynasties, the colonial years, the Japanese invasion and the return of Hong Kong to Chinese sovereignty. There's a historical trail through casements, tunnels and observation posts almost down to the coast.

The small **Law Uk Folk Museum** (☎ 2896 7006; http://hk.history.museum; 14 Kut Shing St, Chai Wan; admission free; ⏲ 10am-1pm & 2-6pm Mon-Wed, Fri & Sat, 1-6pm Sun; Ⓜ Chai Wan, exit B) offers a simple but charming presentation of traditional rural life from two restored Hakka village houses that have been declared a historic monument. The quiet courtyard and surrounding bamboo groves are peaceful and evocative.

Rd, Causeway Bay; 🕑 11am-3pm & 6-11.30pm; Ⓜ Causeway Bay (Exit F); Ⓥ 🚼

If cholesterol-rich Shanghainese classics, such as braised pork leg in brown sauce, weigh a little heavy on your gut and your conscience, keep it healthy with a side of chopped Indian aster or vegetarian dumplings. They're all delicious.

SUSHI HIRO 壽司廣

Japanese $$$

☎ 2882 8752; 10th fl, Henry House, 42 Yun Ping Rd, Causeway Bay; 🕑 12.30-2.30pm & 6.30-11.30pm; Ⓜ Causeway Bay

One of several excellent, if low-key, Japanese places hidden in the area's high-rise offices, Sushi Hiro offers seasonal choices of fish that change on a weekly basis. Set lunch starts from $130 per head (nine pieces) and set dinner $320 (12 pieces). Very reasonable value given the quality.

TAI PING KOON 太平館餐廳

International, Chinese $$$

☎ 2576 9161; 6 Pak Sha Rd, Causeway Bay; 🕑 11am-midnight; Ⓜ Causeway Bay

This place has been around since 1860 and offers an incredible mix of Western and Chinese flavours – what Hong Kong people called 'soy sauce restaurants' in pre-fusion days. Try the borscht and the smoked pomfret or some roast pigeon, all specialities of the house.

Join Causeway Bay's retail crush (p93)

WASABISABI 山葵日本料理

Japanese $$$

☎ 2506 0009; Shop 1301, 13th fl, Food Forum, Times Sq, 1 Matheson St, Causeway Bay; 🕑 noon-3pm & 6pm-midnight; Ⓜ Causeway Bay

Excellent Japanese cuisine, impeccable service and an over-the-top interior. From cable vines through to lipstick reds and into the sweeping sushi bar of palm leaves and ostrich feathers, this is eclectic magnificence. The bar turns into a club at night.

Brecht's Circle is good for a quiet, relaxed conversation over drinks

WEST VILLA 西苑酒家

Cantonese *$$*

☎ 2882 2110; Shops 101-102, 1st fl, Lee Gardens Two, 28 Yun Ping Rd, Causeway Bay; meals from $250; 11am-midnight Mon-Sat, from 10am Sun; M Causeway Bay (exit E); V

Though best known for its *char siu* (叉燒, barbecued pork), which comes slightly charred at the edges and sporting a golden lean-to-fat ratio, this modern establishment also makes delicious soy-sauce chicken with secret ingredients its competitors would kill to know. Book ahead.

DRINK

Unlike Wan Chai, Central or Soho, Causeway Bay is hardly the life and soul. The bars tend to be sparsely frequented here (unless the Rubgy Sevens crowds are in town). Look out for developments at boutique hotel JIA, which will host a cool little bar following a recent fit-out.

BRECHT'S CIRCLE *Bar*

☎ 2577 9636, 2576 4785; ground fl, Rita House, 123 Leighton Rd, Causeway Bay; 4pm-2am Sun-Thu, 4pm-4am Fri & Sat, happy hr 4-8pm; M Causeway Bay

This is a very small and fairly unusual clublike bar. It's a place given more to intimate, cerebral conversation than serious raging. A good place to seek out if you don't fancy the peanut-shell cracking bustle of the East End Brewery.

DICKENS BAR *Pub*

☎ 2837 6782; basement, Excelsior Hong Kong, 281 Gloucester Rd, Causeway Bay; 11am-1am Sun-Thu, 11am-2am Fri & Sat, happy hr 5-8pm; M Causeway Bay

It's ill-lit, the decor is heavy and it's in a basement. The perfect ingredients for that old-fashioned British-pub atmosphere. This long-standing institution remains a popular spot for expats and Hong Kong Chinese alike. There's a very popular curry buffet lunch and lots of big-screen sports.

EXECUTIVE B.A.R. *Bar*

☎ 2893 2080; 27th fl, Bartlock Ctr, 3 Yiu Wa St, Causeway Bay; 5.30pm-3am Mon-Sat; M Causeway Bay (exit B)

In addition to the legendary cocktails ceremoniously crafted by Ichiro, the Japanese owner, there are several dozen varieties of whisky on offer. Friendly reminder: rowdy revellers are not welcome at this understated address.

>HONG KONG ISLAND: ISLAND SOUTH

In complete contrast to the frantic northern shore of Hong Kong Island, its southern extent affords space and relaxation. From Big Wave Bay and Shek O in the east to Aberdeen and Ap Lei Chau in the west, the area is full of attractions and things to do. This is Hong Kong Island's backyard playground – from the good beaches of Repulse Bay, Deep Water Bay and Shek O, to shoppers' paradise Stanley Market and the excellent Ocean Park amusement park near Aberdeen, which packs in enough entertainment for a whole day. The island also has its own little bit of wilderness threaded through by one of Hong Kong's most enjoyable long-range walks, the 78km Wilson Trail, which starts just north of Stanley. In general, the best way to get around this part of Hong Kong Island is by the excellent and extensive bus service. Ride up front on the upper deck and you get a white-knuckle ride thrown in free as the bus navigates narrow, twisting mountain roads. If time is short, taxis are not too cripplingly expensive.

ISLAND SOUTH

SEE

Hong Kong Maritime Museum 1 F4
Ocean Park 2 D2
Repulse Bay 3 E2

SHOP

Horizon Plaza 4 B2
Stanley Market 5 F4

EAT

Ap Lei Chau Market Cooked Food Centre ... 6 B2
Top Deck at the Jumbo ... 7 C2
Verandah 8 E2

Aberdeen Country Park
Peel Rise
Aberdeen Lower Reservoir
Aberdeen
Wong Nai Chung Reservoir
Tai Tam Reservoir
Shek O Country Park
Tai Tam Country Park
Tai Tam Intermediate Reservoirs
Tai Tam Tuk Reservoir
Sandy Bay
Shek Pai Wan Rd
Chinese Cemetery
Aberdeen Praya Rd
Wong Chuk Hang Rd
Aberdeen Harbour
Welfare Rd
Ocean Park
Island Rd
Repulse Bay Rd
Magazine Island
Sham Wan
Cable Car
Deep Water Bay
East Lamma Channel
Ap Lei Chau
Kwun Yam Shrine
Longevity Bridge
Wilson Trail
Repulse Bay
Aberdeen Channel
Middle Island
Middle Bay
Ap Lei Pai
Luk Chau
Tam Rd
Tai Tam Bay
Murray House
Ngan Chau
Stanley Bay
Lamma

SEE

HONG KONG MARITIME MUSEUM 香港海事博物館

2813 2322; www.hkmaritimemuseum.org; ground fl, Murray House, Stanley Plaza, Stanley; adult/child $20/10; 10am-6pm Tue-Fri & Sun, 10am-7pm Sat; 6, 6A, 6X, 260;

This small but worthwhile museum in Stanley's **Murray House** (Hong Kong's oldest colonial building, moved to this location in the mid-1990s) is well worth a look when you're in Stanley. Highlights include some wonderful mock-ups of Tang dynasty seagoing vessels, a nice collection of trade art (including sketches by celebrated 19th-century painter George Chinnery) and a fair amount of hands-on exhibits, including a simulator that allows you to sit on the bridge of a container ship and guide it (maybe) into Victoria Harbour.

OCEAN PARK 香港海洋公園

2552 0291; www.oceanpark.com.hk; Ocean Park Rd, Aberdeen; adult/child $208/103; 10am-6pm; 6X, 73, 629 (Ocean Park Citybus), green minibus 6;

Don't miss Hong Kong's biggest home-grown theme park. It amuses and educates with roller coasters, giant pandas, the world's largest aquarium and an atoll reef. The two-part complex is linked by a scenic (slightly hair-raising) cable-car ride. The park entrance is on the lowland side southeast of Aberdeen and the main section is on the headlands, with terrific views of the South China Sea.

REPULSE BAY 淺水灣

6, 6A, 6X or 260

Though it can get packed at weekends, and even during the week in summer, the long beach at Repulse Bay is a good place if you like people-watching. At its southeastern end is an unusual shrine to

DRAGON BOAT

Hong Kong is the home of modern dragon-boat racing (p26), an activity that originated 2000 years ago in Tanka culture as a ceremony for worshipping deities of the sea. The city has the most teams (some 400) and the most races (over 20 a year) in the world per square metre. It's a sport zealously embraced by fishermen, students and professionals alike. The most spectacular events during the racing season (March to October) are the fishermen's races from late April to May. You'll see junks moored in the harbour, decked out with flags, and people casting paper offerings into the water. The Dragon Boat Association (www.hkdba.com.hk) and Hong Kong Tourist Board (www.discoverhongkong.com) have information on major events.

The colourful stalls at Stanley Market can cause sensory overload

Kwun Yam, the deity of Mercy. The surrounding area has an amazing assembly of mosaics, gods and figures – goldfish, rams, statues of Tin Hau and other southern Chinese icons. In front of the shrine, to the left as you face the sea, is Longevity Bridge; crossing it is supposed to add three days to your life. See also boxed text, p105.

SHOP

HORIZON PLAZA

新海怡廣場 *Furniture, Clothing*

2 Lee Wing Street, Ap Lei Chau, Aberdeen; 10am-7pm; 90 from Central (Exchange Sq terminus)

Dozens of warehouses and factory outlets selling discounted Western- and Chinese-style furniture and designer clothing. Most will pack and ship too. Get a directory from the lift lobby. Take Bus 90 and disembark at Ap Lei Chau Estate terminus; from there take a cab.

STANLEY MARKET 赤柱市集

Market

Stanley Village Rd, Stanley; 9am-6pm; 6, 6A, 6X, 260

No big bargains or big stings, just reasonably priced casual clothes (plenty of large sizes and children's clothes), linens, bric-a-brac, toys and formulaic art, all in a maze of alleys running down to Stanley Bay. It's best to go during the week if possible.

EAT

AP LEI CHAU MARKET COOKED FOOD CENTRE 鴨脷洲街市熟食中心

Cantonese $

1st fl, Ap Lei Chau Municipal Services Bldg, 8 Hung Shing St, Ap Lei Chau, Aberdeen; 6pm-midnight; 36X from Causeway Bay (Lee Garden Rd)

Hawkers, including **Pak Kee** (☎ 2555 2984) and **Chu Kee** (☎ 2555 2052), cook for noisy neighbours and dragon-boaters above a wet market. Order there or buy fresh seafood from the market and have them cook it for you.

Getting there is half the fun – sampan is the only way to go to the Jumbo Floating Restaurant

HOLE IN THE SOUL

The executives' playground of **Repulse Bay** (p102) is surrounded by swanky high-rise apartment blocks. Among them is a giant pink, blue and yellow wavy structure with a giant square hole in the middle called the Repulse Bay. Apparently this design feature was added on the advice of a feng shui expert.

The place to go for local flair and great seafood. You can get there by sampan ($1.80) from Aberdeen Promenade.

TOP DECK AT THE JUMBO

Chinese $$$

☎ 2552 3331; www.cafedecogroup.com; Jumbo Kingdom, Shum Wan Pier Dr, Wong Chuk Hang, Aberdeen; 5pm-midnight Tue-Fri, 11am-late Sat & Sun; 70, 73, 973

This new spin on a Hong Kong institution sits atop the Jumbo Kingdom, the larger of two floating restaurants moored in Aberdeen Harbour. But while the restaurant below offers lacklustre seafood and a 'Beijing's Imperial Palace meets Las Vegas casino' decor, the Top Deck promises grown-up food and delightful surrounds. The Sunday unlimited seafood and champagne buffet is a great splurge. There's free transport for diners from the pier on Aberdeen Promenade.

VERANDAH

International, Asian $$$

☎ 2292 2822; 1st fl, the Repulse Bay, 109 Repulse Bay Rd, Repulse Bay; noon-2.30pm & 3-5.30pm (tea) & 6.30-10.30pm Tue-Sat, 11am-3pm & 3.30-5.30pm (tea) & 6.30-10.30pm Sun; 6, 6A, 6X, 260

This place is housed in a replicated colonial structure in front of the wavy Repulse Bay condos (see boxed text, left), which is meant to recall the stunning Repulse Bay Hotel, which was bulldozed in 1982. Wooden ceiling fans swooshing away, palms in their pots and a sea-facing outlook all lend a tropical feel. The Verandah is hushed and formal with heavy white tablecloths and demurely clinking cutlery. The brunch is famous (book well ahead), and the afternoon tea is the south side's best.

>KOWLOON: TSIM SHA TSUI & TSIM SHA TSUI EAST

Vibrant Tsim Sha Tsui (Sharp Sandy Point) holds one big trump card: an unforgettable view of Hong Kong Island. This is also the part of town for sucking up some culture – the area is thick with museums and performance spaces – and to shop: stores, shopping malls and hotels are crammed into an area not much bigger than 1 sq km. But beware: Nathan Rd, the main drag, is one of the very few places where you'll find merchants poised to rip you off, especially when buying electronic goods or photographic equipment. Above all, Tsim Sha Tsui is Hong Kong's most eclectic district, with a population comprising Chinese, Indians, Filipinos, Nepalese, Africans and Europeans, and the glamorous often charmingly close to the pedestrian.

TSIM SHA TSUI & TSIM SHA TSUI EAST

SEE

- Avenue of the Stars **1** D4
- Chungking Mansions **2** C3
- Former Kowloon British School **3** C1
- Former Marine Police Headquarters **4** C4
- Hong Kong Museum of Art **5** C4
- Hong Kong Museum of History **6** E1
- Hong Kong Space Museum **7** C4
- Kowloon Mosque & Islamic Centre **8** C2
- Kowloon Park **9** C2
- Middle Rd Children's Playground **10** D3
- Peninsula Hotel Hong Kong **11** C3
- Tsim Sha Tsui East Promenade **12** C4
- Tsim Sha Tsui East Waterfront Podium Garden **13** E3

SHOP

- Alan Chan Creations .. (see 11)
- Chinese Arts & Crafts .. **14** B4
- I.T. **15** B3
- Initial **16** D2
- Lane Crawford **17** B4
- Onesto Photo Company **18** D2
- Page One **19** B2
- Premier Jewellery **20** C3
- Pro Cam-fis .... (see 17)
- Rise Shopping Arcade ... **21** D2
- Star Computer City **22** B4
- Swindon Book Co. Ltd ... **23** C3
- www.izzue.com .... (see 15)

EAT

- Aqua **24** B3
- Chang Won Korean Restaurant **25** D2
- Din Tai Fung **26** B3
- Fook Lam Moon **27** D2
- Gaddi's .... (see 11)
- Gaylord **28** C3
- Hokahoka **29** E3
- Hutong .... (see 24)
- Sabatini **30** E2
- Spring Deer **31** D3
- Sweet Dynasty **32** B2
- Swiss Chalet **33** D2
- T'ang Court **34** C3
- Woodlands **35** E3
- Wu Kong Shanghai Restaurant **36** C3
- Ye Shanghai **37** B3

DRINK

- Bar .... (see 38)
- Felix **38** C3
- King Ludwig Beer Hall .. **39** D3
- Phonograph **40** E1
- Tapas Bar **41** E3

PLAY

- Dada **42** D1
- Hong Kong Cultural Centre **43** C4
- Khoob Surat **44** C3
- T'ai Chi **45** C4
- Vibes **46** C2

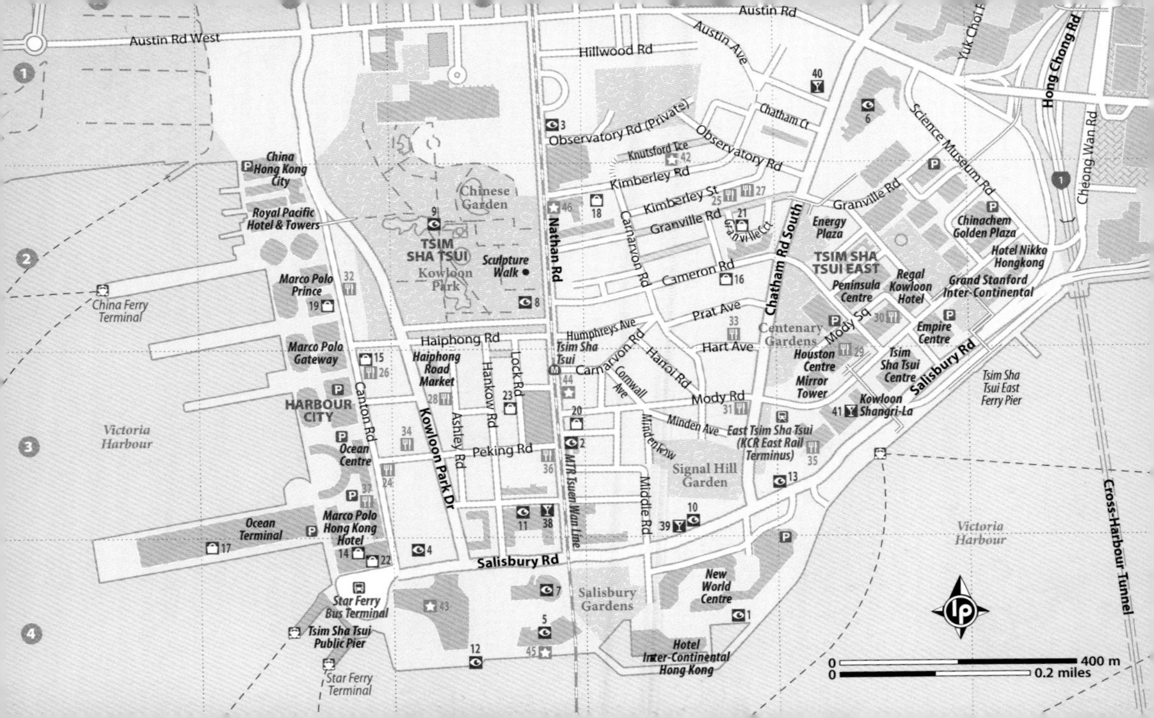
Austin Rd
Austin Rd West
Austin Ave
Hillwood Rd
Yuk Choi Rd
Hong Chong Rd
Cheong Wan Rd
Science Museum Rd
Chatham Ct
Observatory Rd (Private)
Observatory Rd
Knutsford Tce
Kimberley Rd
Kimberley St
Granville Rd
Granville Ct
Carnarvon Rd
Cameron Rd
Chatham Rd South
Nathan Rd
Energy Plaza
TSIM SHA TSUI EAST
Chinachem Golden Plaza
Hotel Nikko Hongkong
Grand Stanford Inter-Continental
Regal Kowloon Hotel
Peninsula Centre
Empire Centre
Mody Sq
Centenary Gardens
Prat Ave
Hart Ave
Houston Centre
Mirror Tower
Tsim Sha Tsui Centre
Salisbury Rd
Tsim Sha Tsui East Ferry Pier
Kowloon Shangri-La
Mody Rd
Minden Ave
Minden Row
East Tsim Sha Tsui (KCR East Rail Terminus)
Signal Hill Garden
Middle Rd
Victoria Harbour
Cross-Harbour Tunnel
New World Centre
Hotel Inter-Continental Hong Kong
Salisbury Gardens
0
400 m
0
0.2 miles
China Hong Kong City
Royal Pacific Hotel & Towers
Chinese Garden
TSIM SHA TSUI
Kowloon Park
Sculpture Walk
China Ferry Terminal
Marco Polo Prince
Marco Polo Gateway
Haiphong Rd
Haiphong Road Market
Humphreys Ave
Tsim Sha Tsui
Hanoi Rd
Cornwall Ave
Hankow Rd
Lock Rd
Ashley Rd
Peking Rd
Kowloon Park Dr
Canton Rd
HARBOUR CITY
Ocean Centre
MTR Tsuen Wan Line
Ocean Terminal
Marco Polo Hong Kong Hotel
Star Ferry Bus Terminal
Tsim Sha Tsui Public Pier
Star Ferry Terminal
1
2
3
4

SEE

CHUNGKING MANSIONS
重慶大廈

36-44 Nathan Rd, Tsim Sha Tsui; admission free; M Tsim Sha Tsui (exit D1)

Say 'budget accommodation' and 'Hong Kong' in one breath and everyone thinks of Chungking Mansions, a place like no other in the world. This huge, ramshackle high-rise dump in the heart of Tsim Sha Tsui caters to virtually all needs – from finding a bed and a curry lunch to changing your Burmese kyat and getting your hair cut – but you may be put off by the undercurrent of sleaze and the peculiar odour of cooking fat, incense and sewage. The building's infamy is fuelled by tales both tall and true of conflagrations, crimes and unclaimed bodies; everyone should come here once. The entrance to Chungking Mansions is via Chungking Arcade, a parade of shops that faces Nathan Rd. See also p17.

FORMER KOWLOON BRITISH SCHOOL
前九龍英童學校

2208 4400; www.lcsd.gov.hk/ce/Museum/Monument/en/main.php; 136 Nathan Rd, Tsim Sha Tsui; M Tsim Sha Tsui (exit B2)

Hong Kong's oldest former school for expatriate children is an Edwardian building that now houses the **Antiquities and Monuments Office**, the official authority on the city's built heritage. Constructed in 1902, the school was subsequently modified to incorporate verandahs and high ceilings, prompted perhaps by the frequent fainting spells suffered by its delicate occupants.

FORMER MARINE POLICE HEADQUARTERS 前水警總部

2926 8000; www.1881heritage.com; 2A Canton Rd, Tsim Sha Tsui; exhibition hall 10am-10pm

The beautiful Victorian former Marine Police Headquarters is now a glitzy hotel and shopping complex, which was deliberately misnamed '1881 Heritage' (the building had had the bad luck to be constructed in 1884: '4' has a similar pronunciation to 'death').

HONG KONG MUSEUM OF ART 香港藝術博物館

2721 0116; http://hk.art.museum; 10 Salisbury Rd, Tsim Sha Tsui; adult/child $10/5, free Wed; 10am-6pm Sun-Wed & Fri, to 8pm Sat, closed Thu; M Tsim Sha Tsui (exit E) Star Ferry (Tsim Sha Tsui)

This museum does a credible job of showing classical Chinese art, paintings and lithographs of old Hong Kong and (mostly) calligraphy in the Xubaizhi collection in a

HONG KONG MUSEUMS PASS

The **Hong Kong Museums Pass** (admission 7 days $30, adult/senior & student 6 months $50/25, 1 yr $100/50) allows multiple entries to six of Hong Kong's museums: **Hong Kong Museum of Coastal Defence** (see boxed text, p96), Hong Kong Science Museum, **Hong Kong Museum of History** (below), **Hong Kong Museum of Art** (opposite), **Hong Kong Space Museum** (below), excluding the Space Theatre, and the **Hong Kong Heritage Museum** (p138). They are available from any Hong Kong Tourism Board (HKTB) outlet (p194) and the participating museums.

total of seven galleries spread over six floors. There are also exquisite ceramics and gold artefacts plus a few worthwhile international exhibitions.

HONG KONG MUSEUM OF HISTORY 香港歷史博物館

☎ 2724 9042; http://hk.history.museum; 100 Chatham Rd South, Tsim Sha Tsui East; adult/child $10/5, free Wed; 10am-6pm Mon & Wed-Sat, 10am-7pm Sun; M Tsim Sha Tsui (exit A2) 5, 8

Hong Kong's best museum after the Hong Kong Heritage Museum (p138) focuses on the territory's archaeology, natural history, ethnography and local history. It's well worth a visit to understand how Hong Kong presents its history to itself and the world (p21). Free guided tours of the museum are available in English at 10.30am and 2.30pm on Saturday and Sunday.

HONG KONG SPACE MUSEUM 香港太空館

☎ 2721 0226; 10 Salisbury Rd, Tsim Sha Tsui; adult/child $10/5, free Wed; 1-9pm Mon & Wed-Fri, 10am-9pm Sat & Sun; M East Tsim Sha Tsui (exit J)

Despite the dated feel, simulators such as the virtual paraglider hold a timeless fascination for overaged nerds and the gift shop sells dehydrated 'astronaut' ice cream. The space theatre screens 'sky shows' and Omnimax films.

KOWLOON MOSQUE & ISLAMIC CENTRE 九龍清真寺

☎ 2724 0095; 105 Nathan Rd, Tsim Sha Tsui; admission free; 5am-10pm; M Tsim Sha Tsui (exit A1)

Hong Kong's largest mosque, completed in 1984, occupies the site of a previous mosque built in 1896 for Muslim Indian troops garrisoned in barracks at what is now known as Kowloon Park (p110). The mosque has a handsome dome, minarets and a carved marble exterior. It is capable of accommodating 7000 worshippers. Muslims are welcome to attend services at the mosque but non-Muslims should ask permission to enter. If you do visit, remove your shoes before entering.

KOWLOON PARK 九龍公園

☎ 2724 3344; www.lcsd.gov.hk/parks/kp/en/index.php; 22 Austin Rd, Tsim Sha Tsui; admission free; 🕑 6am-midnight; Ⓜ Tsim Sha Tsui (exit A1), Jordan (exit C1)

Built on the site of a barracks for Muslim Indian soldiers in the colonial army, Kowloon Park is an oasis of greenery and a refreshing escape from the hustle and bustle of Tsim Sha Tsui. Pathways and walls criss-cross the grass, birds hop around in cages, and towers and viewpoints dot the landscape. The Sculpture Walk features works by local and international sculptors. While it's not a must-visit, the modest Hong Kong Discovery Centre is worth a look if you're interested in Hong Kong's architectural heritage.

MIDDLE RD CHILDREN'S PLAYGROUND 中間道兒童遊樂場

Middle Rd, Tsim Sha Tsui; 🕑 7am-11pm; Ⓜ East Tsim Sha Tsui (exit K)

This leafy playground with views of the waterfront has a breezy spontaneity not often seen in Hong Kong's parks. It's usually quiet, but at weekends children, parents and picnickers of as many ethnicities as there are ways to go down a slide come here to enjoy themselves. The park sits atop the roof of the Tsim Sha Tsui East MTR station. Connected to its eastern exit is the handsome **Tsim Sha Tsui East Waterfront Podium Garden** (尖沙咀東海濱平台花園), where you can read under white shade sails, watch youngsters hone their capoeira moves or head over to Tsim Sha Tsui East.

PENINSULA HOTEL HONG KONG 香港半島酒店

☎ 2920 2888; www.peninsula.com; cnr Salisbury & Nathan Rds, Tsim Sha Tsui; Ⓜ Tsim Sha Tsui (exit E)

More than a Hong Kong landmark, the Peninsula, in the thronelike building opposite the Hong Kong Space Museum, is one of the world's great hotels. Land reclamation has robbed the hotel of its top waterfront location, but the breathtaking lobby of the original building is well worth a visit. And it's by far the classiest place in town to take tea. See also p17.

SIGNAL HILL GARDEN & BLACKHEAD POINT TOWER 訊號山公園

Minden Row, Tsim Sha Tsui; 🕑 tower 9-11am & 4-6pm; Ⓜ East Tsim Sha Tsui (exit K)

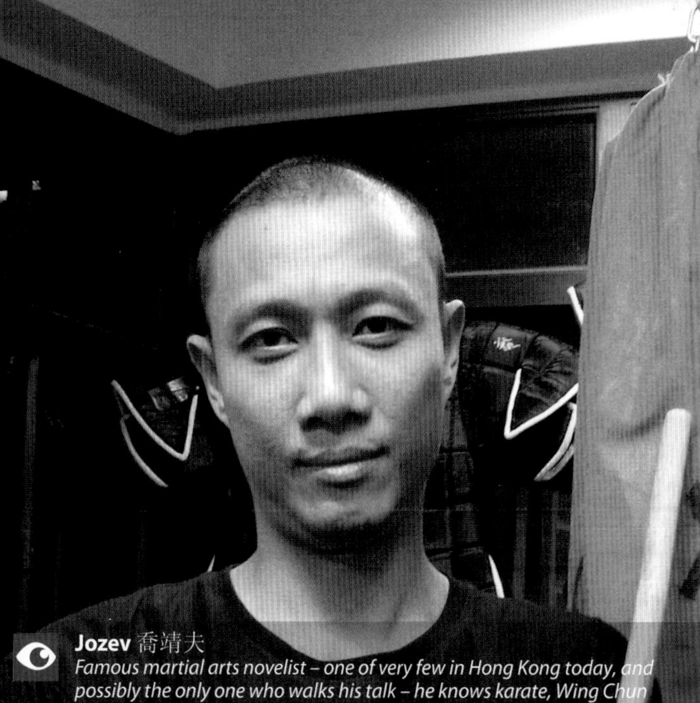

Jozev 喬靖夫

Famous martial arts novelist – one of very few in Hong Kong today, and possibly the only one who walks his talk – he knows karate, Wing Chun and Kali.

Chinese v Western chivalry The Chinese have historically been mistrustful of autocratic regimes so we pin our hopes for justice on folk heroes, rather than members of the ruling class. This is different from Western or Japanese ideas of chivalry. You can see it today in Hong Kong's commemoration of 4 June victims and our support for Liu Xiaobo, the jailed Nobel peace laureate. **Recommended translated martial arts novels** Those of Jin Yong (aka Louis Cha); set in ancient China but full of references to 1960s Hong Kong politics. **Hong Kong's martial arts scene** Political stability has allowed us to preserve traditional forms of Wing Chun, Shaolin, Praying Mantis, t'ai chi etc. We also have Kali from the Philippines, Brazilian Jiu-jitsu, Krav-Maga from Israel, and Systema – which is Russian. Check out the Hong Kong branch of Chin Woo Athletic Association (see p124). **Your idea of a good time** I hunt for Japanese manga, video games and action figures in Sino Centre (see p127). I love Mong Kok's energy.

The views at the top of this knoll are spectacular, and in the 1900s all the ships in the harbour might have returned your gaze – a copper ball in the handsome Edwardian tower was dropped at 1pm daily so that seafarers could adjust their chronometers. The garden is perched above the Middle Rd Children's Playground. Enter from Minden Row (off Mody Rd).

TSIM SHA TSUI EAST PROMENADE 尖東海旁

South of Salisbury Rd along Victoria Harbour, Tsim Sha Tsui; admission free; M Tsim Sha Tsui (exit E)

Stretching along what is arguably the world's most dramatic harbour, this walkway offers superb views of Hong Kong Island. Begin your journey at the old **Kowloon-Canton Railway clock tower** (c 1915), a landmark of the Age of Steam, near the Star Ferry concourse. To your left is the windowless **Cultural Centre**, passing which you'll arrive at the **Avenue of the Stars**, Hong Kong's underwhelming tribute to its film industry. This is a good vantage point for the **Symphony of Lights**, a nightly (8pm) 20-minute laser light show projected from atop skyscrapers.

CULTURAL KALEIDOSCOPE

One of the more interesting offerings of the **Hong Kong Tourism Board** (HKTB; ☎ 2508 1234; www.discoverhongkong.com) is a series of a dozen free cultural programs in English called 'Meet the People'. Run by local experts in their fields, topics covered include antiques, architecture, Cantonese opera, Chinese medicine, Chinese cake-making, Chinese tea, diamonds, feng shui, kung fu, jade and pearl shopping and t'ai chi.

SHOP

ALAN CHAN CREATIONS

東西坊 *Gifts & Souvenirs*

☎ 2723 2722; www.alanchancreations.com; Shop 5A, Basement, Peninsula Hotel Hong Kong, cnr Salisbury & Nathan Rds, Tsim Sha Tsui; 9.30am-7pm; M Tsim Sha Tsui (exit E) Star Ferry (Tsim Sha Tsui)

Alan Chan has designed everything – from airport logos to soy-sauce bottles – and now lends his name to stylish souvenirs, such as clothing and ceramic pieces. Some items he has a direct hand in, others he simply approves of. Cool, contemporary Chinese design that should inspire plenty of gift ideas.

CHINESE ARTS & CRAFTS

中藝 *Gifts & Souvenirs*

☎ 2735 4061; www.cachk.com; 1st fl, Star House, 3 Salisbury Rd, Tsim Sha Tsui; 10am-9.30pm; M Tsim Sha Tsui Star Ferry (Tsim Sha Tsui)

BUYER BEWARE

Hong Kong is a trustworthy place to shop, but it's worth bearing a couple of things in mind. Most shops are loath to give refunds but they can usually be persuaded to exchange purchases that can be resold; just make sure you get a receipt. When buying electronic goods, always beware of merchandise imported by an unauthorised agent, as this may void your warranty. A good marker of trustworthy merchants is the Quality Tourism Services logo (which should be displayed on the front door). If you experience problems, call the **Hong Kong Consumer Council** (☎ 2929 2222; www.consumer.org.hk).

From silk cushions to jade earrings, the pricey traditional-style gifts here show you can keep your head and your poise while swimming in tourist cliches.

GRANVILLE RD FACTORY OUTLETS 加連威老道出口店

Clothing & Accessories

Map p107, D2; Granville Rd, Tsim Sha Tsui; Ⓜ Tsim Sha Tsui

If you have the time and inclination to rifle through racks and piles of factory seconds, the dozen or so factory outlets selling slightly premium mainstream casual and leisure brands along Granville Rd should reward you with costs a fraction of store price. Hotspots include **UNO OUN** (No 29), **Sample Moon** (No 30) and the **Baleno Outlet Store** (No 24B).

I.T. *Clothing & Accessories*

☎ 2730 7681; www.ithk.com; Shop LG01 & LG16-17, Basement, Silvercord, 30 Canton Rd, Tsim Sha Tsui; noon-10pm; Ⓜ Tsim Sha Tsui (exit A1)

This trendy shop carries a selection of first-to-third-tier designer brands from Europe and Japan – similar to DMop (p93) but less edgy and with more choices from Japan. Prices are high but not outrageous. The I.T. group has shops in all the major shopping areas.

INITIAL *Clothing & Accessories*

☎ 2311 4223; www.initialfashion.com; Shop 2, 48 Cameron Rd, Tsim Sha Tsui; 11.30am-11.30pm; Ⓜ Tsim Sha Tsui (exit B2)

This attractive shop and café carries stylish, multifunctional urbanwear with European and Japanese influences. The clothes created by local designers are complemented by imported shoes, bags and costume jewellery.

LANE CRAWFORD 連卡佛

Department Store

☎ 2118 3428; www.lanecrawford.com; ground & 1st fl, Ocean Terminal, Harbour City, Salisbury Rd; 10am-9pm; Ⓜ Tsim Sha Tsui Star Ferry (Tsim Sha Tsui)

Swindon Book Co. Ltd has tomes to suit all tastes at its Tsim Sha Tsui store

Hong Kong's first (and most successful) Western-style department store is still a very upmarket place – rather like the British department store Harvey Nichols (which has opened across the harbour in the Landmark mall).

ONESTO PHOTO COMPANY 忠誠 *Photographic Equipment*

☎ 2723 4668; Shop 18, block B, ground fl, Champagne Crt, 16 Kimberley Rd, Tsim Sha Tsui; 11am-8pm Mon-Sat, 3.30-7pm Sun; M Tsim Sha Tsui

This retail outlet, which stocks mostly film cameras, has price tags on its equipment (a rarity in Tsim Sha Tsui) but there's always a bit of latitude for bargaining.

PAGE ONE *Books*

☎ 2730 6080; www.pageonegroup.com; Shop 3202, 3rd fl, Gateway Arcade, Harbour City, Canton Rd, Tsim Sha Tsui; 10.30am-10pm Mon-Thu, 10.30am-10.30pm Fri-Sun; M Tsim Sha Tsui Star Ferry (Tsim Sha Tsui)

A chain, yes, but a good one. Page One has Hong Kong's best selection of art and design magazines and books, and it's also strong on photography, literature, film and children's books.

PREMIER JEWELLERY 愛寶珠寶 *Jewellery*

☎ 2368 0003; Shop G14-15, ground fl, Holiday Inn Golden Mile Shopping Mall, 50 Nathan Rd, Tsim Sha Tsui; 10am-

7.30pm Mon-Sat, 10.30am-4pm Sun; Ⓜ Tsim Sha Tsui
This family business is directed by a qualified gemologist and is a firm favourite. If you're looking for something in particular, give them a day's notice to have a selection ready for you. They can also help you design your own piece.

PRO CAM-FIS *Outdoor Gear*

☎ 3188 4271; www.procam-fis.com.hk; Shop 267-269, 2nd fl, Ocean Terminal, Harbour City, Salisbury Rd; 10am-9pm; Star Ferry
Pro Cam-fis sells both lightweight and cold-weather outdoor gear; kids sizes are available. There's a good range of travel wear for men and women.

RISE SHOPPING ARCADE

利時商場 *Clothing*

☎ 2363 0301; www.rise-hk.com; 5-11 Granville Circuit, Tsim Sha Tsui; noon-9pm; Ⓜ Tsim Sha Tsui (exit B2)
Bursting the seams of this minimall is cheap streetwear from Hong Kong, Korea and Japan, with a few quasi-hip brands chucked in for good measure. Patience and a good eye could land you purchases fit for a *Vogue* photo shoot.

STAR COMPUTER CITY

星光電腦城 *Computers*

☎ 2736 2608; 2nd fl, Star House, 3 Salisbury Rd, Tsim Sha Tsui; 10am or 10.30am-7.30pm or 8pm; Ⓜ Tsim Sha Tsui Star Ferry (Tsim Sha Tsui)
This is the largest complex of computer outlets in Tsim Sha Tsui, with two dozen shops selling laptops, personal organisers and Apple computers. It's not as cheap as the computer malls in Mongkok or New Kowloon, but it is better set up for international buyers.

SWINDON BOOK CO LTD

辰衝 *Books*

☎ 2366 8001; www.swindonbooks.com; 13-15 Lock Rd, Tsim Sha Tsui; 9am-6.30pm Mon-Thu, 9am-7.30pm Fri & Sat, 12.30-6.30pm Sun; Ⓜ Tsim Sha Tsui
This is one of the best 'real' (as opposed to 'supermarket') bookshops. Its sister store is Central's Hong Kong Book Centre (p48).

SHIPPING NEWS

Goods can be mailed home by post, and some shops will package and post the goods for you. It's a good idea to find out whether you will have to clear the goods through customs at the other end. If the goods are fragile, it's sensible to buy 'all risks' insurance. Smaller items can be shipped from the post office. **United Parcel Service** (UPS; ☎ 2735 3535) also offers services from Hong Kong to some 200 destinations. **DHL Express** (☎ 2400 3388), with outlets in many MTR stations, is another option.

WWW.IZZUE.COM

Clothing & Accessories

www.izzue.com; ☎ 2314 2556; LG64, Silvercord Centre, 30 Canton Rd, Tsim Sha Tsui; noon-10pm

You'll find simple, contemporary and comfortable styles, much like a slightly hipper Gap, in this chain of modish boutiques. There are almost two dozen outlets throughout the territory.

EAT

AQUA

Italian, Japanese $$$

☎ 3427 2288; www.aqua.com.hk; 29th fl, One Peking, 1 Peking Rd, Tsim Sha Tsui; noon-2.30pm & 6-11.30pm; M Tsim Sha Tsui

This ultraminimalist place, just below a fabulous bar called Aqua Spirit, has a split personality, made up of Aqua Roma and Aqua Tokyo. The food is fine, but the views are simply astonishing.

CHANG WON KOREAN RESTAURANT 莊園韓國料理

Korean $$

☎ 2368 4606; 1G Kimberley St; 11.30am-midnight; M Tsim Sha Tsui

If you're looking for truly authentic Korean food, head for this place, just one of several restaurants along a stretch that makes up Tsim Sha Tsui's 'Little Korea'. Try the excellent *bibimbab* (vegetables in sauce atop rice; $100).

DIN TAI FUNG *Shanghainese* $

☎ 2730 6928; www.dintaifung.com.tw; Shop 130, 3rd fl, 30 Canton Rd; 11.30am-10.30pm; M Tsim Sha Tsui (exit C1); V

The dumpling, noodle and other Shanghainese classics at this famous Taiwanese chain can be anyone's comfort food. There's always a line at the door and they don't take reservations; it's best to go in the afternoon.

FOOK LAM MOON 福臨門

Cantonese $$$

☎ 2366 0286; Shop 8, 1st fl, 53-59 Kimberley St; 11am-11pm; M Tsim Sha Tsui

Cheongsam-clad hostesses will guide you through the extensive, expensive and unusual menu – think shark's fin, frog, abalone. The pan-fried lobster balls are a house speciality. One of Hong Kong's top Cantonese restaurants.

GADDI'S *French* $$$

☎ 2315 3171; www.peninsula.com/Hong_Kong; 1st fl, the Peninsula, 19-21 Salisbury Road, Tsim Sha Tsui; noon-2.30pm & 7-10.30pm; M East Tsim Sha Tsui (exit L3)

Don't dismiss Gaddi's just because half a century ago it was the only thinkable place to celebrate a birthday if you were anyone at all.

The classical decor may be a tad stuffy and the live Filipino band gratuitous, but the food – traditional French with contemporary touches – is definitely still among the best in town.

GAYLORD 爵樂印度餐廳

Indian $$

☎ 2376 1001; 1st fl, Ashley Centre, 23-25 Ashley Rd, Tsim Sha Tsui; noon-3pm & 6-11pm; M Tsim Sha Tsui; V

The dim lighting and live Indian music set the scene for enjoying the excellent rogan josh, dhal and other favourite dishes at Hong Kong's oldest Indian restaurant, which has been operating since 1972. There are lots of vegetarian choices as well.

HOKAHOKA *Japanese* $$

☎ 2366 1784; 51-52 Houston Ctr, 63 Mody Rd, Tsim Sha Tsui East; set lunch from $58; M East Tsim Sha Tsui (exit P2)

At this deliciously low-key izakaya, you can make a meal of sake and all manner of nibbles, or feast on raw fish and grilled meat.

HUTONG 胡同

Northern Chinese $$$

☎ 3428 8342; 28th fl, One Peking, 1 Peking Rd, Tsim Sha Tsui; noon-3pm & 6pm-midnight; M Tsim Sha Tsui Star Ferry (Tsim Sha Tsui)

Strategically muted lighting and interiors just this side of kitsch lend Michelin-starred Hutong a dramatic air. Like the decor, the tasty contemporary dishes with northern leanings are a tad contrived, but never mind, the real jewel is outside the window – the Kowloon waterfront in all its majestic splendour.

SABATINI *Italian* $$$

☎ 2733 2000; 3rd fl, Royal Garden Hotel, 69 Mody Rd, Tsim Sha Tsui East; noon-2.30pm & 6-11pm; M Tsim Sha Tsui Tsim Sha Tsui East Ferry Pier 5, 8

Fine food and elegant surrounds (think frescoes and terracotta tiles) give Sabatini that classic Italian feel. Traditional offerings, such as fettuccine carbonara, are light in the best possible sense, leaving room to sample the exquisite desserts. The wine list is excellent but expensive.

SPRING DEER 鹿鳴春

Northern Chinese $

☎ 2366 4012; 1st fl, 42 Mody Rd, Tsim Sha Tsui; 11am-2.30pm & 6-10.30pm; M Tsim Sha Tsui (exit N2); V

Hong Kong's most famous Peking duck is served here and the roast lamb is impressive, but the service can be about as welcoming as a Beijing winter, c 1967. Spring Deer comes recommended by Michelin inspectors. Booking essential.

Enjoy an astonishing view of the skyline from the 29th floor at Aqua (p116)

SWEET DYNASTY 糖朝

Cantonese, Dessert $

☎ 2199 7799; 100 Canton Rd, Tsim Sha Tsui; 8pm-midnight Mon-Thurs, 8am-11pm Fri & Sat, 7.30am-11pm Sat, 7.30am-midnight Sun; M Tsim Sha Tsui (exit A1); V

This mini empire with locations in Shanghai, Taiwan and Japan has an ambitious menu featuring all dishes casual and Cantonese, but we think the desserts, noodles and congee win hands-down. The clean and modern Hong Kong shop is packed during peak hours.

SWISS CHALET *Swiss* $$

☎ 2191 9197; 12-14 Hart Av, Tsim Sha Tsui; noon-midnight Mon-Sat, 6pm-midnight Sun; M East Tsim Sha Tsui (N1);

At any time here you'll see half the tables vigorously dunking and swirling in a pot of fondue. The excellent cheese swamp comes in 13 varieties ($188 to $280); there is also a wide selection of solid meat dishes. A word of caution: drinking water with fondue can cause indigestion.

T'ANG COURT 唐閣

Cantonese $$$

☎ 2375 1133; http://hongkong.langhamhotels.com; Langham Hotel, 8 Peking Rd, Tsim Sha Tsui; 11am-2.30pm & 6-10.30pm Mon-Fri, noon-2.30pm & 6-10.30pm Sat & Sun; M East Tsim Sha Tsui (exit L4); V

As befitting a restaurant named after the greatest dynasty in China, T'ang Court has raised its speciality, Cantonese cooking, to an art. The atmosphere is plush and hushed, with deep-pile carpets and heavy silks, and the only noise you'll hear is that of yourself talking. If that seems too formal, rest assured, the polished service will make you feel right at home, like an emperor in his palace.

WOODLANDS

Vegetarian, Indian $

2369 3718; upper ground fl, 16 & 17 Wing On Plaza, 62 Mody Rd, Tsim Sha Tsui; meals $55-100; noon-3.30pm & 6.30-10.30pm; M East Tsim Sha Tsui (exit P1); V

A favourite of Tsim Sha Tsui's Indian community, Woodlands comes highly recommended for its excellent South Indian fare and modest charm. Dithering gluttons should order the thali meal, a metal tray with samplings of curries, rice and dessert.

WU KONG SHANGHAI RESTAURANT 滬江飯店

Shanghainese $$

2366 7244; www.wukong.com.hk; basement, Alpha House, 27-33 Nathan Rd, Tsim Sha Tsui; 11.30am-midnight; M Tsim Sha Tsui; V

The specialities at this Shanghainese restaurant – cold pigeon in wine sauce and crispy fried eels – are worth a trip across town. Dim sum is served all day.

YE SHANGHAI 夜上海

Shanghainese $$$

2376 3322; www.elite-concepts.com; 6th fl, Marco Polo Hotel, Harbour City, Canton Rd, Tsim Sha Tsui; 11.30am-3pm & 6-11pm; M East Tsim Sha Tsui (exit L4); V

At 'Shanghai nights', dark woods and subtle lighting inspired by 1920s Shanghai fill the air with romance. The modern culinary creations, which are lighter than traditional Shanghainese fare, are also exquisite. The only ripples on the silk screen are the Cantonese dim sum being served at lunch, though that too is wonderful.

DRINK

Kowloon generally has more of a local Chinese scene than Hong Kong Island. There are four basic clusters of bars in Tsim Sha Tsui: along Ashley Rd; within the Hanoi Rd, Prat Ave and Chatham Rd triangle; along Knutsford Tce, Kowloon's tame answer to Lan Kwai Fong; and most recently along Minden Ave behind the Holiday Inn. Further towards the east it's mainly hostess-bar territory.

BAR *Bar*

2315 3163; 1st fl, Peninsula Hotel Hong Kong, cnr Salisbury & Nathan Rds, Tsim Sha Tsui; 5pm-2am Mon-Wed, 5pm-3am Thu-Sun; M Tsim Sha Tsui (exit E) Star Ferry (Tsim Sha Tsui)

For mellow 1940s and '50s jazz,

take your smoking jacket along and sip cognac at the Peninsula's most stylish watering hole. Your fellow tipplers will be serious business types, coutured couples and new money trying to look old(er).

FELIX *Bar*

☎ 2315 3188; 28th fl, Peninsula Hotel Hong Kong, cnr Salisbury & Nathan Rds, Tsim Sha Tsui; 6pm-2am; M Tsim Sha Tsui (exit E) Star Ferry (Tsim Sha Tsui)

Enjoy the fabulous view at this Philippe Starck–designed bar connected to Felix restaurant, one of the swankiest dining rooms in Hong Kong's poshest hotel. Guys, brace yourselves for a dramatic view through the gents' urinals.

KING LUDWIG BEER HALL *German Bar*

☎ 2369 8328; www.kingparrot.com; 32 Salisbury Rd, Tsim Sha Tsui; noon-1am Sun-Thu, to 2am Fri & Sat; M East Tsim Sha Tsui (Exit J)

This busy place with antler lighting fixtures is popular with visiting Germans and others hankering after pork knuckle, sauerkraut and German beer on tap, including Maisel's Weiss. It's located just under Middle Road Children's Playground (p110).

A VERY CLOSE SHAVE

Among the oft-told tales about the hotel affectionately known as 'the Pen' is the one about the spy with the razor. After the capitulation of British forces in Hong Kong to the Japanese on Christmas Day 1941, it was learned that the manager of the hotel barbershop had been a Japanese spy (and naval commander to boot), taking advantage of the chatty, informal atmosphere of the surrounds to collect useful information about troop movements and so on.

PHONOGRAPH *Bar*

☎ 2730 6622; ground fl, 2 Austin Ave, Tsim Sha Tsui; 7pm-4am; M Tsim Sha Tsui (exit B2)

With dark, moody interiors opening onto postwar residences in a quiet corner of Tsim Sha Tsui, Phonograph is a breath of fresh air on Kowloon's bar scene. Indie musicians and artist types come here to lose themselves in the shadows and the eclectic music selection. If you don't see them at this location, they have probably moved to another spot in the neighbourhood. Call **Angel** (☎ 93500094) to find out the new address.

TAPAS BAR *Tapas Bar*

☎ 2733 8756; www.shangri-la.com/en/property/hongkong/kowloonshangrila; Lobby, Kowloon Shangri-la, 64 Mody Rd, Tsim Sha Tsui East; 3.30pm-1am; M East Tsim Sha Tsui (exit P1)

New World bottles, harbour views and an appetising tapas menu make this bar inside a hotel a great venue for some light drinking, people watching or, if you're into posing – a bit of that too.

PLAY

DADA *Live Music*

☎ 3763 8778; 2nd fl, Luxe Manor, 39 Kimberley Rd, Tsim Sha Tsui; 🕒 2.30pm-1am Sun-Wed, to 2am Thu-Sat; Ⓜ Tsim Sha Tsui (exit B1)

It may look a bit over the top (and naming yourself Dada is a convenient excuse for that), but this live music venue is surprisingly relaxing in an unconventional sort of way. Live 'jazz' Thursday, R&B Friday and Saturday.

HONG KONG CULTURAL CENTRE 香港文化中心

Concert Hall, Theatre

☎ 2734 2009; www.hkculturalcentre.gov.hk; 10 Salisbury Rd, Tsim Sha Tsui; tickets $100-500; Ⓜ Tsim Sha Tsui (exit E) ⛴ Star Ferry (Tsim Sha Tsui)

Clad in pink ceramic tiles and lacking a single window in one of the most dramatic spots on earth, this building's shell is an aesthetic stinker. However, inside you'll find Hong Kong's premier venue – with a 2000-seat concert hall with an impressive Rieger pipe organ, two theatres, rehearsal studios and a grand main lobby. It's home to the Hong Kong Philharmonic and the Hong Kong Chinese Orchestra, and major touring companies play here. There are daily **tours** (adult/child $10/5); phone ahead for bookings.

KHOOB SURAT

Indian Beauty Treatment

☎ 2367 7742; www.khoobsuratbeautyparlour.com; Shop 25, 1st fl, Mirador Mansion, 54-64B Nathan Road, Tsim Sha Tsui; 🕒 10.30am-7.30pm Mon-Sat; Ⓜ Tsim Sha Tsui (exit M2)

This Indian beauty parlour offering facials, waxing services, henna 'tattoos' and 'threading' has a hair removal 'happy hour' (2pm to 4pm, Monday to Saturday).

T'AI CHI *T'ai Chi*

☎ 2508 1234; www.discoverhongkong.com; Tsim Sha Tsui East Promenade; free; 🕒 8-9am Mon, Wed & Fri; Ⓜ Tsim Sha Tsui (exit J)

Let a spritely master show you how to 'Spread your wings like a stork' and 'Wave hands like clouds' against the views of Victoria Harbour in front of the Museum of Art. T'ai chi or shadow boxing is supposed to give you a sharper mind and a fitter heart. Pre-registration required (see the boxed text, p112).

VIBES *Live Music*

☎ 2315 5999; www.themirahotel.com; 5th fl, the Mira Hong Kong, 118 Nathan Road, Tsim Sha Tsui; 🕒 3pm-midnight; Ⓜ Tsim Sha Tsui (Exit B1)

A cross between Bali and Kowloon Park (p110), this al fresco bar comes with resident DJ, cabanas and tropical greenery. Try their 'molecular cocktails', which involve liberal uses of liquid nitrogen and foam.

>KOWLOON: YAU MA TEI & MONG KOK

Just north of Tsim Sha Tsui the narrow byways of Yau Ma Tei (yow-ma-day) – meaning place (*tei*) where fishermen waterproofed boats with oil (*yau*) and repaired hemp ropes (*ma*) – reward the explorer with a close-up look at a more traditional Hong Kong. The streets running east to west between Kansu St and Jordan Rd include Nanking St (mahjong shops and parlours), Ning Po St (paper kites and votives, such as houses, mobile phones and hell money, to burn for the dead) and Saigon St (herbalist shops, old-style tailors, pawnshops). On Shanghai St you'll find Chinese bridal and trousseau shops. Mong Kok (Prosperous Point) is one of Hong Kong's most congested working-class residential areas, as well as one of its busiest shopping districts. Traditionally the place locals came to buy everyday items, such as clothes, shoes, computer accessories and kitchen supplies, the area is rapidly getting a facelift.

YAU MA TEI & MONG KOK

SEE

- Chin Woo Athletic Association 1 C6
- Jade Market 2 B5
- Temple Street Night Market 3 B4
- Temple Street Night Market 4 B5
- Tin Hau Temple 5 C5
- Tung Choi St (Ladies') Market 6 C3
- Wholesale Fruit Market 7 B4
- Yuen Po St Bird Garden & Flower Market 8 C1

SHOP

- Bruce Lee Club 9 C4
- Protrek 10 C4
- Sino Centre 11 B3
- Tak Hing Dried Seafood 12 C5
- Yue Hwa Chinese Products Emporium ..13 C6

EAT

- Good Hope Noodle 14 B2
- Kubrick Bookshop Café 15 B5
- Mido 16 B5
- Tim Ho Wan 17 C3

PLAY

- Broadway Cinematheque 18 B4

A
B
C
D
Boundary St
Boundary Street Recreation Ground
Mong Kok Stadium
Embankment Rd
Sycamore St
Lai Chi Kok Rd
Cedar St
Portland St
Playing Field Rd
Flower Market Rd
Prince Edward
Prince Edward Rd West
Yuen Po St
Tung Chau St
Queen Elizabeth School
Royal Plaza Hotel
Bedford Rd
Nullah Rd
Arran St
Sai Yeung Choi St South
Tung Choi St
Fa Yuen St
Sai Yee St
Luen Wan St
Fuk Tsun St
Bute St
MTR Tsuen Wan Line
Mong Kok East (MTR East Station)
MONG KOK
Kadoorie Av
Ivy St
Mong Kok Rd
Argyle St
Anchor St
Fife St
Man Fuk Rd
Anchor St Park
Soares Ave
Victory Ave
MA TAU WAI
Mong Kok
Waterloo Rd
Peace Ave
West Kowloon Corridor
Macpherson Playground
Yim Po Fong St
Nelson St
Nathan Rd
Shantung St
OLYMPIC CITY
Reclamation St
Shanghai St
Canton Rd
Soy St
Oi Sen Path
PARK AVENUE
Kwong Wa St
Princess Margaret Rd
Dundas St
Hoi Wang Rd
HOI FU COURT
Kwong Wah Hospital
HO MAN TIN
Wah Yan College
Ferry St
Tung On St
Hamilton St
Wylie Rd
Chung Hau St
Pitt St
Yau Ma Tei
YAU MA TEI
Lai Cheung Rd
Shek Lung St
King's Park
Tung Kun St
Man Ming La
Arthur St
Hi Lung La
King's Park Rise
Ching Ping St
Wing Sing La
Public Square St
Market St
Queen Elizabeth Hospital
Hoi Wang Rd
Kansu St
Gascoigne Rd
Man Cheong St
Pak Hoi St
Shanghai St
Temple St
Woo Sung St
Saigon St
King's Park Sports Ground
Man Yuen St
Man Wui St
Lin Cheung Rd
Wai Ching St
Battery St
Ning Po St
Chi Wo St
Cheong Lok St
Nanking St
Jordan Rd
Jordan Path
Jordan
Bowring St
Woosung St
Parkes St
Pilkem St
Tak Shing St
Kowloon Cricket Club Ground
Chatham Rd South
Austin Rd
0 400 m
0 0.2 miles

SEE

CHIN WOO ATHLETIC ASSOCIATION 精武體育會

☎ 2384 3238; Flat B & C, 13th fl, Wah Fung Bldg, 300 Nathan Rd, Yau Ma Tei; 🕑 2.30-9pm; Ⓜ Jordan (exit B1)
This is an 88-year-old branch of Chin Woo Athletic Association, founded 100 years ago in Shanghai by the famed kungfu master Huo Yuanjia. The Shanghai Chin Woo was featured in Bruce Lee's *Fist of Fury* and Jet Li's *Fearless*.

JADE MARKET 玉器市場

Kansu & Battery Sts, Yau Ma Tei; admission free; 🕑 10am-6pm; Ⓜ Yau Ma Tei (exit C), Jordan (exit A) 🚌 9
The jade knick-knacks, including Buddha charm necklaces and delicately carved zodiac animals, on sale at this market make great mementos and presents. The market is split into two parts by the loop formed by Battery St and has hundreds of stalls. Unless you really know your nephrite from your jadeite, though, it's not wise to buy expensive pieces here.

SHANGHAI ST 上海街

Ⓜ Yau Ma Tei (exit C)
Once Kowloon's main drag, Shanghai St is lined with stores selling Chinese wedding gowns, sandlewood incense, kitchenware, herbal medicine, Buddhist provisions, a pawn shop (at the junction with Saigon St) and mahjong companies where only the seasoned dare to tread.

TEMPLE ST NIGHT MARKET 廟街夜市

Temple St, Yau Ma Tei; admission free; 🕑 4pm-midnight; Ⓜ Jordan (exit C2), Yau Ma Tei (exit C)
Temple St, which extends from Man Ming Lane in the north to Nanking St in the south and is cut in two by the Tin Hau temple complex, is the place to go for cheap clothes, *dai pai dong* (open-air street stalls) food, Chinese memorabilia, watches, pirate CDs and DVDs, fake labels, footwear, cookware and everyday items. Any marked prices should be considered mere suggestions – this is definitely a place to bargain. It's

A CONSUMER HEAVEN IN HELL

In the more old-fashioned streets of Kowloon and Sheung Wan, you'll find clusters of shops selling paper votive offerings that are burned for the dead. The most popular are Hell bank notes, handy currency for the departed, but you can also buy them other little things to make eternity that bit more comfortable: paper Big Mac meals, cameras, Rolexes and, of course, that Hong Kong essential item, the mobile phone.

Find trinkets and talismans at the Jade Market

also a place to catch some entertainment (p25).

TIN HAU TEMPLE 天后廟

☎ 2332 9240; cnr Public Square St & Nathan Rd, Yau Ma Tei; admission free; 8am-5pm; M Yau Ma Tei (exit C)
A couple of blocks northeast of the Jade Market (left) is this temple, dedicated to Tin Hau, the goddess of seafarers. You'll find a row of fortune tellers, some of whom speak English, if you head through the last doorway on the right from the main entrance on Public Square St. To buy and light one of the incense spirals you see hanging from the ceiling (they last 10 days) costs a mere $130.

TUNG CHOI ST (LADIES') MARKET 通菜街(女人街)

Tung Choi St, Mong Kok; admission free; noon-10.30pm; M Mong Kok (exit D3)
Also known as Ladies' Market, the Tung Choi St market is a cheek-by-jowl affair offering cheap clothes and trinkets. Vendors start setting up their stalls as early as noon, but it's best to get here between 1pm and 6pm when there's much more on offer. Beware, the sizes stocked here tend to suit the lissom Asian frame. See also p25.

WHOLESALE FRUIT MARKET 油麻地果欄

Cnr Shek Lung St & Reclamation Sts; 2-6am; M Yau Ma Tei (exit D)
When the rest of the city is asleep, this listed historic market (1913) comes alive with trucks offloading fresh fruit, wholesalers and vendors barking out prices and bare-backed workers manoeuvring mountains of boxes in front of two-storey brick-and-stone buildings wielding pre-WWII signboards.

YUEN PO ST BIRD GARDEN & FLOWER MARKET 園圃街雀鳥花園及花墟

Yuen Po St, Mong Kok; admission free; 7am-8pm; M Prince Edward (exit B1) Mong Kok MTR East Rail 1, 1A, 2C, 12A

Kubrick Bookshop Café (p128) in Yau Ma Tei devotes its shelf space to all things film-related

There are hundreds of birds for sale at Yuen Po St Bird Garden, between Boundary St and Flower Market Rd, along with elaborate teak and bamboo birdcages (see boxed text, p127). If you carry on walking south along Yuen Po St, you'll reach the daily flower market, where some 50 florists sell blooms and plants. To see the flower market at its busiest, head there after 10am, especially on Sunday.

SHOP

Streets specialising in just one or two types of goods abound in Mong Kok and Yau Ma Tei. Fife St, for example, has an amazing collection of stalls selling old vinyl, books, ceramics, machinery and music scores. The northern end of Tung Choi St, on the other hand, is awash in shops selling goldfish (useful for soaking up bad feng shui) and bicycles. The street markets in Yau Ma Tei and Mong Kok also have the cheapest clothes in town.

BRUCE LEE CLUB 李小龍會

Kungfu Memorabilia

☎ 2771 7093; www.bruceleeclub.com; Shop 160-161, In's Point, 530 Nathan Road; 1-9pm; M Yau Ma Tei (exit A1)

Founded by Bruce Lee's fans, this mini-museum–souvenir-shop has action figures, film publications and other memorabilia related to the kungfu icon.

PROTREK *Outdoor Gear*

www.protrek.com.hk; 522 Nathan Rd, Yau Ma Tei; noon-8pm Mon-Sat, 11.30am-9.30pm; M Yau Ma Tei (exit C)

This reliable shop with branches all over town is arguably your best bet for outdoor gear that will see you through from sea to summit. They run training courses on outdoor activities as well. The English-speaking staff are very helpful.

SINO CENTRE 信和中心 *Mall*

582-592 Nathan Road, Mong Kok; M Yau Ma Tei (exit A2)

This shabby mall in the heart of Mong Kok will give you a taste of local youth culture, with its shops selling CDs (new and used), magazines, comics, action figures, computer games and other kidult bait. There are also fly-by-night bootleg DVD vendors.

SINGING FOR LUCK

The Chinese have long favoured songbirds as pets, and a bird's singing prowess will often determine its price. Some species of birds are also considered harbingers of good fortune, which is why you'll sometimes see them being taken to the races. Enthusiasts gathering at Yuen Po St Bird Garden (p125) in Mong Kok can often be seen feeding their caged prizes grasshoppers and other juicy insect treats through the bars of the cages with chopsticks.

TAK HING DRIED SEAFOOD 德興海味 *Dried Seafood*

☎ 2780 2129; 1 Woosung St, Yau Ma Tei; 9am-7.30pm; M Yau Ma Tei (exit C)

One of very few honest dried seafood stores, this delightful corner establishment has glass jars stuffed with dried scallops, crocodile meat, bird's nest and oysters, though you might prefer their figs, cashews, candied lotus seeds and ginseng.

YUE HWA CHINESE PRODUCTS EMPORIUM 裕華國貨 *Department Store*

☎ 3511 2222; www.yuehwa.com; 301-309 Nathan Rd, Yau Ma Tei; 10am-10pm; M Jordan

This cavernous place offers pretty much everything that a visiting souvenir hunter could ask for – seven packed floors of ceramics, furniture, souvenirs and clothing, as well as bolts of silk, herbs, clothes, porcelain, luggage, umbrellas and kitchenware. It's the biggest and best of some 18 branches of Yue Hwa across Hong Kong.

Catch an art-house flick at the Broadway Cinematheque

EAT

GOOD HOPE NOODLE

好旺角粥麵家 *Noodle Bar* $

☎ 2394 5967; 146 Sai Yeung Choi St South, Mong Kok; 🕒 11am-3am; Ⓜ Mong Kok

This busy noodle stop is known far and wide for its terrific wonton soups and shredded pork noodles with spicy bean sauce. It's an eat-and-go sort of place, so don't come here if you feel like lingering.

KUBRICK BOOKSHOP CAFÉ

Café $

☎ 2384 5465; Shop H2, Prosperous Garden, 3 Public Square St, Yau Ma Tei; 🕒 11.30am-10pm; Ⓜ Yau Ma Tei

This café and bookshop next to the Broadway Cinematheque (p129) has a great range of film-related books, magazines and paraphernalia, and serves good coffee and decent pre-flick food, such as sandwiches ($33 to $42) and pasta dishes ($35 to $45).

MIDO 美都餐室

Hong Kong Fast Food $

☎ 2384 6402; 63 Temple St, Yau Ma Tei; 🕒 7.30am-10pm; Ⓜ Yau Ma Tei

This ultimate version of a *cha chan tang*, a uniquely Hong Kong café with local dishes, in a 1950s building opposite the Tin Hau Temple (p125) serves meals throughout the day, but it's best to come at breakfast ($15 to $30) or in the afternoon for such oddities as *yuan yang* (equal parts coffee and black tea with milk), *ling lok* (boiled cola with lemon and ginger) and toast smeared with condensed milk. See also p25.

TIM HO WAN 添好運

Dim Sum $

2332 2896; Shop 8, 2-20 Kwong Wa St, Mong Kok; meals $30-50; 10am-9.15pm

A former Four Seasons dim-sum chef recreates his magic in the world's cheapest Michelin-starred eatery. Get a ticket when you arrive and check back after an hour.

PLAY

BROADWAY CINEMATHEQUE

百老匯電影中心 *Cinema*

☎ 2388 3188; www.cinema.com.hk; Ground fl, Prosperous Garden, 3 Public Square St, Yau Ma Tei; tickets $32-55; Ⓜ Yau Ma Tei

Yau Ma Tei may seem like an unlikely place for an alternative cinema, but it's worth checking out for new art-house releases and re-runs here. The Kubrick Bookshop Café (opposite) next door serves good coffee and light bites.

>KOWLOON: NEW KOWLOON

Before high-rises give way to mountains and scrub, you'll find the so-called New Kowloon (no one in town uses this purely administrative phrase). A sprawling conurbation and a slice of unvarnished Hong Kong urban living, it's not a beautiful part of town and lacks the glamour of the central districts, with the exception of Kowloon Tong, which is home to much 'old money' and some of the city's best schools and most expensive residences. But there are some worthwhile places of interest worth seeking out in New Kowloon, including a serenely beautiful nunnery and the most vibrant temple in Hong Kong. Most places of interest lie along the MTR stations of (from west to east) Sham Shui Po, Kowloon Tong, Lok Fu, Wong Tai Sin and Diamond Hill.

NEW KOWLOON

SEE

Cattle Depot Artist Village 1 D4
Chi Lin Nunnery 2 F2
Jockey Club Creative Arts Centre 3 A3
Kowloon Walled City Park 4 D3
Sik Sik Yuen Wong Tai Sin Temple 5 D2

SHOP

Ap Liu St Flea Market 6 A3
Golden Computer Arcade 7 A3

EAT

Cheong Fat 8 D3
Golden Orchid Thai Restaurant 9 D3

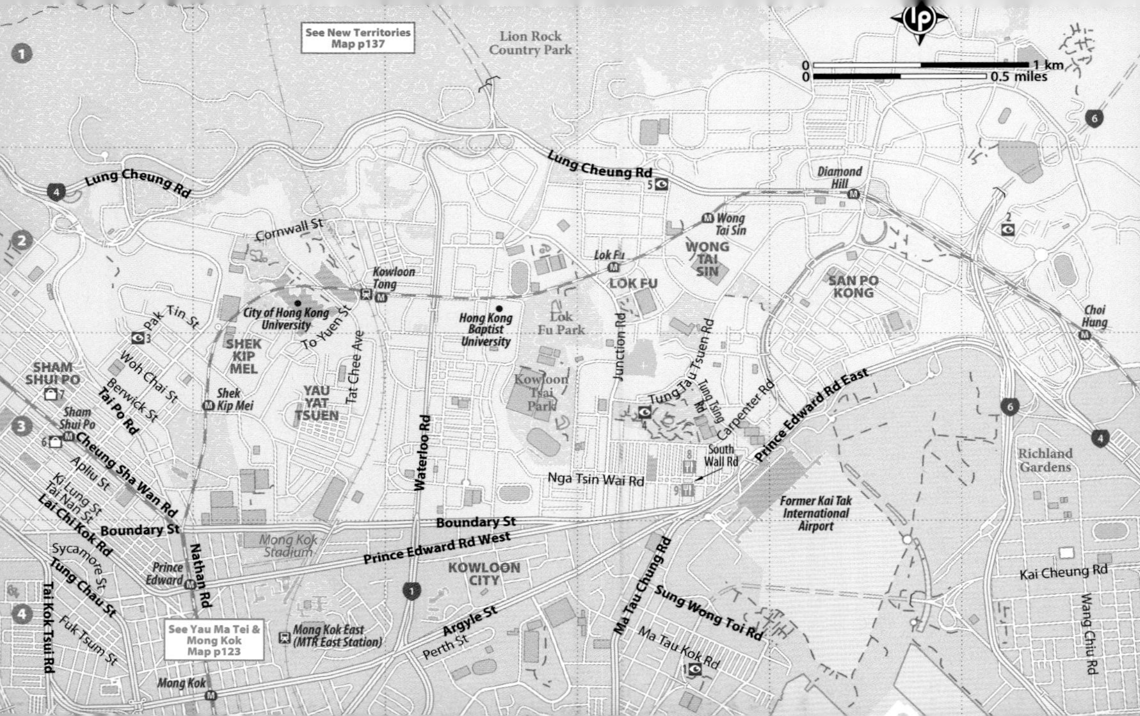

See New Territories Map p137
Lion Rock Country Park
0 1 km
0 0.5 miles
Lung Cheung Rd
Lung Cheung Rd
Diamond Hill
Wong Tai Sin
WONG TAI SIN
Lok Fu
LOK FU
SAN PO KONG
Choi Hung
Cornwall St
Kowloon Tong
City of Hong Kong University
Hong Kong Baptist University
Lok Fu Park
Junction Rd
Tung Tau Tsuen Rd
Tung Tsing Rd
Carpenter Rd
Prince Edward Rd East
Pak Tin St
To Yuen St
Tat Chee Ave
SHEK KIP MEI
YAU YAT TSUEN
Kowloon Tsai Park
SHAM SHUI PO
Woh Chai St
Berwick St
Tai Po Rd
Shek Kip Mei
Sham Shui Po
Cheung Sha Wan Rd
Apliu St
Ki Lung St
Tai Nan St
Lai Chi Kok Rd
Boundary St
Waterloo Rd
South Wall Rd
Nga Tsin Wai Rd
Richland Gardens
Former Kai Tak International Airport
Boundary St
Mong Kok Stadium
Prince Edward Rd West
KOWLOON CITY
Sycamore St
Tung Chau St
Prince Edward
Nathan Rd
Kai Cheung Rd
Tai Kok Tsui Rd
Fuk Tsum St
See Yau Ma Tei & Mong Kok Map p123
Mong Kok East (MTR East Station)
Argyle St
Perth St
Ma Tau Chung Rd
Sung Wong Toi Rd
Ma Tau Kok Rd
Wang Chiu Rd
Mong Kok

SEE

CHI LIN NUNNERY

志蓮淨苑

☎ 2354 1888; 5 Chi Lin Dr, Diamond Hill; admission free; nunnery 9am-4.30pm, garden 6.30am-7pm; M Diamond Hill (exit C2, then 5min walk along Fung Tak Rd)

This Tang-style wooden complex, built in 1998 without a single nail, is a serene place with lotus ponds, bonsai, and silent nuns delivering offerings to Buddha and arhats (Buddhist disciples freed from the cycle of birth and death). Designed to show the harmony of humans with nature, the complex is a visual, architectural and spiritual balm amid the severe high-rises nearby.

KOWLOON WALLED CITY PARK

九龍寨城公園

☎ 2716 9962; www.lcsd.gov.hk/parks/kwcp/en; Tung Tsing Rd, Kowloon City; admission free; 6.30am-11pm; M Lok Fu (exit B, then 15min walk south on Junction & Tung Tau Tsuen Rds) 1, 10, 113

The walls that enclose this beautiful park were once the perimeter of a notorious village that technically remained part of China throughout British rule. The enclave was known for its vice, prostitution, gambling and –

Chi Lin Nunnery makes a striking contrast to the city's skyscrapers

HONG KONG'S OWN BLOSSOM

The flower on Hong Kong's flag is the *Bauhinia blakeana*, also called the Hong Kong orchid. This species of bauhinia exists nowhere else. From early November to March you may see the purple blossoms on bauhinia trees, a species unique to the territory, in Victoria Park (p92), Kowloon Walled City Park (opposite) or outside the Foreign Correspondent Club (Map p55, D4) in Central.

worst of all – illegal dentists. In 1984 the Hong Kong government acquired the area, rehoused the residents, bulldozed the tenements and replaced them with pavilions, ponds, turtles, goldfish and exquisite flora in this attractive park.

SIK SIK YUEN WONG TAI SIN TEMPLE

嗇色園黃大仙祠

☎ 2854 4333; www.siksikyuen.org.hk; Lung Cheung Rd, Wong Tai Sin; donation requested; 7am-5.30pm; M Wong Tai Sin (exit B2)

A sensory whirl of colourful pillars, roofs, lattice work, flowers and incense, this busy and hugely atmospheric temple is a destination for all walks of Hong Kong society, from pensioners to businessmen, parents and young professionals. Some come simply to pray, others to divine the future with *chim*, bamboo 'fortune sticks' that are shaken out of a box on to the ground and then read by a fortune teller (they're available for free to the left of the main temple). For more see the boxed text, p139, and p20.

SHOP

AP LIU ST FLEA MARKET 鴨寮街 *Electronics*

Ap Liu St, Sham Shui Po; noon-midnight; M Sham Shui Po (exit A2)

This street has vendors of every electronic/electrical appliance imaginable (new and used), from cameras to satellite dishes. It's very local.

WORTH THE TRIP

Many of Hong Kong's artist communes are housed in interesting locations, making them worth a visit even though many of their tenants' studios are closed during the day. Red-bricked **Cattle Depot Artist Village** (63 Ma Tau Kok Rd, To Kwa Wan; 106, 12A & 5C) is a disused century-old slaughterhouse. Former factory premises **Jockey Club Creative Arts Centre** (JCCAC; www.jccac.org.hk; 30 Pak Tin St, Shek Kip Mei) contains artists' studios, exhibition space and shops (see p94). **Fotan Art Studios** (www.fotanian.com) features breezy lofts in vacated industrial buildings. Check their websites for special events and open days.

Head to Kowloon Walled City Park (p132) to enjoy some tranquillity away from the city's hectic centre

GOLDEN COMPUTER ARCADE 黃金電腦商場

Computers

Basement & 1st fl, 146-152 Fuk Wa St, Sham Shui Po; M Sham Shui Po (exit D2)

The cramped stalls inside are pretty much the cheapest places in Hong Kong for computers and components as well as cheap software and accessories, such as keyboards, ink cartridges, CDs and DVDs. Most shops open daily from 10am to 10pm but some don't open until noon. It's packed at weekends.

EAT

The neighbourhood of Kowloon City is Hong Kong's Thai quarter, and it's worth a journey if you're looking for a *tom yum* (Thai hot and sour soup) or green-curry fix. The surrounding neighbourhood is packed with herbalists, jewellers, tea merchants and bird shops; it's worth having a postprandial meander to take a look.

CHEONG FAT 昌發 *Thai* $

☎ 2382 5998; 27 South Wall Rd, Kowloon City; 11.30am-11.30pm; M Kowloon Tong (exit B2), minibus 25M; V

Cheong Fat serves tasty if thirst-inducing Chiang Mai noodles, salads, pork knuckle stew, chicken curry, skewers and grilled fish.

GOLDEN ORCHID THAI RESTAURANT 金蘭花 *Thai* $

☎ 2383 3076; 12 Lung Kong Rd, Kowloon City; noon-midnight; 5C, 101

This eatery has spill-over rooms for when its restaurant fills up.

>NEW TERRITORIES

Along with Lantau, the New Territories contains the rural and wild places of Hong Kong. Given the very close proximity of seven million people, that might sound like an odd claim, but you really can get away from the city in the New Territories (so called because the land was leased to Britain in 1898, half a century after Hong Kong Island and Kowloon). Extensive country parks, including the spectacular and unspoiled Sai Kung Peninsula, are not the only appeal of the sprawling area bordering China proper. A world-class museum, one of Hong Kong's most interesting monasteries and a new wetland centre are among the other worthwhile attractions in this diverse chunk of Hong Kong. Getting to and around the New Territories is easy. The area is well served by the main east and west rail lines, light rail services in the west and a regular and reliable bus network. Taxis are plentiful and catching one from the main towns and stations to go the last kilometre or so to a place of interest is a worthwhile and relatively inexpensive investment.

NEW TERRITORIES

SEE

Hong Kong Heritage Museum 1 D3
Hong Kong Wetland Park 2 B2
Ping Shan Heritage Trail 3 B2
Sai Kung 4 E3

EAT

Chuen Kee Seafood Restaurant ....(see 4)
Dah Wing Wah 5 B2
Sha Tin 18 ....6 D2

SHENZHEN SPECIAL ECONOMIC ZONE (SEZ)
SHENZHEN
0 5 km
0 3 miles
Lo Wu
Lok Ma Chau
Lok Ma Chau Spur Line
Sheung Shui
Fanling
Mai Po Marsh & Nature Reserve
Long Ping
Tin Shui Wai
Lam Tseun North Country Park
NEW TERRITORIES
Lam Tsuen River
Kam Sheung Rd
Siu Hong
Tuen Mun
Castle Peak
Tai Lam Country Park
Tai Lam Tunnel
Tai Mo Shan Country Park
Tai Lam Chung Reservoir
Tai Mo Shan
Shing Mun Country Park
Shing Mun Reservoir
Tsuen Wan West
Shing Mun Tunnel
Kam Shan Country Park
Tsing Yi
Mei Foo
Nam Chung Reservoir
Hok Tan Reservoir
Hok Tau Reservoir
Pat Sin Leng Country Park
Wong Leng Shan
Plover Cove Country Park
Plover Cove Reservoir
Kat O Hoi
Yan Chau Tong
Double Island
Crescent Island
Kat O & Port Island Country Parks
Tai Pang Wan (Mirs Bay)
Port Island
Tap Mun Chau
Hoi Ha Wan Marine Park
Chek Chau Hau (Middle Channel)
Tai Tan Hoi Hap
Tolo Channel
Ma Shi Chau Protected Area
Tai Po Market
Tolo Harbour
Tai Po Kau Nature Reserve
University
Racecourse
Fo Tan
Wu Kai Sha
Ma On Shan
Sai Kung West Country Park
Sai Kung Peninsula
Sai Kung East Country Park
Tai Long Wan
Pak Tam Chung
High Island Reservoir
Ma On Shan Country Park
Sha Tin
Tai Wei
Tate's Cairn Tunnel
Buffalo Hill
Lion Rock Country Park
Lion Rock Tunnel
MacLehose Trail
Kowloon Tong
Kowloon Peak
Tseung Kwan O Tunnel
KWUN TONG
Hung Hom
Victoria Harbour
Habe Haven
Kiu Tsui Chau
Kau Sai Chau
Leung Sheun Wan
Port Shelter
Shelter Island
Tiu Chung Chau
See Chau
Wong Nai Chau
Kong Tau Pai
Lang Ha Wan
Bluff Island
Basalt Island
High Junk Peak
Clearwater Bay Country Park
Clearwater Bay
Junk Bay
Tin Ha Shan
Joss House Bay
Big Wave Bay
Tung Lung Chau
SOUTH CHINA SEA
Chek Lap Kok
AsiaWorld-Expo
Airport
Hong Kong International Airport
East Brother
West Brother
Sunny Bay
Ma Wan
Disneyland Resort
Discovery Bay Tunnel
Tai Pak Wan (Discovery Bay)
Tung Chung
LANTAU
NGONG PING
Cable Car
Siu Kau Yi Chau
Kau Yi Chau
Sunset Peak
Lantau South Country Park
Lantau Peak
Silvermine Bay
Cha Kung To
Hei Ling Chau
Chi Ma Wan Peninsula
West Lamma Channel
Victoria Peak
Aberdeen Tunnel
HONG KONG ISLAND
Ap Lei Chau

NEIGHBOURHOODS NEW TERRITORIES

SEE

HONG KONG HERITAGE MUSEUM 香港文化博物館

2180 8188; www.heritagemuseum.gov.hk; 1 Man Lam Rd, Sha Tin; adult/child $10/5, free Wed; 10am-6pm Mon & Wed-Sat, 10am-7pm Sun; Sha Tin MTR East Rail, then 10min walk west & south along Tai Po & Lion Rock Tunnel Rds

This award-winning, three-storey purpose-built innovator features magnificent displays on Cantonese opera and the cultural heritage of the New Territories, the inspiring Children's Discovery Gallery (which has learning and play zones), the art collection of one Dr TT Tsui and, from time to time, the wonderful works of Hong Kong's little-known but excellent photographers.

HONG KONG WETLAND PARK 香港濕地公園

3152 2666, 2708 8885; www.wetlandpark.com; Wetland Park Rd, Tin Shui Wai; adult/child $30/15; 10am-5pm Wed-Mon; MTR West Rail to Tin Shui Wai then Light Rail 705 or 706, 967

This 61-hectare park in Tin Shui Wai, north of Tuen Mun, focuses on the wetland ecosystems and biodiversity of the northwest New Territories. It's a wonderful place to spend an entertaining (and educational) morning or afternoon. Bus 967 from the Admiralty MTR bus station on Hong Kong Island also serves the park.

One of Hong Kong Wetland Park's four boardwalks

PING SHAN HERITAGE TRAIL 屏山文物徑

Kam Tin, Yuen Long; M West Rail Tin Shui Wai station (exit E)

Hong Kong's first ever heritage trail features historic buildings belonging to the Tangs, the first and the most powerful of the 'Five Clans' (see p16). Highlights of the 1km trail include Hong Kong's oldest **pagoda** (9am-1pm & 2-5pm Wed-Mon), a magnificent **ancestral hall** (9am-1pm & 2-5pm), a temple, a study hall, a well and a **gallery** (10am-5pm Tue-Sun) inside an old police station that was built by the British as much to monitor the coastline as to keep an eye on the clan. Cross Tsui Sing Rd from the ground floor of the MTR station and you'll see the pagoda. Set aside two hours for the trail.

SAI KUNG 西貢

M Choi Hung, then minibus 1A or 1M, 92, Sha Tin MTR East Rail, then bus 299

Apart from the Outlying Islands, the Sai Kung Peninsula is one of the last havens left in Hong Kong for hikers, swimmers and boaters, and most of it is one huge 7500-hectare country park. A short journey to any of the islands off Sai Kung town is rewarding. Hidden away are some excellent beaches that can be visited by *kaido* (small boats), which depart from the waterfront. The **MacLehose Trail**, a 100km route across the New Territories, begins at Pak Tam Chung on the Sai Kung Peninsula. On top of this, Sai Kung town boasts excellent Chinese seafood restaurants, especially along the attractive waterfront.

STICKY FORTUNES

One of the most popular methods of divination in Hong Kong is with the *chim* (fortune sticks), found at temples. The sticks are shaken out of a box on to the ground; each bears a numeral corresponding to a printed slip of paper held by the temple guardian. The paper should be taken to the temple's fortune teller, who can interpret its particular meaning for you.

EAT

CHUEN KEE SEAFOOD RESTAURANT 全記海鮮菜館

Cantonese $$

2792 6938; 87-89 Man Nin St, Sai Kung; 7am-11pm; M Sha Tin, 299;

At Michelin-lauded Chuen Kee you can pick your meal from the tanks of live seafood, agree on a price, and they'll steam, fry or blanch it for you.

DAH WING WAH 大榮華酒樓

Walled Village $

2476 9888; 2nd fl, Koon Wong Mansion, 2-6 On Ning Rd, Yuen Long; 6am-midnight; 968 or N968 from Tin Hau terminus

This famous oldie (c 1950) specialises in walled-village dishes (see p16) such as lemon-steamed mullet and smoked oysters. Cantonese dim sum is served throughout the day.

SHA TIN 18 沙田18

Northern Chinese $$$

3723 7932; www.hongkong.shatin.hyatt.com; Hyatt Regency Hong Kong, 18 Chak Cheung St, Sha Tin; 11.30am-3pm & 5.30-10.30pm; M East Rail University station; V

Lovely desserts and delectable views accompany Hong Kong's best Peking duck (24-hour advance booking required).

>OUTLYING ISLANDS

Even if you're here for only a few days, try to make some time to see one or two of the islands. They offer a greener, slower-paced, less built-up side of Hong Kong compared to the teeming city centre. The largest, Lantau, is almost twice the size of Hong Kong Island, yet it is sparsely populated, offering great areas of wilderness, tranquil monasteries and long stretches of empty beach. Cheung Chau's winding streets afford an insight into a more traditional, low-rise way of life, while the car-free tracks of leafy Lamma lead to seafood restaurants and dramatic views from the ridge of its rocky spine. The islands listed here are all easily accessible from Hong Kong Island daily, and Cheung Chau and Lantau can be reached from Kowloon at the weekend as well.

OUTLYING ISLANDS

SEE

Cheung Chau 1 D3
Cheung Po Tsai Cave 2 D4
Hong Kong Disneyland....3 E1
Kwun Yam Wan (Afternoon) Beach 4 D4
Lamma 5 F4
Lantau Trailhead 6 C2
Lantau Trailhead 7 B3
Ngong Ping Skyrail ......(see 8)
Ngong Ping Village 8 B3
Pak Tai Temple 9 D4
Po Lin Monastery ....(see 8)
Tai O 10 A3
Tian Tan Buddha ....(see 8)

SHOP

Citygate Outlets 11 C2

EAT

Bookworm Café 12 F3
Po Lin Vegetarian Restaurant ....(see 8)
Rainbow Seafood Restaurant 13 F4
Windsurfing Watersports Centre & Cafe 14 D4

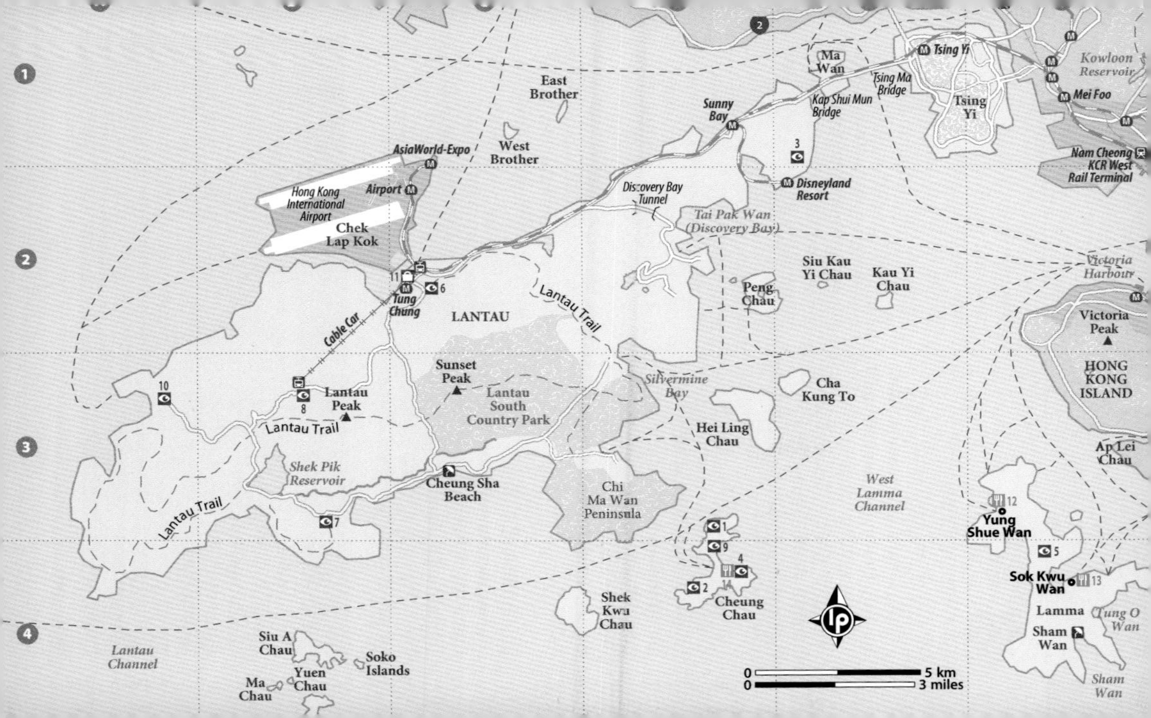

East Brother
West Brother
AsiaWorld-Expo
Airport
Hong Kong International Airport
Chek Lap Kok
Tung Chung
LANTAU
Cable Car
Lantau Trail
Lantau Peak
Sunset Peak
Lantau South Country Park
Shek Pik Reservoir
Cheung Sha Beach
Chi Ma Wan Peninsula
Sunny Bay
Discovery Bay Tunnel
Tai Pak Wan (Discovery Bay)
Ma Wan
Kap Shui Mun Bridge
Tsing Ma Bridge
Tsing Yi
Disneyland Resort
Kowloon Reservoir
Mei Foo
Nam Cheong KCR West Rail Terminal
Siu Kau Yi Chau
Kau Yi Chau
Peng Chau
Victoria Harbour
Victoria Peak
HONG KONG ISLAND
Silvermine Bay
Cha Kung To
Hei Ling Chau
Ap Lei Chau
West Lamma Channel
Yung Shue Wan
Sok Kwu Wan
Lamma
Tung O Wan
Sham Wan
Cheung Chau
Shek Kwu Chau
Siu A Chau
Soko Islands
Yuen Chau
Ma Chau
Lantau Channel
0 5 km
0 3 miles

SEE

CHEUNG CHAU 長洲

Cheung Chau from Central (pier 5, Outlying Islands ferry terminal) or Tsim Sha Tsui (Star Ferry Pier, weekends only)

The houseboats bobbing up and down Cheung Chau's busy harbour are one attraction here, but make sure you also see **Pak Tai Temple** (2981 0663; Pak She Fourth Lane; admission free; 9am-5pm), site of the colourful Bun Festival (see below) in May, swim at **Kwun Yam Wan (Afternoon) Beach** (which is also popular with windsurfers) and visit **Cheung Po Tsai Cave** in the southwest corner, which was an old pirate hideout.

LAMMA 南丫島

Yung Shue Wan or Sok Kwu Wan from Central (pier 4, Outlying Islands ferry terminal) or Aberdeen

The third-largest island after Lantau and Hong Kong, Lamma is known for its lively pubs, seafood restaurants, beaches and hikes. The laid-back lifestyle, strong feeling of community and relatively low rental costs make it a popular place with expats. Climbing the steep trails along the rocky spine of Lamma above Yung Shue Wan affords great views of the shipping lanes. An easier way to see a good portion of the island is to follow the 4km-long Family Trail between the two main villages, Yung Shue Wan and Sok Kwu Wan, which takes a little over an hour.

LANTAU 大嶼山

Mui Wo from Central (pier 6, Outlying Islands ferry terminal) or Tsim Sha Tsui (Star Ferry Pier, weekends only)

More than half of Lantau's surface area is designated country parkland, and there are several superb mountain trails, including the 70km **Lantau Trail**, which passes over Lantau Peak (957m). There

BUN FIGHTS

If you're here in May, make for the bun towers built near Pak Tai Temple (above), an iconic part of the colourful eight-day Cheung Chau Bun Festival. The towers are formed from bamboo scaffolding up to 20m high and covered with sacred rolls. Formerly, people would scramble up the towers on the designated day to grab one of the buns for good luck, but the practice stopped after a fatal accident in 1978. The tower-climbing event has been resurrected as a race with extra safety precautions. On the third day of the festival (a Sunday), there's a lively procession of floats, stilt walkers and colourfully dressed 'floating children', who are carried through the streets on long poles cleverly wired to metal supports hidden under their clothing.

A welcoming sight – Tian Tan Buddha on Lantau

are also some excellent beaches, including long and empty **Cheung Sha**, some interesting traditional villages, such as **Tai O** (famous for its rope-tow ferry and pungent shrimp paste) and several important religious retreats, including the **Po Lin Monastery** (admission free; ⏲ 6am-6pm) and the striking, 23m **Tian Tan Buddha** (admission free; ⏲ 10am-5.30pm). Adjacent to the complex is **Ngong Ping Village** (☎ 2109 9179; www.np360.com.hk; admission free; ⏲ 10am-6pm Mon-Fri, 10am-6.30pm Sat & Sun; 🚼), with several Buddhist-related multimedia attractions, including **Walking with Buddha** and **Monkey's Tale Theatre** (adult/child for both $65/35), shops and food outlets, and served by the **Ngong Ping Skyrail** (adult/child one way $58/28, return $88/45; 🚼) cable car from Tung Chung. Lantau's newest attraction is **Hong Kong Disneyland** (☎ 830 830; www.hongkongdisneyland.com; adult/child Mon-Fri $295/210, Sat & Sun $350/250; ⏲ 10am-9pm Apr-Oct, 10am-7pm Nov-Mar; 🚼), located on the northeast coast and served by its own Mass Transit Rail (MTR) station. In truth, unless you have very young children in tow, Ocean Park (p102) on Hong Kong Island offers more interest and thrills than this rather lame branding exercise aimed at mainland Chinese visitors.

SHOP

CITYGATE OUTLETS 東薈城

Mall

20 Tat Tung Rd, Tung Chung, Lantau; www.citygateoutlets.com.hk; MTR Tung Chung Station (exit B); ⏲ 10am-10pm

A swanky, five-storey mall with dozens of shops selling new and out-of-season branded fashion, sportswear, outdoor gear and electrical appliances. Prices are slightly lower than what you'd find in the city but don't expect mind-blowing deals.

TURTLE OUTRAGE

Sham Wan on Lamma's southern coast has traditionally been the one beach in the whole of Hong Kong where endangered green turtles *(Chelonia mydas)* still struggle onto the sand to lay their eggs from early June to the end of August. Along with developers, a major hurdle faced by the long-suffering turtles is the appetite of Lamma locals for their eggs. In 1994, three turtles laid about 200 eggs, which were promptly consumed by villagers. Today anyone taking, possessing or attempting to sell one of the eggs faces a fine of $100,000 and one year in prison.

EAT

BOOKWORM CAFÉ

Vegetarian $

2982 4838; 79 Main St, Yung Shue Wan, Lamma; 10am-9pm Mon-Fri, 9am-10pm Sat, 9am-9pm Sun; Yung Shue Wan; V

The Bookworm Café is not just a great vegetarian café–restaurant with fruit juices and organic wine, it's also a secondhand bookshop and an internet café. It's a very convivial spot.

PO LIN VEGETARIAN RESTAURANT 寶蓮苑素食

Vegetarian $

2985 5248; Ngong Ping village, Lantau; 11.30am-4.30pm; Mui Wo, then bus 2; V

This simple meatless restaurant on Lantau is located in the covered arcade to the left of the main Po Lin Monastery building. Buy your ticket at the monastery or at the ticket office below the Tian Tan Buddha statue. Sittings occur every 30 minutes.

RAINBOW SEAFOOD RESTAURANT

天虹海鮮酒家

Chinese, Seafood $$

2982 8100; Shops 1A & 1B, ground fl, 16-20 First St, Sok Kwu Wan, Lamma; 11am-10.30pm; Sok Kwu Wan

The Rainbow, which has a couple of waterfront locations, specialises in seafood, especially steamed grouper, lobster and abalone.

WINDSURFING WATERSPORTS CENTRE & CAFE

長洲滑浪風帆中心露天茶座

Western $

2981 8316; www.ccwindc.com.hk; 1 Hak Pai Rd, Cheung Chau; 10am-6pm

Join local and expat watersports enthusiasts for sandwiches and wine at this balmy seaside café owned by Lai Gun, the uncle of Hong Kong's only Olympic royalty, windsurfer Lee Lai-shan.

>MACAU

Enjoy a shady respite at the Lou Lim Ioc Garden (p149)

MACAU

Not long ago a sleepy, Portuguese colony, tiny Macau has in a few short years become a 24/7 gambling megaresort. An hour's boat ride west of Hong Kong, this is China's Las Vegas, a brash, neon-lit magnet for mainland Chinese gamblers. Chunks of Nevada seem to have been helicoptered into the heart of its captivating fusion of Asian and Mediterranean cultures and heritage, creating an extraordinary mix of the paint-still-drying new and the centuries old. Four and a half centuries of Portuguese rule up to 1999 (when China resumed sovereignty) are still written in the territory's older architecture: picture-postcard churches and civic buildings, narrow streets, traditional shops, and Portuguese and Macanese restaurants. The tiny (27.5 sq km) territory consists of the Macau Peninsula, which is attached to China, and across the bridges the 'islands', Taipa and Coloane (now a single land mass dominated by the huge new gambling epicentre of the Cotai Strip). Getting to Macau from Hong Kong has never been easier, with high-speed ferries running between the two territories every half-hour day and night.

MACAU

SEE

AFA 1 A1
Albergue SCM ....(see 16)
A-Ma Temple 2 A2
Bishop's Palace ....(see 3)
Chapel of Our Lady of Guia ....(see 7)
Chapel of Our Lady of Penha 3 A2
Chapel of St Francis Xavier 4 B6
Church of Our Lady of Carmel 5 B4
Church of St Dominic 6 A2
Guia Fort 7 B1
Kun Iam Temple 8 B1
Lou Lim Ioc Garden 9 B1
Macau Museum 10 A1
Macau Museum of Art 11 B2
Mandarin's House 12 A2
Museu do Oriente 13 A1
Old Ladies' House ....(see 16)
Ox Warehouse 14 A1
Penha Hill ....(see 3)
Ruins of the Church of St Paul 15 A1
Saint Lazarus District 16 A2
St Joseph's Seminary Church 17 A2
Taipa House Museum 18 B4
Tam Kong Temple 19 B6
Tap Seac Square 20 A1
Treasury of Sacred Art ....(see 6)

SHOP

Lines Lab ....(see 16)
Macau Creations ....(see 15)
Pinto Livros 21 A2

EAT

A Petisqueira 22 B4
Alfonso III 23 A2
Antonio 24 B4
Café Nga Tim 25 B6
Clube Militar de Macau 26 A2
Restaurante Litoral 27 A2

DRINK

Corner's Wine Bar & Tapas Café ....(see 15)
Jabber Cafe ....(see 16)

PLAY

Blue Frog 28 B4
Grand Lisboa 29 A2
Macau Soul ....(see 15)
Wynn Macau Casino 30 A2

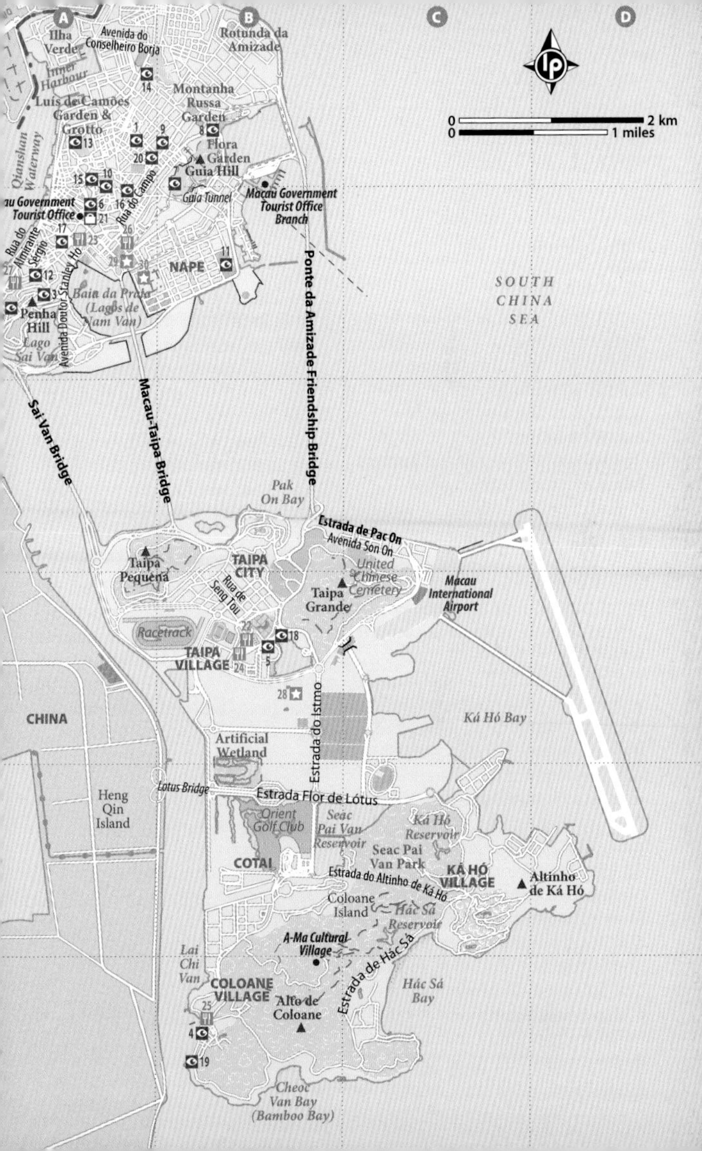

A
B
C
D
Ilha Verde
Avenida do Conselheiro Borja
Rotunda da Amizade
Inner Harbour
14
Luís de Camões Garden & Grotto
Montanha Russa Garden
8
1
9
13
20
Flora Garden
Guia Hill
Qianshan Waterway
15
10
16
Rua do Campo
Guia Tunnel
Macau Government Tourist Office Branch
au Government Tourist Office
6
21
17
23
26
Rua do Almirante Sérgio
Avenida Doutor Stanley Ho
29
30
NAPE
11
27
12
3
Baía da Praia (Lagos de Nam Van)
Penha Hill
Lago Sai Van
Avenida Doutor Stanley Ho
0
2 km
0
1 miles
SOUTH CHINA SEA
Ponte da Amizade Friendship Bridge
Macau-Taipa Bridge
Sai Van Bridge
Pak On Bay
Estrada de Pac On
Avenida Son On
Taipa Pequena
TAIPA CITY
Rua de Seng Tou
United Chinese Cemetery
Taipa Grande
Macau International Airport
Racetrack
22
18
TAIPA VILLAGE
24
5
28
Estrada do Istmo
CHINA
Ká Hó Bay
Artificial Wetland
Lotus Bridge
Estrada Flor de Lótus
Heng Qin Island
Orient Golf Club
Seac Pai Van Reservoir
Ká Hó Reservoir
Seac Pai Van Park
COTAI
KÁ HÓ VILLAGE
Estrada do Altinho de Ká Hó
Altinho de Ká Hó
Coloane Island
Hác Sá Reservoir
A-Ma Cultural Village
Estrada de Hác Sá
Lai Chi Van
COLOANE VILLAGE
Alto de Coloane
Hác Sá Bay
25
4
19
Cheoc Van Bay (Bamboo Bay)

MACAU PENINSULA

SEE

A-MA TEMPLE 媽閣廟

Templo de A-Ma; Rua de São Tiago da Barra; admission free; 10am-6pm
Behind Macau's oldest temple (1488), which is named after the Goddess of the Sea, is picturesque **Penha Hill** (主教山; Colina da Penha), which contains **Bishop's Palace** and **Chapel of Our Lady of Penha** (Capela de Nostra senora da Penha).

ART SPACES

Excellent classical and modern art can be viewed at **Macau Museum of Art** (澳門藝術博物館; Museu de Arte de Macau; ☎ 8791 9814; www.artmuseum.gov.mo; Macau Cultural Centre, Av Xian Xing Hai; $5; 10am-6.30pm Tue-Sun) and **Museu do Oriente** (東方基金會博物館; www.foriente.pt; 13 Praça de Luís de Camões; 10am-5.30pm Mon-Fri, 10am-7pm during special exhibitions). The group **AFA** (全藝社; Art for All Society; ☎ 2836 6064; www.afamacau.com; 3rd fl, Lun Hing Knitting Factory, 45 Rua de Francisco Xavier Pereira; 2.30-6pm Mon-Fri, 10am-6pm Sat & Sun) has a gallery inside a knitting factory showing some of Macau's best contemporary art; it also holds exhibitions all over town. Former slaughterhouse **Ox Warehouse** (牛房倉庫; ☎ 2853 0026; http://oxwarehouse.blogspot.com; cnr Avenida Coronel Mesquita & Avenida do Almirante Lacerda; noon-7pm Wed-Mon) specialises in experiential art.

CHURCH OF ST DOMINIC 玫瑰堂

Igreja de São Domingos; Largo de São Domingos; admission free; 8am-6pm
This 17th-century baroque church with a beautiful altar and a timber roof (see p153) contains the **Treasury of Sacred Art** (Tesouro de Arte Sacra; admission free; 10am-6pm), a three-storey Aladdin's cave of ecclesiastical art.

GUIA FORT 東望洋山堡壘

Fortaleza de Guia; 9am-5.30pm
The highest point on the peninsula, Macau's most significant fort is home to the oldest lighthouse on the China coast (1865) and the stunning **Chapel of Our Lady of Guia** (聖母雪地殿教堂; Capela de Nossa

JUST THE FACTS

Passport You need it to visit Macau.
Telephone code ☎ 853
Currency Pataca (MOP$), which is divided into 100 avos. Hong Kong dollars are accepted everywhere.
Information Macau Government Tourist Office (Map p147, A2; MGTO; ☎ 2831 5566; www.macautourism.gov.mo; 9 Largo do Senado; 9am-6pm); ferry terminal branch (Map p147, B2; ☎ 2872 6416; 9am-10pm).

Señora da Guia; 10am-5pm Tue-Sun), built in 1622 and retaining almost 100% of its original features, including some of Asia's most valuable mural paintings.

KUN IAM TEMPLE 觀音堂

Templo de Kun Iam; Av do Coronel Mesquita; 10am-6pm

In the main hall of Macau's oldest temple (1627) is a statue of a bearded *arhat* rumoured to represent Marco Polo. The first treaty of trade and friendship between the USA and China was signed in the temple's gardens (1844).

LOU LIM IOC GARDEN 盧廉若公園

Jardim de Lou Lim Ioc; 10 Estrada de Adolfo de Loureiro; admission free; 6am-9pm

This wonderful garden has huge shade trees, lotus ponds, bamboo groves, grottoes and a bridge with nine turns to escape from evil spirits (who apparently can only move in straight lines). Locals use the park to practise t'ai chi or play traditional Chinese musical instruments.

MACAU MUSEUM 澳門博物館

Museu de Macau; 2835 7911; www.macaumuseum.gov.mo; Praceta do Museu de Macau, Fortaleza do Monte; adult/child $15/8, free on 15th of month; 10am-6pm Tue-Sun

Incense coils hanging above the altar, A-Ma Temple

Housed in 17th-century Monte Fort, this worthwhile museum tells an engaging multimedia tale of the history of the hybrid territory of Macau and is perhaps the best introduction to its traditions and culture.

MANDARIN'S HOUSE 鄭家大屋

Caso do Mandarim; 2896 8820; www.wh.mo/mandarinhouse; 10 Travessa de Antonio da Silva; free; 10am-5.30pm Fri-Tue

This sprawling (c 1869) complex with over 60 rooms was the ancestral home of Zheng Guanying, an author–merchant whose readers included emperors and Chairman Mao. The stunning compound features a moon gate, a passageway for sedans, courtyards and halls in a labyrinthine layout typical of Chinese architecture.

RUINS OF THE CHURCH OF ST PAUL 大三巴牌坊

Ruinas de Igreja de São Paulo; Rua de São Paulo; admission free

The weathered facade and majestic stairway are all that remain of this church, which was designed by an Italian Jesuit and built by exiled Japanese Christians in the early 17th century. However, with its wonderful statues, portals and engravings, some consider it to be the greatest monument to Christianity in Asia (see p153).

ST JOSEPH'S SEMINARY CHURCH 聖若瑟修院及聖堂

Capela do Seminario São Jose; Rua do Seminario; 10am-5pm

One of Macau's most beautiful models of tropicalised baroque architecture (see p153), the church (1746–58) features a scalloped entrance canopy (European), a system of triangular beams and rafters (Chinese) in its roof, and China's oldest dome.

TAP SEAC SQUARE 塔石廣場

Praca do Tap Seac

This new square lined with important historic buildings (the Cultural Affairs Bureau, Central Library of Macau and Library for Macau's Historical Archives) was designed by Macanese architect Carlos Marreiros, who also created the Tap Seac Health Centre (adjacent to the Cultural Affairs Bureau), a contemporary interpretation of Macau's neo-classical buildings, featuring a verandah and wavy glass suggestive of windblown cheongsams.

> **THIS WAY AROUND**
> For information on getting to and from Macau from Hong Kong, see p184. Central Macau is best explored on foot; taxis are cheap for attractions further afield. The *Macau Tourist Map*, available from any Macau Government Tourist Office branch, has a full list of bus routes.

SHOP

MACAU CREATIONS

澳門佳作 *Gifts*

☎ 2835 2954; www.macaucreations.com; 5a Rua da Ressurreicao; 10am-10pm

Excellent Macau-themed clothes, stationery and other memorabilia designed by 30 artists living in the city, including one of Asia's most celebrated painters, Russian Konstantin Bessmertny. Your best choice for gifts. It's right under the Ruins of St Paul.

PINTO LIVROS 邊度有書

Books

☎ 2833 0909; http://blog.roodo.com/pintolivros; 3rd fl, 1a Veng Heng Bldg, 31 Largo do Senado; 11.30am-11pm

This reading room overlooking Largo do Senado features interesting titles in art and culture, and esoteric CDs.

EAT

ALFONSO III 亞豐素三世餐廳

Macanese $

☎ 2858 6272; 11a Rua Central; noon-3pm & 6-10.30pm, Mon-Sat

With a diverse menu featuring liver and tripe dishes in addition to popular classics, all fabulously executed, it's clear this low-key eatery doesn't just cater for the weekend crowds. Book ahead – it's always packed.

CLUBE MILITAR DE MACAU 澳門陸軍俱樂部

Portuguese $$$

☎ 2871 4000; www.clubemilitardemacau.net; 975 Avenida da Praia Grande; noon-3pm & 7-11pm

The Military Club is one of Macau's most distinguished colonial buildings and its Portuguese restaurant is as atmospheric as you'll find. The food is very good, if perhaps not the best in town.

RESTAURANTE LITORAL 海灣餐廳

Macanese $$

☎ 2896 7878; 261A Rua do Almirante Sérgio; noon-3pm & 5.30-10.30pm

This is arguably the best Macanese restaurant on the peninsula, and offers superb duck and baked rice dishes.

HISTORY SHOPPING

The markets and traditional shops of the narrow streets of the Macau Peninsula are great for hunting down mementoes of your visit. Rua de Madeira is a charming market street, with many shops selling carved Buddha heads and other religious items. Rua dos Mercadores will lead you past tailors, wok sellers, tiny jewellery shops, incense and mahjong shops, and other traditional businesses. At the far end of Rua da Tercena, where the road splits, is a flea market where you can pick up baskets and other rattan ware, jade pieces and old coins. Great streets for antiques, ceramics and curios (such as traditional Chinese kites) are Rua de São Paulo, Rua das Estalagens and Rua de São António, and the lanes off them. Saint Lazarus (see the boxed text, p154) has many interesting shops, including – inside **Albergue SCM** (www.albcreativelab.com; 8 Calçada da Igreja de São Lazaro) – **Lines Lab** (www.lineslab.com; Shop A3; 1-8pm Tue-Sun) where two Portuguese designers sell edgy, Macau-inspired clothes and accessories.

DRINK

CORNER'S WINE BAR & TAPAS CAFÉ *Wine Bar*

☎ 2848 2848; 3 Travessa de Sa\~o Paulo; café noon-5pm daily, bar 5pm-midnight Sun-Thu & to 1am Fri & Sat

This roof-top bar and tapas joint has a great location just across from the Ruins of the Church of St Paul (p150) and serves decent tapas dishes. At night it's a perfect place to come for some chilled-out drinks amid soft lighting and soothing music.

JABBER CAFE *Boutique Café*

☎ 2835 3618; 34-38; Rua de São Roque, Ferreira de Almeida; noon-7pm Tue-Fri & 3-7pm Sat & Sun

Located in the St Lazarus district, this sexy subterranean café with hot-pink walls belongs to a fashion designer who also lends her talent to the tasty and creative menu. The cocktails will give you a nice afternoon buzz.

PLAY

Macau's nightlife may be dominated by the ever-expanding casino scene, but if you don't fancy playing the tables (in many the minimum bet is $100 or more, and punters must be over 18 and properly dressed: no shorts or flipflops), there are a number of interesting live-music venues to choose from.

GRAND LISBOA *Casino*

☎ 2838 2828; www.grandlisboa.com; Avenida de Lisboa; 24hr

Packed with rare artworks and precious stones inside, the lavish and spectacular Grand Lisboa's towering, flaming-torch-shaped megastructure has become the landmark you navigate the peninsula streets by.

COLORFUL COLOANE

A haven for pirates until the early 20th century, Coloane (路環; Lo Wan in Cantonese), considerably larger than Taipa, is the only part of Macau that doesn't seem to be changing at a headspinning rate. All buses stop at the roundabout in Coloane Village on the muddy western shore, which overlooks mainland China just across the water. The highlight in the village is the **Chapel of St Francis Xavier** (聖方濟各教堂; Capela de São Francisco Xavier; Av de Cinco de Outubro; 10am-8pm), built in 1928, which contains paintings of the infant Christ with a Chinese Madonna, and other reminders of Christianity and colonialism in Asia. There are also a handful of interesting temples in the village, including **Tam Kong Temple** (譚公廟; Templo Tam Kong; Largo Tam Kong Miu; 8.30am-6pm), which has a dragonboat made of whale bone. To the north of the village on Estrada da Lai Chi Vun are photogenic old **junk-building sheds**, which have been the centre of a heated development-versus-preservation debate.

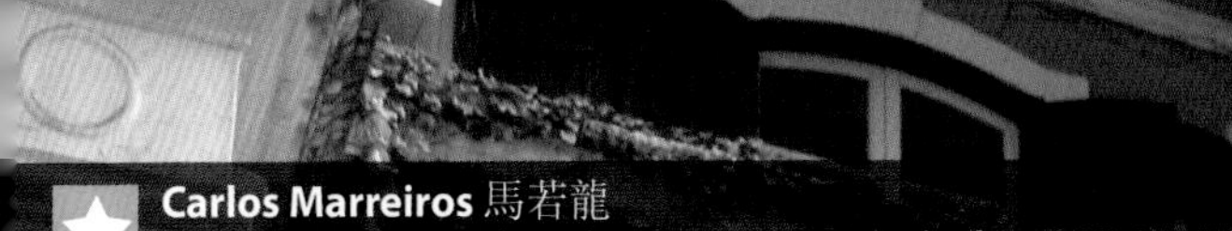

Carlos Marreiros 馬若龍

Macanese architect, urban planner, painter, poet; also former Minister of Culture of Macau and drafter of Macau's decree law for heritage preservation

Portuguese architecture Macau buildings that appear 'Portuguese' are actually a fusion of Portuguese and Chinese styles, techniques and materials, with contributions from Goa, the Philippines, Malacca, Italy and Spain. I call this 'Mediterrasianness'. St Paul's (p150) was designed by an Italian Jesuit, but has Chinese, Japanese and Indochinese features. The gargoyles include (boldly, for a Jesuit) Chinese lions, the kind guarding temples. The Mandarin's House (p149) has Western arches and Indian mother-of-pearl window panels. Churches feature baroque architecture adapted for the tropical climate, and timber is often used in place of stone because the Chinese are experts in carpentry. The only structures that are 100% Portuguese or Chinese are fortresses and temples.

MACAU SOUL 澳感廊
Live Music

☎ 2836 5182; www.macausoul.com; 31A Rua de Sao Paulo; 🕘 9.30am-8.30pm Mon-Thu, to midnight Fri-Sun
Huddled in the shadows of the Ruins of the Church of St Paul (p150), Macau Soul is elegantly decked out in woods and stained-glass windows, with a basement where blues bands perform to packed audiences. Opening hours vary so phone ahead.

WYNN MACAU CASINO
Casino

☎ 2888 9966; www.wynnmacau.com; Rua Cidade de Sintra; 🕘 24hr
The Vegas-style Wynn Macau Casino is arguably the most upmarket of the lot, with every game imaginable (up to $2500 minimum bet) and original Matisse and Renoir paintings on the premises.

TAIPA & COLOANE ISLANDS

SEE

TAIPA HOUSE MUSEUM
龍環葡韻 *Museum*

Casa Museum da Taipa; Av da Praia; $5; 🕘 10am-5.30pm Tue-Sun
Five waterfront villas below the **Church of Our Lady of Carmel** (嘉模聖母堂; Igreja de Nossa Senhora de Carmo; Rue da Restauração) show how the Macanese middle class lived in the early 20th century.

EAT

A PETISQUEIRA
葡國美食天地 *Portuguese* $

☎ 2882 5354;15D, 15C Rua de S. Joao, Taipa Village; 🕘 noon-2.15pm & 7-10.15pm Tue to Fri, noon-2.45pm & 7-10.15pm Sat & Sun
This unassuming eatery favoured by the Macanese community has been whipping up authentic Portuguese dishes for almost two decades. Book ahead.

ANTONIO 安東尼奧
Portuguese $$$

☎ 2899 9998; www.antoniomacau.com; 3 Rua dos Negociantes, Taipa; 🕘 noon-

> **ST LAZARUS ART SPACE**
> The lovely St Lazarus District, centred around cobbled Calçada da Igreja de São Lazaro (瘋堂斜巷), is where you'll find artists and designers setting up shop in historic houses. The highlight here is **Old Ladies' House** (仁慈堂婆仔屋; ☎ 2852 2550; www.albcreativelab.com; 8 Calcada da Igreja de Sao Lazaro; 🕘 noon-7pm Wed-Mon), a former shelter for Portuguese refugees from Shanghai and, later, for homeless elderly women, which is now run by one of Macau's most active art organisations, Albergue SCM. There's a poetic courtyard out front with two gorgeous old trees.

Keep an eye out for the Chinese-lion gargoyles at the Ruins of the Church of St Paul (p150)

3pm & 6.30-10.30pm Mon-Fri, noon-10.30pm Sat & Sun
Dark mahogany and blue-and-white azulejo tiles prepare you for an authentic Portuguese meal at this Michelin-recommended restaurant known for its goat's cheese with olive oil and honey, and seafood stew.

CAFÉ NGA TIM
雅憩花園餐廳 *Macanese* $$

☎ 2888 2086; 8 Rua Caetano, Coloane; ⏰ noon-1am
We love Nga Tim's simple and traditional Chinese–Portuguese food, the laid-back atmosphere, the location (opposite the Chapel of St Francis Xavier), the prices and the owner, Feeling – a guitar- and erhu-strumming former cop.

PLAY

BLUE FROG *Live Music*

☎ 2882 8281; www.bluefrog.com.cn; The Venetian Macao-Resort-Hotel, Estrada da Baía de N. Senhora da Esperança, Taipa; ⏰ 11am-late
Almost every weekend this bar transforms into a stage for indie gigs with psych-rockers or synth-punkers, who look completely out of place in a casino, having the time of their lives. And it's awesome.

>SNAPSHOTS

All that high-rise urban bustle you've seen from afar is just one side to Hong Kong. This is also a city with green escapes, wild ocean shores, diverse culinary options and cultural attractions. Locate the highlights of what this compelling city has to offer with this easy-to-use rundown of what makes Hong Kong such a memorable destination.

ACCOMMODATION

OK, so the first choice you need to make is whether to stay Hong Kong Island side or Kowloon side. Many of the cool sights await and much of the nightlife goes down on the Island, but Tsim Sha Tsui (p106) has much to recommend it, not least that amazing view of Hong Kong Island (plus a profusion of museums and galleries).

If you're on a tight budget, your options on the Island side are limited more or less to busy Causeway Bay (p90), which is great for parks and shopping but is hardly Hong Kong's beating social heart. Over the water, Tsim Sha Tsui is rammed with budget places, mostly tiny guesthouses, some in shabby tenement blocks. It's livelier, too.

For those seeking a mid-priced stay, Wan Chai (p78) on Hong Kong Island has plenty of midrange places, some at very reasonable rates. Tsim Sha Tsui and Kowloon (p122), however, offer by far the most bang for your midrange buck.

If you have cash, or an expense account to splash, Hong Kong really is your playground and the very acme of luxury can be yours. The finer hotels here really are up there with the best in the world, from the old-school charm of the Peninsula (p110) in Tsim Sha Tsui, to the sleek modernity of the Four Seasons, your average oligarch's home away from home. Just name it, helicopter airport transfers maybe, or shopping by Rolls Royce Phantom, your wish is the concierge's command.

Hong Kong's two accommodation high seasons are from March to April and October to November, though things can be tight around Chinese New Year (late January or February) as well. Outside these periods, rates drop (sometimes substantially) and little extras can come your way: room upgrades, late checkout, free breakfast and complimentary cocktails.

WEB RESOURCES

If you fly into Hong Kong without having booked accommodation, the **Hong Kong Hotels Association** (www.hkha.org) can secure you a deal of up to 50% off more than 100 midrange to high-end hotels. Local travel agent www.taketraveller.com can get you similar deals.

BEST DELUXE HOTELS

- Four Seasons Hotel Hong Kong (www.fourseasons.com)
- Grand Hyatt Hotel (pictured above; www.hongkong.hyatt.com)
- Island Shangri-La (www.shangri-la.com)
- Mandarin Oriental (www.mandarinoriental.com)
- Peninsula Hong Kong (www.peninsula.com)

BEST BOUTIQUE HOTELS

- Hotel LKF (www.hotel-lkf.com.hk)
- Fleming (www.thefleming.com)
- Jia (www.jiahongkong.com)
- Upper House (www.upperhouse.com)

BEST FOR STYLE ON A BUDGET

- Bishop Lei International House (www.bishopleihtl.com.hk)
- Ice House (www.icehouse.com.hk)
- Salisbury (www.ymcahk.org.hk)
- Stanford Hillview Hotel (www.stanfordhillview.com)
- Traders Hotel (www.shangrila.com/en/property/hongkong/traders)

BEST GUESTHOUSES & HOSTELS

- Alisan Guest House (http://home.hkstar.com/~alisangh)
- Booth Lodge (http://boothlodge.salvation.org.hk)
- Golden Island (www.gig.com.hk)
- Hop Inn (www.hopinn.hk)
- YWCA Building (www.ywca.org.hk)

ARCHITECTURE

Over the centuries Hong Kong has played host to everything from Tao temples and Qing dynasty forts to Victorian churches and Edwardian hotels (see www.heritage.gov.hk for a list of historic structures and the latest in Hong Kong's preservation efforts). But Hong Kong's ceaseless cycle of deconstruction and rebuilding means that few structures have survived the wrecking ball, at least in the central parts of the city. The best places for pre-colonial Chinese architecture still extant are the ancestral halls and walled villages of the New Territories (p136) and Outlying Islands (p140). A good way to see these is on an organised tour run by the Hong Kong Tourism Board (p194). Central (p40) on Hong Kong Island is a good hunting ground for surviving colonial architecture, though Tsim Sha Tsui (p106) can boast a few classic examples. Needless to say, enthusiasts of modern architecture will have a field day here. Central and Wan Chai (p78) on Hong Kong Island are especially rich showcases for the modern and contemporary buildings.

BEST PRE-COLONIAL CHINESE BUILDINGS

> Law Uk Folk Museum Buildings (p96)
> Man Mo Temple (p44)
> Ping Shan Heritage Trail (p138)
> Tin Hau Temple (p92)

BEST COLONIAL STRUCTURES

> Central Police Station Compound (p42)
> Former French Mission Building (p42)
> Former Marine Police Headquarters (p108)
> Murray House (p102; pictured right)
> Old Kowloon-Canton Railway Clock Tower (p112)

MOST INTERESTING 20TH-CENTURY STRUCTURES

> Hongkong & Shanghai Bank (p44)
> Lippo Centre (p78)
> Mandarin Oriental Hotel (Map p41, E3)
> Shanghai Street (p124)
> Wholesale Fruit Market (p125)

DRINKING

Drinking venues in Hong Kong fall into two main categories: buzzing bars jammed with revellers shouting over the music and each other in the main nightlife districts, and quieter, plush hotel bars with smooth service, sensational views and some elbow room. This 24/7 city doesn't really do cosy little neighbourhood bars or pubs unless you visit some of the remote island (p140) or New Territories (p136) destinations.

Lan Kwai Fong (p65) in Central and, increasingly, the streets spilling up from it towards Soho are the best areas for bars. The stomping grounds of expat and Chinese suits and professionals, it's full of life and revellers almost every night. Pubs in Wan Chai (p86) are cheaper and more relaxed, though a number of sleek addresses have sprung up in the Star Street neighbourhood, and those in Tsim Sha Tsui (p119) generally more local.

MOST STYLISH BARS & CLUBS

- > Dragon-I (p66; pictured above)
- > Executive B.A.R. (p99)
- > Red Bar (p51)
- > Sevva (p53)
- > Tazmania Ballroom (p73)

BEST FOR MEETING NONPOSEURS

- > Barco (p65)
- > Classified Mozzarella Bar (p87)
- > Club 71 (p65)
- > Phonograph (p120)
- > Yumla (p73)

BEST FOR LIVE MUSIC

- > Grappa's Cellar (p53)
- > Makumba (p70)
- > Peel Fresco (p71)
- > Skylark Lounge (p73)

BEST FOR SEEING & BEING SEEN

- > Club Feather Boa (p66)
- > Dragon-I (p66; pictured above)
- > Drop (p69)
- > Propaganda (p71)
- > Tazmania Ballroom (p73)

FOOD

It is hard to have a conversation in Hong Kong without mentioning food, especially when many still greet each other by asking, 'Have you eaten yet?' The vast majority of Hong Kong's 10,000-odd restaurants serve Chinese food, of course. Cantonese is by far the most popular Chinese cuisine in Hong Kong, but Chiu Chow, Shanghainese, Sichuanese and Northern Chinese are also widely available. Cantonese cuisine is famously fresh: there's an emphasis on freshly slaughtered meat (mostly pork and chicken) and seafood. It is common to see tanks in seafood restaurants full of creatures of the finned or shelled persuasion enjoying their final moments on *terra infirma*. Simple techniques such as steaming and stir-frying allow the ingredients to retain their delicate and well-balanced flavours (for information on dim sum, see p22). Chiu Chow cuisine, a kind of Cantonese cuisine that's managed to distinguish itself from the crowd, makes liberal use of garlic, vinegar and condiments; it's famous for braised goose and seafood dishes, such as cold crab and shark's fin soup. Shanghainese cooking and its lighter cousin Hangzhou cuisine use a lot of wine, sugar and cured meat, and rely on stewing, braising and frying. Sichuanese is the most fiery, making great use of chillies and pungent peppercorns. Northern Chinese food uses a lot of oils (eg sesame and chilli) coupled with such ingredients as vinegar, garlic, spring onions, bean paste and dark soy sauce. Steamed bread, dumplings and noodles are preferred to rice, and lamb and mutton, seldom seen on other Chinese menus, are also popular.

The full range of international fare is on your doorstep, too: Italian, Japanese, Brit pub grub, French, Korean, Indian and Mediterranean food is all well represented across most price ranges. Central (p49) is the best pick for Western restaurants, especially Soho (p61), though you'll also find a fair few in Tsim Sha Tsui (p116), Admiralty and Wan Chai (p83).

BEST DIM SUM RESTAURANTS

> City Hall Maxim's Palace (p50)
> Lin Heung Tea House (p62)
> Luk Yu Tea House (p62)
> Lung King Heen (p51)
> T'ang Court (p118)

BEST FOR NON-CANTONESE CHINESE FOOD

> Carrianna Chiu Chow Restaurant (p83)
> Hang Zhou Restaurant (p84)
> San Xi Lou (p84)
> Spring Deer (p117)
> Ye Shanghai (p119)

BEST FOR LATE-NIGHT BITES

> Chang Won Korean Restaurant (p116)
> Tsui Wah Restaurant (p64)

BEST FOR LOCAL FLAIR

> ABC Kitchen (p49)
> Ap Lei Chau Market Cooked Food Centre (p104)
> Lan Fong Yuen (p61)
> Mido (p128)
> Tai Ping Koon (p97)

Opposite Barbecued ducks ready to be enjoyed at Yung Kee (p65) **Above** Luk Yu Tea House interior (p62)

WORKOUT OR PAMPER

Aside from walking, hiking and t'ai chi, most activity options will be of the indoor variety. Several fitness club chains in Hong Kong allow short-term memberships for $150 to $200 a day, and both Kowloon Park (p110) and Victoria Park (p92) have swimming pools that are for leisure as well as laps. Yoga is also popular, stretching from the sweaty hot variety to the more meditation-based practices.

If you're after sedentary relaxation, massage and pampering treats, there are some amazing spas in the high-end hotels – notably the Four Seasons, the Peninsula (p110), the InterContinental and the Grand Hyatt – and in dedicated places in Central (p40).

For a more local experience, try deep-tissue massage and foot massage, both available at Happy Foot Reflexology Centre (p70). Different from the 'feel-good' massages you get at spas, the former entails intense kneading and pushing of acupuncture points. Similarly, the latter involves applying focused pressure to reflex points located in the soles of the feet to cure or prevent illness. The Chinese believe that our nerve zones travel from the bottom of our feet to the top of our head, encompassing all vital organs in between. Both can be quite painful for the uninitiated, but converts swear that they are addictive.

BEST HOTEL SWIMMING POOLS

- Four Seasons (www.fourseasons.com)
- Grand Hyatt Hotel (www.hongkong.hyatt.com)
- Renaissance Harbour View Hotel (www.renaissancehotels.com)
- Royal Garden Hotel (www.rghk.com.hk)

BEST FOR PAMPERING

- Elemis Day Spa (p69)
- Happy Foot Reflexology Centre (p70)
- Khoob Surat (p121)
- Sense of Touch (p71)

BEST FOR JOGGING & T'AI CHI

- Kowloon Park (p110)
- Middle Rd Children's Playground (p110)
- Tsim Sha Tsui East Promenade (p112)
- Victoria Park (p92)

BEST FOR GAIN THROUGH PAIN

- Pure Fitness (p71)
- Happy Foot Reflexology Centre (p70)
- Khoob Surat (p121)

GAY & LESBIAN

Travellers to Hong Kong will find a small but vibrant and growing gay-and-lesbian scene. It may not compete with the likes of New York or London, but Hong Kong has come a long way all the same.

It was, after all, only in 1991 that the Crimes (Amendment) Ordinance removed criminal penalties for homosexual acts between consenting adults over the age of 18 (the criminal laws against male homosexuality were initially a product of British colonialism, with a maximum sentence of life imprisonment). Since then gay groups have been lobbying for legislation to address the issue of discrimination on the grounds of sexual orientation. Despite these changes, however, Hong Kong Chinese society remains fairly conservative, and it can still be risky for gays and lesbians to come out to their family members or employers.

The bilingual website http://hkpride.net has information on the annual **Hong Kong Pride Parade**. Be sure to get hold of a copy of the free monthlies *Gmagazine* or the more comprehensive *Q Guide*, or log on to **GayStation** (www.gaystation.com.hk), **Gay Hong Kong** *(www.gayhk.com)* or **Utopia Asia** *(www.utopia-asia.com)*. **Horizons** (☎ 2815 9268; www.horizons.org.hk) is a phone service that provides information and advice to local and visiting gays, lesbians and bisexuals.

BEST FOR CLUBBING

> Propaganda (p71)
> T:ME (p67)
> Works (p71)

BEST FOR SHOPPING

> DMop (p93)
> G.O.D. (p94)
> Horizon Plaza (p103)
> Vintage HK (p60)
> Spy Henry Lau (p95)

KIDS

With its mad cityscapes, Cantonese kids sporting Japanese-style fashions and spiky hair, thrill rides up mountains and dozens of novel ways to get around, Hong Kong is a great travel destination for kids. Food and sanitation is of a high standard, the locals make a big fuss of younger kids and the territory is jam-packed with things to entertain. As a starting point for ideas, get a copy of the Hong Kong Tourism Board's *Hong Kong Family Fun Guide* (www.discoverhongkong.com).

Business travellers and tourists alike are bringing their children in increasing numbers to Hong Kong, and many deluxe and top-end hotels, including the Peninsula (p110), the Island Shangri-La and the Mandarin Oriental, have special programs for children, ranging from art workshops to Chinese cookery lessons.

Children are generally welcome in Hong Kong's restaurants – especially Chinese ones. Few restaurants have highchairs, however, so bring your own if you can't do without. Though most restaurants don't do special children's servings, Chinese food is generally shared and it's easy to create your own munchkin-sized portion.

Most hotels will be able to recommend babysitters if you have daytime appointments or are considering a night out without the kid(s). Otherwise contact **Rent-a-Mum** (☎ 2523 4868; www.rent-a-mum.com) and expect to pay $130 to $180 per hour.

BEST CHILDREN'S ATTRACTIONS

- Middle Rd Children's Playground (p110)
- Ngong Ping Skyrail (p143)
- Ocean Park (p102)
- The Peak (p74)

BEST EDUCATIONAL FUN

- Hong Kong Maritime Museum (p102)
- Hong Kong Museum of History (p109)
- Hong Kong Space Museum (p109)
- Hong Kong Wetland Park (pictured right; p138)
- Hong Kong Zoological & Botanical Gardens (p43)

MACAU

Macau (p145) is a dichotomy. On the one hand, the fortresses, churches and food of its former colonial master, Portugal, speak to a uniquely Mediterranean style on the South China Coast. On the other, Macau is now the self-styled Las Vegas of the East, which is why the vast majority of Chinese visit the place. But there's a lot more to Macau than just gambling. The tiny peninsula and the islands of Coloane (p154) and Taipa (p154) constitute a colourful palette of pastels and ordered greenery. The Portuguese influence is everywhere – cobbled back streets, baroque churches, ancient stone fortresses, art-deco apartment buildings, and restful parks and gardens – and there are several world-class museums plus an active and growing independent art and music scene. Having said that, it is worth making some time for a gawp at the casinos even if you're not here for the gambling. The buildings alone compete to outdazzle each other, while inside, the casino complexes offer an evermore enticing mix of entertainment, including big-name musicians, its own Cirque du Soleil troupe, some excellent fine dining and lashings of opulence.

MOST BEAUTIFUL

- > Chapel of Our Lady of Guia (p148)
- > Coloane (p152)
- > Mandarin's House (p149)
- > Ruins of the Church of St Paul (p150)
- > Tap Seac Square (p150)

BEST ART

- > Albergue SCM (p151)
- > AFA (p148)
- > Macau Museum of Art (p148)
- > Museu do Orient (p148)

BEST SHOPPING

- > Macau Creations (p150)
- > St Lazarus District (p154)

BEST RELIGIOUS ARCHITECTURE

- > Church of St Dominic (p148)
- > Kun Iam Temple (p149)
- > Ruins of the Church of St Paul (p150)
- > St Joseph's Seminary Church (p150)

MUSEUMS & GALLERIES

Hong Kong boasts some two dozen museums scattered across the territory, exploring everything from tea ware (p80) and space exploration (p109) to Hong Kong cinema (see p96) and the history of medicine (p76). Among the most worthwhile cultural experiences are the excellent Hong Kong Museum of History (p109) in Tsim Sha Tsui East, and the Hong Kong Heritage Museum (p138) in the New Territories, both of which do a fine job of explaining Hong Kong's history and culture. The Hong Kong Museum of Art (p108) offers a good introduction to Chinese fine and applied arts through its worthwhile temporary exhibitions and its diverse and dazzling permanent collection of painting, ceramics, calligraphy and antiquities. At the same time, Hong Kong counts twice as many galleries that show everything from cutting-edge home-grown art to old photographs and 'decorative' pieces created to blend in. More than 60 galleries, both commercial and government-supported, take part in the annual Hong Kong Art Walk (p29) in March.

MOST INFORMATIVE

- > Hong Kong Film Archive (p96)
- > Hong Kong Heritage Museum (p138)
- > Hong Kong Museum of Art (p108)
- > Hong Kong Museum of History (p109)
- > Law Uk Folk Museum (p96)

BEST BUYABLE ART

- > Grotto Fine Art (p58)
- > Hanart TZ Gallery (p48)

BEST 'PEOPLE'S' ART SPACES

- > Cattle Depot Artist Village (p133)
- > Fotanian (p133)
- > Para/Site Art Space (p45)
- > Jockey Club Creative Arts Centre (p133)

PARKS & GARDENS

Hong Kong's precious green spaces are surprisingly profuse and varied. The territory counts almost two dozen country parks (mostly in the New Territories, p136, and the Outlying Islands, p140) where you can walk, hike, bird-watch etc. But you don't have to travel great distances in Hong Kong in order to commune with nature; the urban areas of Hong Kong Island and Kowloon are hardly devoid of parks and gardens. Some, such as Hong Kong Park (p80), are laid out to 'reflect' rather than 'represent' nature, and are awash in fake waterfalls and stone 'mountains', while others, such as Hong Kong Wetland Park (p138), embrace Mother Nature with open arms. As well as these managed havens, Hong Kong offers a wilder side. It's easy to imagine you've left the city behind at places like the Sai Kung Peninsula (p139). Relatively hard to get to and almost uninhabited, it offers great promise for hikers, beach bums and boat lovers alike. A more challenging way to experience these wilder open spaces is to tackle one of the great trails, such as the MacLehose Trail (p139), which traverses the New Territories, or the 78km Wilson Trail (p100), which snakes through Hong Kong Island's hilly, green backyard.

BEST FOR WILDLIFE
> Hong Kong Park (p80)
> Hong Kong Wetland Park (p138)
> Hong Kong Zoological & Botanical Gardens (p43)

BEST FOR VIEWS
> Hong Kong Park (p80)
> Middle Rd Children's Playground (p110)
> Signal Hill Garden and Blackhead Point Tower (p110)
> Tsim Sha Tsui East Waterfront Podium Garden (p110)

BEST FOR PEOPLE-WATCHING
> Hong Kong Park (p80)
> Kowloon Park (p110)
> Victoria Park (p92)

MOST HAPPENING
> Hong Kong Park (p80)
> Hong Kong Wetland Park (p138)
> Ocean Park (p102)

SHOPPING

Hong Kong may not be the bargain basement it once was, but it still wins hands-down in the region for variety and competitive consumerism. Any international brand worthy of its logo sets up at least one shop here, and a handful of local brands are worth spending your money on. Clothing (ready made or tailored), shoes, jewellery, luggage and, to a lesser a degree nowadays, electronic goods are the city's strong suits.

There is no sales tax (for the moment at least), so the marked price is the price you'll pay. Credit cards are widely accepted, except in markets. It's rare for traders to accept travellers cheques or foreign currency as payment. Sales assistants in department or chain stores rarely have any leeway to give discounts, but you can try bargaining in owner-operated shops and certainly in markets.

You can count on shops in Central (p47) to be open from 10am to 6pm or 7.30pm daily. In Causeway Bay (p93) and Wan Chai (p81) many will stay open until 9.30pm or 10pm. In Tsim Sha Tsui (p112), Yau Ma Tei (p126) and Mong Kok (p126) they close around 9pm.

BEST FOR LOCAL EDIBLES
- Graham St Market (p56)
- Kowloon Soy Company (p59)
- Tak Hing Dried Seafood (p127)
- Yiu Fung Store (p95)

MOST UNUSUAL
- Ap Liu St Flea Market (p133)
- Eu Yan Sang (p58)
- Golden Computer Arcade (p135)
- Rise Shopping Arcade (p115)
- Sino Centre (p127)

BEST FOR SOUVENIRS
- G.O.D. (p94)
- Shanghai Tang (p49)
- Yue Hwa Chinese Products Emporium (p127)

BEST FOR PERIOD PIECES
- Amours Antiques (p56)
- Wattis Fine Art (p61)

VEGETARIAN

Beware: there are a hundred ways to eat meat on the seemingly meat-free menu items in ordinary restaurants, meat-stock simmered vegetables being the most common problem. Stick to the specialists and you'll be fine.

Chinese vegetarian food has undergone a renaissance in recent years, and is consumed by devout Buddhists and the health conscious alike. Large monasteries in Hong Kong, including Po Lin Monastery (p144) on Lantau, often have vegetarian restaurants, though you will also find many vegetarian restaurants in Kowloon and on Hong Kong Island. For the most part they are Cantonese or Shanghainese and strictly vegetarian as they are owned and operated by Buddhists.

Meatless dishes can be found elsewhere: vegetarian congee is available in most noodle shops, and dim sum houses serve a number of vegetarian treats, including *chongyau beng* (onion cakes) and *fu pei gun* (crispy tofu roll), but be cautious.

Western vegetarian food is less easy to come by if you want anything more complex than a salad, but there are a few options in Central (p49) and on Lamma (p144). Some Indian restaurants are exclusively vegetarian, but most in Hong Kong offer a combined menu.

BEST FOR VEGAN FOOD
> Life (p61)
> Lock Cha Tea Shop (p89)

BEST FOR VEGETARIAN FOOD
> Bookworm Café (p144)
> Kung Tak Lam (p95)
> Pure Veggie House (p84)
> Woodlands (p119)

BEST FOR VEGETARIAN TREATS
> Honeymoon Desserts (p50)
> Kowloon Soy Company (p59)
> Sweet Dynasty (p118)
> Yiu Fung Store (p95)

MOST VEGETARIAN FRIENDLY
> Dumpling Yuan (p61)
> Loshan Snow Garden (p96)
> Spring Deer (p117)
> Ye Shanghai (p119)

VIEWS

Skyscrapers march up steep jungle-clad slopes and blaze neon by night across a harbour forever crisscrossed by freighters and motor junks. Nothing quite matches the vistas from the Peak (p18) in Hong Kong, but then it's difficult to get things wrong with mountains on one side, water on the other and a mixed bag of modern skyscrapers and ageing tenement buildings in the middle to provide the platform. It's not just for thrill seekers; fantastic views of the harbour form the backdrop of some excellent restaurants, hotels, bars and clubs.

Remember, too, that it's not just about Hong Kong from the top down. Some of the most dramatic sights in the territory are those of Hong Kong from the ground up. Just stand at the water's edge on the promenade in Tsim Sha Tsui (p112) and you'll understand. Views on the move are another good way to soak up Hong Kong's uniquely energetic vistas, whether it means boarding a Star Ferry (p10), partaking of a movable feast on the Midlevels Escalator (p56), or watching an urban panorama scroll by aboard a clanking, ancient tram (p13).

BEST VANTAGE POINTS

- Hong Kong Monetary Authority Information Centre (p46)
- Ocean Park (p102)
- Sevva (p53)
- The Peak (p74)
- Tsim Sha Tsui East Promenade (p112)

BEST RESTAURANTS WITH A VIEW

- Aqua (p116)
- Caprice (p49)
- Hutong (p117)
- Lung King Heen (p51)

>BACKGROUND

Pay homage to the god of wealth in Repulse Bay (p102)

BACKGROUND

HISTORY

Until British marines clambered ashore to plant the Union Jack on Hong Kong Island in the mid-19th century, this was a neglected corner of the Chinese empire inhabited by farmers, fishermen and, on 'remote' islands such as Cheung Chau (p142), pirates. Trade between China and Britain had commenced around 1683, but the balance was unfavourable to the Europeans – until they began bringing opium into China in the late 18th century.

Despite bans issued by Chinese Emperor Jiaqing and his son and successor, Dao Guang, trade in opium continued until 1839 when the commissioner of Guangzhou, Lin Zexu, destroyed 20,000 chests – almost half a tonne – of the 'foreign mud' at Humen (Taiping). This gave Britain the pretext it needed to take military action against China. British gunboats besieged Guangzhou and then sailed north, forcing the Chinese to negotiate. Captain Charles Elliot, the chief superintendent of trade, demanded that a small, hilly island near the mouth of the Pearl River be ceded 'in perpetuity' to the English crown. Hong Kong formally became a British possession in June 1843.

The so-called Second Anglo-Chinese War (1856–60) won the Kowloon peninsula – and control of Victoria Harbour – for the British. Less than 40 years later, China agreed to lease the much larger 'New Territories' to Britain for a period of 99 years.

Steady numbers of Chinese refugees fleeing war and famine entered the colony from the early 20th century up to the late 1930s. In 1941 Japanese forces swept down from Guangzhou and occupied Hong Kong for four years, imprisoning both local Chinese and foreigners at Stanley Fort.

The communist revolution in China in 1949 sent more refugees pouring into Hong Kong. On a paltry, war-scarred foundation, local and foreign businesses built an immense manufacturing (notably textiles and garments) and financial services centre that transformed Hong Kong into one of the world's great economic successes. By 1960 Hong Kong was home to about 3 million people, up from a population of 600,000 at the end of WWII.

In 1967, at the height of the so-called Cultural Revolution in China, violent riots and bombings by pro-communist groups rocked the colony. Panic spread for months before the Chinese premier, Chou Enlai, inter-

CHINA'S INVASION PLAN

The peaceful agreement that eventually settled the status of Hong Kong after 1997 could have gone another way.

Margaret Thatcher, the British prime minister who negotiated the deal, said Deng Xiaoping, then China's leader, told her he 'could walk in and take the whole lot this afternoon'.

Lu Ping, the top Chinese negotiator, recently confirmed this was no bluff on Deng's part. Deng feared that announcing the date for the 1997 handover would provoke serious unrest in Hong Kong, thus compelling China to invade.

vened. The colonial government subsequently introduced reforms and social welfare to pacify discontent.

Few gave much thought to Hong Kong's future until the late 1970s, when the British and Chinese governments started meeting to decide what would happen in (and after) 1997. Though Britain was legally bound to hand back only the New Territories, and not Hong Kong Island and Kowloon, which had been ceded 'in perpetuity', most of the population lived there; it would have been an untenable division. In December 1984 Britain formally agreed to hand back the entire territory, and a joint declaration affirmed that the 'Hong Kong Special Administrative Region' would retain its social, economic and legal systems for 50 years after the handover.

Nervousness increased as the handover date drew closer, especially after 1989 when Chinese troops opened fire on and killed pro-democracy demonstrators in Beijing's Tiananmen Square, and both people and capital moved to safe havens overseas. A belated attempt by Britain to increase the number of democratically elected members of Hong Kong's Legislative Council spurred China to set up a pro-Beijing Provisional Legislative Council across the border in Shenzhen. On 1 July 1997 this body took office in Hong Kong, and Shanghai-born shipping magnate Tung Chee Hwa was named chief executive.

Hong Kong has weathered many storms in the period since becoming a part of China again, including a severe economic downturn and an outbreak of deadly Severe Acute Respiratory Syndrome (SARS).

Sir Donald Tsang, who became chief executive in 2005, enjoyed a short period of popularity, but has found his support dwindling as he is caught between the public who yearn for more democracy and Beijing, which is unwilling to loosen its grip over the former colony.

HONG KONG IN PRINT

- *Hong Kong: Epilogue to an Empire* (Jan Morris) Anecdotal and very readable history of Hong Kong.
- *Myself a Mandarin* (Austin Coates) Very charming and highly recommended memoir of a special magistrate in the New Territories of the 1950s.
- *Old Hong Kong* (Formasia) If you like old pictures with your history, this three-volume work is for you.

GOVERNMENT & POLITICS

Hong Kong 'constitution' is the Basic Law, published in 1988, which in theory guarantees Hong Kong's freedom in everything except foreign affairs. Hong Kong's government is a complicated hybrid of a quasi-presidential system combined with a quasi-parliamentary model. An 800-member election committee chooses the chief executive, the leader of the executive branch of power, in an election that can go uncontested (and often does), giving rise to complaints by democracy advocates that the system does not represent the people.

The 60-seat Legislative Council considers and passes legislation. Half of its seats are returned by the voting public, the other half by occupationally based groups, or 'functional constituencies', groups the democracy campaigners accuse of being dominated by big business and of rendering the Legislative Council a mere rubber stamp for the executive.

The current chief executive, Donald Tsang, replaced Tung Chee Hwa in 2005. With the economy once again booming, and the withdrawal of Anson Chan, Hong Kong's most popular political figure, from the contest, Tsang was assured re-election in March 2007.

ECONOMY

Business is Hong Kong's heart and soul. The monopolies in certain sectors of the economy (eg transport and power generation) notwithstanding, the territory remains a capitalist's dream and the most economically free in the world, with trade virtually unrestricted, a hard-working labour force, excellent telecommunications and very low taxes (the maximum personal income tax is 17% while company profits tax is capped at 16.5%).

Service industries now employ about 85% of Hong Kong's workforce and make up 90% of its GDP; the manufacture of textiles, toys and other commodities now takes place over the border. Mainland China supplies almost half of Hong Kong's total imports and exports. Other important trading partners are the USA (8%), Japan (7%), Taiwan (5%), Singapore (4%) and South Korea (3%).

Hong Kong maintained an average GDP growth of 4% from the 1990s to 2008, notwithstanding the economic downturn during the Asian financial crisis in 1997 and the outbreak of SARS in 2003. The phenomenal growth of China is taking Hong Kong along with it: about 40% of the listed companies on the Hong Kong stock exchange are Chinese companies; mainland tourists to the territory now outnumber visitors from all other countries combined. By 2009 GDP had reached US$42,800 per capita. Hong Kong's economy was hit by the global financial crisis in 2009, but it soon began to recover, thanks to resilient Chinese economic growth. Politically and economically, the future of Hong Kong is increasingly reliant on its motherland.

ENVIRONMENT

Pollution has been, and remains, a serious problem in Hong Kong.

Hong Kong people are proud of their harbour, but it has suffered from years of industrial and sewage pollution. However, a disposal system in Victoria Harbour is now collecting up to 75% of the sewage, and water quality has improved in the harbour and at Hong Kong's 41 gazetted beaches.

Air pollution, responsible for an estimated 2000 premature deaths a year, is an even more serious concern. Mounting public pressure has forced the government to take more decisive measures in recent years to control emissions from vehicles and power plants, the major source of air pollution. The governments of Hong Kong and Guangdong, where most of the air pollution originates, have jointly committed to reducing regional emissions of major air pollutants. Nonetheless, most travellers to Hong Kong will find it hard to breathe in congested areas in Central, Causeway Bay and Mong Kok. An hourly update of Hong Kong's air pollution index can be found on www.epd.gov.hk.

SOCIETY & CULTURE

While Hong Kong may seem very Westernised on the surface, Chinese beliefs and traditions persist at every level of society. Buddhism and

WHERE THE GRASS IS GREEN(ER)

Not all of Hong Kong is concrete and glass. Some 425 sq km – 38% of the total land area – has been designated as protected country parkland. These 23 parks and 15 'special areas' – for the most part in the New Territories and on the Outlying Islands, but also encompassing the slopes of Hong Kong Island – comprise uplands, woodlands, coastlines, marshes and all of Hong Kong's 17 freshwater reservoirs. In addition, there are four protected marine parks and one marine reserve.

Taoism – mixed with elements of Confucianism, traditional ancestor worship and animism – are the dominant religions. In general, though, Chinese people are much less concerned with high-minded philosophies than they are with the pursuit of worldly success, the appeasement of spirits and predicting the future. Visits to temples are usually made to ask the gods favours for specific things, such as a loved one's health or the success of a business.

FENG SHUI

Literally 'wind water', feng shui (or geomancy) aims to balance the elements of nature to create a harmonious environment. It's been in practice since the 12th century, and it continues to influence the design of buildings, highways, parks, tunnels and other sites in Hong Kong. To guard against evil spirits, who can move only in straight lines, doors are often positioned at an angle. For similar reasons, beds cannot face doorways. Ideally, homes and businesses should have a view of calm water (even a fish tank helps). Corporate heads shouldn't have offices that face west: otherwise profits will go in the same direction as the setting sun.

FORTUNE TELLING

There are any number of props and implements that Chinese use to predict the future but the most common method of divination in Hong Kong are *chim* – the 'fortune sticks' (see boxed text, p139) found at Buddhist and Taoist temples.

NUMEROLOGY

In Cantonese the word for 'three' sounds similar to 'life', 'nine' like 'eternity' and the ever-popular number 'eight' like 'prosperity'. Lowest on the totem pole is 'four', which shares the same pronunciation as the word for 'death'. As a result the right (or wrong) number can make (or break) a business or relationship. The Bank of China Tower (p42) officially opened on 8 August 1988; August is always a busy month for weddings.

ZODIAC

The Chinese zodiac has 12 signs like the Western one, but their representations are all animals. Your sign is based on the year of your birth (according to the lunar calendar). Being born or married in a particular year is believed to determine one's fortune, so parents often plan for their children's sign. The year of the dragon sees the biggest jump in the birth rate, closely followed by the year of the tiger.

ARTS

The phrase 'cultural desert' can no longer be used for Hong Kong. There are philharmonic and Chinese orchestras, Chinese and modern dance troupes, a ballet company and several theatre companies. And the number of international arts festivals seems to grow each year.

CHINESE OPERA

Chinese opera, an unusual hybrid of song, dialogue, mime, acrobatics and dancing, is a world away from the Western variety and many foreigners find it hard to appreciate. Performances can last up to five or six hours, and the audience makes an evening of it – eating, chatting among themselves and playing musical chairs when bored, laughing at the funny parts, crying at the sad bits.

Costumes, props and body language reveal much of the meaning in Chinese opera – check out the enlightening display on Cantonese opera at the Hong Kong Heritage Museum (p138). For a better understanding of this art form join the Cantonese Opera Appreciation Class in the Hong Kong Tourism Board's 'Meet the People' program (see boxed text, p112).

CINEMA

Hong Kong cinema became widely known to the West when Bruce Lee unleashed his high-pitched war cry in *The Big Boss* (Fists of Fury;

CATCH IT WHERE YOU CAN

The best time to see and hear Chinese opera is during the Hong Kong Arts Festival (p28) in February, and outdoor performances are staged in Victoria Park during the Mid-Autumn Festival (p30). At other times you might take your chances at catching a performance at the Temple St Night Market (p25) or Hong Kong City Hall (p53).

1971), but the kung fu genre had been very much alive before that. Signature directors of the period included Chang Cheh, whose macho aesthetics seduced Quentin Tarantino, and King Hu, who favoured a more refined style of combat. Their works continue to influence the films of today.

The late '70s and '80s saw the rise of the New Wavers, a group of filmmakers who grew up in Hong Kong and studied film overseas. Their works were more artistically adventurous and had a more contemporary sensibility. Ann Hui, Asia's top female director, and Wong Kar-wai are New Wavers who have won overseas film awards.

Due to changes in the market, the Hong Kong film industry sank into a gloom in the mid-'90s, from which it's slowly recovering. But there have been sunny patches too. *Infernal Affairs* (2002), directed by Andrew Lau and Alan Mak, was such a hit that Martin Scorsese remade it as *The Departed*. *Election* (2005) and *Election 2* (2006), by master of Hong Kong noir Johnnie To, also enjoyed immense critical and box office success.

The Hong Kong International Film Festival (p29), with its laudable balance of art house and mainstream titles, is Asia's best film festival.

DANCE

Hong Kong's professional dance companies are the **Hong Kong Dance Company** (www.hkdance.com), for Chinese traditional and folk, and **City Contemporary Dance Company** (www.ccdc.com.hk) and the **Hong Kong Ballet** (www.hkballet.com), for classical and contemporary.

One traditional form of Chinese dance that lives on in Hong Kong is the lion dance. A dance troupe under an elaborately painted Chinese lion costume leaps around to the sound of clanging cymbals, giving the dancers a chance to demonstrate their acrobatic skills.

MUSIC

Western classical music is very popular in Hong Kong. The territory boasts the Hong Kong Philharmonic Orchestra, Hong Kong Sinfonietta and City Chamber Orchestra of Hong Kong. Opportunities to see big-name soloists and major orchestras abound, especially during the Hong Kong Arts Festival (p28).

The best time to experience world-class jazz is during the Hong Kong International Jazz Festival (p30) and the Hong Kong Arts Festival (p28). You can sample traditional Chinese music, albeit in a form adapted to a symphony orchestra model, at concerts given by the **Hong Kong Chinese Orchestra** (www.hkco.org). Hong Kong's home-grown popular music scene is dominated by 'Canto-pop' – compositions that often blend Western rock, pop and R&B with Chinese melodies and lyrics.

PAINTING

Painting in Hong Kong falls into three broad categories: contemporary local, classical Chinese and classical Western. Contemporary local art differs from that of mainland China, as Hong Kong artists are largely the offspring of refugees and the products of a cultural fusion; they blend East and West and are concerned with finding their orientation in the metropolis through personal statement. The best places to see examples of this art are the Hong Kong Museum of Art (p108), Hanart TZ Gallery (p48) and Para/Site Art Space (p45).

HONG KONG ON FILM

> *Chungking Express* (1994) – Director Wong Kar Wai's portrait of two cops dealing with love and relationships. Powerful (and, at times, funny) stuff.

> *Infernal Affairs* (2002) – Andrew Lau and Alan Mak's star-studded, utterly gripping and multi-award winning thriller about a cop (Tony Leung) and a Triad member (Andy Lau) is way better than Scorsese's Oscar-winning remake *The Departed*.

> *In the Mood for Love* (2000) – Wong Kar Wai's stylish tale of infidelity and obsession stars Maggie Cheung and Tong Leung as two neighbours in 1960s Hong Kong who discover their spouses are having an affair.

> *Made in Hong Kong* (1997) – Fruit Chan's low budget award winner about a moody young gang member who finds the suicide note of a young girl is a bleak take on modern Hong Kong youth.

NO-NOS & DO-DOS

There aren't many unusual rules of etiquette to follow in Hong Kong; in general, common sense will take you as far as you'll need to go. But on matters of identity, appearance and gift giving, local people might see things a little differently from you. For pointers on how to conduct yourself at the table, see the boxed text on p62.

- Clothing – Beyond the suited realm of business, smart casual dress is acceptable even at swish restaurants. On the beach topless is a local turn-off and nudity a no-no.
- Colours – These are often symbolic to Chinese people. Red symbolises good luck, virtue and wealth (though writing in red can convey anger or unfriendliness). White symbolises death, so avoid giving white flowers (except at funerals).
- Face – Think status and respect (both receiving and showing): keep your cool, be polite and order a glass of vintage Champagne at an expensive hotel. You've arrived.
- Gifts – If you want to give flowers, chocolates or wine to someone (a fine idea if invited to their home), they may appear reluctant for fear of seeming greedy, but insist and they'll give in and accept. Money enclosed in little red envelopes *(laisee)* is given at weddings and the lunar new year.
- Name Cards – Hong Kong is name-card crazy and in business circles they are a must. People simply won't take you seriously unless you have one (be sure to offer it with both hands). Bilingual cards can usually be printed within 24 hours; try printers along Man Wa Lane in Central (Map p41, C1) or ask your hotel to direct you.

THEATRE

Nearly all theatre in Hong Kong is Western in form and staged in Cantonese. Theatre groups include the **Hong Kong Repertory Theatre** (www.hkrep.com) and the more experimental **Chung Ying Theatre Company** (www.chungying.com).

DIRECTORY

TRANSPORT

ARRIVAL & DEPARTURE

Most international travellers arrive and depart via Hong Kong International Airport. Travellers to and from mainland China can use ferry, road or rail links to Guangdong and points beyond. Hong Kong is accessible from Macau via ferry or helicopter.

AIR

Sleek **Hong Kong International Airport** (Map p141, B2; ☎ 2181 8888; www.hkairport.com) is on Chek Lap Kok, an island flattened and extended by reclaimed land off the northern coast of Lantau. Highways, bridges (including the 2.2km-long Tsing Ma Bridge) and a fast train on 35km of track link the airport with Kowloon and Hong Kong Island.

The **Airport Express** (☎ 2881 8888; www.mtr.com.hk) departs from Hong Kong station ($100) in Central every 12 minutes from 5.50am to 1.15am daily, calling at Kowloon station ($90) in Jordan and at Tsing Yi island ($60) en route; the full trip takes 24 minutes. Vending machines dispense tickets at the airport and train stations en route. You can also use an Octopus card (p185). If you are booked on a scheduled flight and are taking the Airport Express to the airport, you can check in your bags and receive your boarding pass from one day to 90 minutes before your flight at Hong Kong or Kowloon Airport Express stations (open 5.30am to 12.30am).

There are also good bus links to/from the airport. Major hotel and guesthouse areas on Hong Kong Island are served by the A11 ($40) and A12 ($45) buses; the A21 ($33) does similar areas in Kowloon. Buses run every 10 to 30 minutes from about 6am to between midnight and 1am; the 'N' buses follow the same route after that. Buy your ticket at the booth near the airport bus stand.

OTHER WAYS TO GO

As noted in the introduction to this chapter, you don't have to take to the skies to reach Hong Kong – at least from the north (China) and the west (Macau). Travellers to/from mainland China make use of ferries, buses and trains. Indeed, the celebrated Trans-Mongolian and Trans-Manchurian trains will get you from Beijing to Moscow while very much on the ground; contact **Monkey Shrine** (www.monkeyshrine.com) or **Russia Experience** (www.trans-siberian.co.uk) for details. It's also possible to drive or take a bus to Macau and then catch a ferry to Hong Kong from there.

A taxi from the airport to Tsim Sha Tsui/Central costs around $230/300. **Parklane Limousine Service** (☎ 2730 0662; www.hongkonglimo.com) and **Trans-Island Limousine Service** (☎ 3193 9333; www.trans-island.com.hk) charge $570/650 to the same destination for up to four people.

TRAIN

Getting to/from Shenzhen over the border in mainland China is a breeze. Just board the **Mass Transit Railway** (MTR; ☎ 2881 8888; www.mtr.com.hk) East Rail (p186) at Hung Hom (Map p107, F1) or East Tsim Sha Tsui stations (Map p107, E3) and ride it for 40 minutes to Lo Wu (2nd/1st class $33/66); Shenzhen is a couple of hundred metres away.

The Kowloon–Guangzhou express train departs from the Hung Hom station a dozen times daily (from $190, 1¾ hours). Tickets can be booked in advance at MTR stations in Hung Hom, Kowloon Tong and Sha Tin; from China Travel Service (CTS) agents; or over the phone through the **Intercity Passenger Services Hotline** (☎ 2947 7888).

Another rail line links Kowloon with both Shanghai and Beijing. Trains to Beijing (hard/soft sleeper from $574/934, 24 hours) via Guangzhou, Changsha and Wuhan leave on alternate days. Trains to Shanghai ($508/825, 19 hours) via Guangzhou and Hangzhou leave on the other days.

BUS

Several transport companies in Hong Kong offer bus services to Guangzhou, Shenzhen airport and other destinations in the Pearl River Delta:

CTS Express Coach (☎ 2764 9803, 2261 2472; http://ctsbus.hkcts.com)

Trans-Island Limousine Service (☎ 3193 9333: www.trans-island.com.hk)

BOAT

Services to/from the Hong-Kong Macau Ferry Terminal (Map p41, C1) run around the clock. Ferry tickets ($142 from Hong Kong Island; higher prices from about 6pm to 6am and at weekends) can be purchased at the terminals or by calling local carrier **Turbojet** (☎ 2921 6688; www.turbojet.com.hk). The **Cotai Jet** (☎ 2359 9990; www.cotaijet.com.mo) departs from the Hong-Kong Macau Ferry Terminal (economy/superclass Monday to Friday $134/236, Saturday and Sunday $146/252, night crossing $168/267) and connects with the new strip of casinos on Taipa Island in Macau.

Jet catamarans and hovercraft depart from the China Ferry Terminal (Map p107, A2) to destinations in Guangdong.

CLIMATE CHANGE & TRAVEL

Travel – especially air travel – is a significant contributor to global climate change. At Lonely Planet, we believe that all travellers have a responsibility to limit their personal impact. As a result, we have teamed with Rough Guides and other concerned industry partners to support Climate Care, which allows travellers to offset the greenhouse gases they are responsible for with contributions to energy-saving projects and other climate-friendly initiatives in the developing world. Lonely Planet offsets all staff and author travel.

For more information, turn to the responsible travel pages on www.lonelyplanet.com. For details on offsetting your carbon emissions and a carbon calculator, go to www.climatecare.org.

VISA

Visas are not required for citizens of the UK (up to 180 days), of other EU countries, Australia, Canada, Israel, Japan, New Zealand, the USA (90 days) and South Africa (30 days). Others should check visa regulations at www.immd.gov.hk before leaving home.

RETURN/ONWARD TICKET

Visitors requiring visas have to show that they have adequate funds for their stay (a credit card should do the trick) and that they hold an onward or return ticket.

DEPARTURE TAX

The Hong Kong airport departure tax ($120 for everyone over 12 years) is almost always included in the price of the air ticket.

GETTING AROUND

Hong Kong is small and crowded, and public transport is the only practical way to move people.

The ultramodern Mass Transit Railway (MTR; p186) subway is the quickest way to get to most urban destinations. The bus system is extensive and as efficient as the traffic allows, but it can be bewildering for short-term travellers. Ferries are fast and economical and throw in spectacular harbour views at no extra cost. Trams are really just for fun.

In this guide we include icons – MTR, bus, train/tram or ferry – to indicate the most practical and convenient form of transport for each listing.

In this book, the nearest metro, bus, train/tram or ferry route is noted after the M, bus, tram or ferry icons in each listing. See also the transport map on the inside back cover.

TRAVEL PASSES

The **Octopus card** (☎ 2929 2222; www.octopuscards.com), a rechargeable 'smart card' valid on most forms of public transport in Hong Kong, costs $150. This includes a $50

Local Travel

	Central	Peak	Causeway Bay
Central	n/a	Peak, 10min	M Island line, 6min
Peak	Peak, 10min	n/a	M Island line, 6min & Peak, 10min
Causeway Bay	M Island line, 6min	M Island line, 6min & Peak, 10min	n/a
Tsim Sha Tsui	M Tsuen Wan line, 5min	M Tsuen Wan line 5min & Peak,	M Island & Tsuen Wan lines, 8min
Sha Tin	M Island line, 6min & East Rail line, 16min	M Island line, 6min, East Rail line, 16min & Peak, 10min	170, 50min
Lantau	Lantau, 31-48min	Lantau, 31-48min & Peak, 10min	M Island line, 8min & Lantau, 31-48min

refundable deposit and $100 worth of travel. Octopus fares are 5% to 10% cheaper than ordinary ones on the MTR.

For shorter stays there's the new **MTR Tourist Day Pass** ($55), valid on the MTR for 24 hours after the first use.

TRAIN

Mass Transit Railway

The **Mass Transit Railway** (MTR; ☎ 2881 8888; www.mtr.com.hk) is clean, fast and safe and transports around 3.7 million people daily. Tickets cost $4 to $26 ($3.80 to $23.10 if purchased with an Octopus card; see p185). Trains run every two to 10 minutes from around 6am to between 12.30am and 1am daily on ten lines including the Airport Express line (p183). Ticket machines accept notes and coins and dispense change.

The longer distance MTR East Rail line, which runs from Hung Hom station to Lo Wu on the mainland border, and West Rail line, which links Hung Hom with Tuen Mun in the New Territories, offer the fastest route to the New Territories. The 30-minute rides from Hung Hom to Sheung Shui on the East Rail and Tuen Mun on the West Rail, for example, cost just $8.50 and $18.50 respectively.

BUS

Hong Kong's extensive bus system will take you just about anywhere in the territory. Most

Tsim Sha Tsui	Sha Tin	Lantau
M Tsuen Wan line, 5min	182, 1hr	Lantau, 31-48min
M Tsuen Wan line, 5min & Peak, 10min	182, 1hr & Peak, 10min	Lantau, 31-48min & Peak, 10min
M Island & Tsuen Wan lines, 8min	170, 50min	M Island line, 8min & Lantau, 31-48min
n/a	East Rail line, 16min & Lantau, 31-48min, Sat & Sun 35min	M Tsuen Wan line, 5min
MTR East Rail, 16min	n/a	Lantau, 31-48min & 182, 1hr
M Tsuen Wan line, 5min & Lantau, 31-48min, at weekends Lantau, 35min	Lantau, 31-48min, & 182, 1hr	n/a

buses run from 5.30am or 6am until midnight or 12.30am, though there are a handful of night buses that run from 12.45am to 5am or later. Bus fares cost $2.50 to $40, depending on the destination. You will need exact change or an Octopus card (p185).

Central's most important terminal for buses is below Exchange Square (p42). From here you can catch buses to Aberdeen, Repulse Bay, Stanley and other destinations on the southern side of Hong Kong Island. In Kowloon the Star Ferry bus terminal (Map p107, B4) has buses heading up Nathan Rd and to the Hung Hom train station.

Figuring out which bus you want can be difficult, but **City Bus** and **First Bus** (www.nwstbus.com.hk), owned by the same company, and **Kowloon Motor Bus** (www.kmb.hk) provide user-friendly route searching on their websites.

MINIBUS

Also known as 'public light buses' (an official term that no-one ever uses in conversation), minibuses seat up to 16. Small red 'minibuses' ($2 to $20) don't run regular routes; you can get on or off unless restricted by road rules. Green 'maxicabs' operate on some 350 set routes and make designated stops. Two popular routes are the 6 ($4.70) from Hankow Rd in Tsim Sha Tsui to Tsim Sha Tsui East and Hung Hom station in Kowloon, and the 1 ($8.40) to Victoria Peak from next to Hong Kong station.

TRAM

Hong Kong Island's double-decker trams are not fast but are fun and cheap and a great way to explore the northern coast. For a flat fare of $2 (dropped in a box beside the driver as you disembark) you can rattle along as far as you like over 16km of track, 3km of which wends its way into Happy Valley. Trams operate from around 6am to as late as 12.30am and run every two to 10 minutes.

There are six routes (west to east): Kennedy Town–Western Market, Kennedy Town–Happy Valley, Kennedy Town–Causeway Bay, Sai Ying Pun (Whitty St)–North Point, Sheung Wan (Western Market)–Shau Kei Wan and Happy Valley–Shau Kei Wan. The longest run (Kennedy Town–Shau Kei Wan, with a change at Western Market) takes about 1½ hours. For more tram information, see p13.

Strictly speaking a funicular, the Peak Tram (one way/return adult $25/36, senior and child 3 to 11 years $9/16) departs for Victoria Peak about every 10 to 15 minutes from 7am to midnight. The tram's

NEED TO KNOW

Electricity The standard voltage is 220V, 50Hz AC. Most electric outlets are designed to accommodate the British variety with three square pins.
Metric System The metric system is officially used, but traditional Chinese weights and measures persist at local markets, including leung (37.8g) and gan (catty; about 605g). There are 16 leung to the gan.
Newspapers & Magazines The local English-language newspapers are the *South China Morning Post* (www.scmp.com) published daily ($7), and *The Standard* (www.thestandard.com.hk) Monday to Saturday ($6). The Beijing mouthpiece *China Daily* (www.chinadaily.com.cn) prints a Hong Kong English–language edition ($6). The *Asian Wall Street Journal* as well as regional editions of *USA Today*, the *International Herald Tribune* and the *Financial Times* are printed in Hong Kong.
Radio Popular English-language stations in Hong Kong are RTHK Radio 3 (current affairs and talkback; 567AM, 1584AM, 97.9FM and 106.8FM), RTHK Radio 4 (classical music; 97.6FM-98.9FM), RTHK Radio 6 (BBC World Service relays; 675AM), AM 864 (hit parade; 864AM) and Metro Plus (news; 1044AM).
Television The two English-language terrestrial stations are TVB Pearl and ATV World.
Time Hong Kong Standard Time is eight hours ahead of GMT; there is no daylight saving time in summer.

lower terminus (Map p41, E4; 33 Garden Rd, Central) is behind St John's Building, at the northwestern corner of Hong Kong Park. See also p18.

BOAT

There are four Star Ferry routes, but by far the most popular is the one running between its new home (Outlying Islands ferry terminal pier 7; Map p41, F1) in Central and Tsim Sha Tsui (Map p107, B4). Fares are $1.70/2.20 (lower/upper deck) and, quite frankly, there's no other trip like it in the world. Star Ferries also links Central with Hung Hom and Wan Chai with Hung Hom and Tsim Sha Tsui. For more on Star Ferries, see p10.

Two separate ferry companies operate services to the outlying islands, including Lantau, Cheung Chau and Lamma, from ferry terminal piers 4, 5 and 6 (Map p41, E1) in Central.

TAXI

Hong Kong taxis are a bargain compared to taxis in other world-class cities. The flag fall for taxis on Hong Kong Island and Kowloon is $18 for the first 2km plus a metered fare of $1.50 or $1 for every additional 200m respectively below or above $70.50. It's slightly less in the New Territories ($14.50/1.30) and on Lantau ($13/1.30).

CAR & MOTORCYCLE

Hong Kong's maze of one-way streets and dizzying expressways is not for the faint-hearted. Traffic is heavy and finding a parking space is difficult and very expensive.

If you do need to use a vehicle, hire one with a driver from **Ace Hire Car** (☎ 2572 7663, 2893 0541; www.acehirecar.com.hk), which has chauffeur-driven cars for $160 to $250 per hour (minimum two to five hours, depending on location).

PRACTICALITIES

BUSINESS HOURS

Business hours are 9am to 5.30pm or 6pm Monday to Friday and (sometimes) 9am to noon or 1pm on Saturday. Many offices close for lunch between 1pm and 2pm.

Shops catering to the tourist trade keep longer hours, but almost nothing opens before 9am, and many shops don't open until 10am or even 10.30am. Even tourist-related businesses shut down by 10pm.

Most banks, post offices, shops and attractions are closed on public holidays. Restaurants usually open daily, including Sunday.

CLIMATE & WHEN TO GO

October, November and nearly all of December are the best months to visit. Temperatures are moderate in Hong Kong during these months, the skies are clear and the sun shines. January and February are cloudy and cold but dry. It's warmer from March to May but the humidity is high, with lots of fog and drizzle. The sweltering heat and humidity from June to September can make for some sweaty sightseeing; the threat of typhoon looms throughout September.

Travel in and out of Hong Kong can be especially difficult during Chinese New Year (late January/February).

DISCOUNTS

Children aged three to 11 and seniors over 60 or 65 are generally offered half-price admission at attractions and on most forms of transport, but family tickets are rare.

The International Student Identity Card (ISIC) offers discounts on some forms of transport and cheaper admission to museums and other attractions. If you're under 26 but not a student, you can apply for an International Youth Travel Card (IYTC) issued by the Federation of International Youth Travel Organisations (FIYTO), which gives much the same discounts. Teachers can apply for the International Teacher Identity Card (ITIC).

EMERGENCIES

Hong Kong is generally very safe both night and day but, as with anywhere, things can go wrong.

Ambulance, Fire & Police ☎ 999
Police (crime hotline) ☎ 2527 7177
Rape Crisis Line ☎ 2375 5322

HOLIDAYS

New Year's Day 1 January
Chinese New Year Three days in late January/February
Easter Three days in late March/April
Ching Ming Early April
Buddha's Birthday Late April/May
Labour Day 1 May
Dragon Boat Festival Late May/June
Hong Kong SAR Establishment Day 1 July
Mid-Autumn Festival Mid-September/October
China National Day 1 October
Chung Yeung Festival October
Christmas Day 25 December
Boxing Day 26 December

INTERNET

INTERNET CAFÉS

With the plethora of places offering low-cost or free wi-fi, including most hotels, all of Hong Kong International Airport (p183) and public libraries, you'll have no trouble accessing the internet with your own laptop. If you didn't bring yours along, Hong Kong has plenty of independent options:

Central Library (Map p91, C3; ☎ 3150 1234; www.hkpl.gov.hk; 66 Causeway Rd, Causeway Bay; 10am-9pm Thu-Tue, 1-9pm Wed) Free access.

Pacific Coffee Company (Map p41, E2; ☎ 2868 5100; www.pacificcoffee.com; Shop 1022, 1st fl, IFC Mall, 8 Finance St, Central; 7am-11pm Sun-Thu, to midnight Fri & Sat) Free access with purchase; one of scores of branches in Hong Kong, located within the Two International Finance Centre (p46).

INTERNET RESOURCES

Lonely Planet (www.lonelyplanet.com) A good start for many of Hong Kong's more useful links.
GovHK (www.info.gov.hk)
Hong Kong News.Net (www.hongkongnews.net)
Hong Kong Observatory (www.hko.gov.hk)
Hong Kong Outdoors (www.hkoutdoors.com)
Hong Kong Telephone Directory (www.pccw.com)
Hong Kong Tourism Board (www.discoverhongkong.com)
South China Morning Post (www.scmp.com.hk)
Time Out (www.timeout.com.hk)

LANGUAGE

Chinese and English are Hong Kong's two official languages. While Cantonese is used in Hong Kong in everyday life by most (some 94%) of the population, English is still the primary language of commerce, banking, international trade and the higher courts.

However, there has been a dramatic rise in the number of Mandarin-speaking tourists since the handover, and some locals are now learning Mandarin in addition to English.

BASICS

Hello, how are you?	*nei ho ma?*
Goodbye.	*baai baai/joi gin*
I'm fine.	*ngo gei hou*
Excuse me.	*ng goi*
Yes.	*hai*
No.	*ng hai*
Thank you very much.	*do je saai/ng goi saai*
You're welcome.	*ng sai haak hei*
Do you speak English?	*nei sik ng sik gong ying man a?*
I don't understand.	*ngo ng ming*
How much is this?	*gei do chin a?*
That's too expensive!	*taai gwai la!*

EATING & DRINKING

That was delicious!	*ho mei!*
I'm a vegetarian.	*ngo sik jaai ge*
The bill, please.	*ng goi maai daan*

EMERGENCIES

I'm sick.	*ngo beng jo*
Help!	*gau meng a!*
Call the police!	*giu ging chaat!*
Call an ambulance!	*giu gau seung che!*
Call a doctor!	*giu yi sang!*

TIME & NUMBERS

today	*gam yat*
tomorrow	*ting yat*
yesterday	*kam yat*

0	*ling*
1	*yat*
2	*yi (leung)*
3	*saam*
4	*sei*

5	*ng*
6	*luk*
7	*chat*
8	*baat*
9	*gau*
10	*sap*
11	*sap yat*
12	*sap yi*
20	*yi sap*
21	*yi sap yat*
100	*yat baak*
101	*yat baak ling yat*
110	*yat baak yat sap*
120	*yat baak yi sap*
200	*yi baak*
1000	*yat chin*

MONEY

The local currency is the Hong Kong dollar (HK$). The dollar is divided into 100 cents. Notes are issued in denominations of $10, $20, $50, $100, $500 and $1000. There are coins of 10c, 20c, 50c, $1, $2, $5 and $10.

Hong Kong is a relatively pricey destination. You can survive on $300 a day, but it will require a good deal of self-discipline. Better to budget for around $600.

International travellers can withdraw funds from their home accounts using just about any of the numerous ATMs scattered around the territory. The most widely accepted credit cards in Hong Kong are Visa, MasterCard, American Express, Diners Club and JCB. For 24-hour card cancellations or assistance, try calling the following numbers:

American Express (☎ 2811 6122)
Diners Club (☎ 2860 1888)
MasterCard (☎ 1 636 722 7111)
Visa (☎ 800 900 782)

For currency exchange rates, see the inside front cover of this book.

ORGANISED TOURS

There is a mind-boggling array of tours available via every conceivable conveyance. Some of the best tours are offered by the **Hong Kong Tourism Board** (HKTB; ☎ 2508 1234; www.discoverhongkong.com), and tours run by individual companies can usually be booked at any HKTB branch (p194). The more unusual tours include the Come Horseracing tour available through **Splendid Tours & Travel** (☎ 2316 2151; www.splendidtours.com) during the racing season. The tour includes admission to the Visitors' Box of the Hong Kong Jockey Club Members' Enclosures and buffet with drinks. Tours scheduled at night (Wednesday) last about 5½ hours, while daytime tours (Saturday or Sunday) are about seven hours long.

As well as offering a scenic dolphin-spotting expedition, the four-hour tour (adult/child $360/180) off Lantau offered by **Hong Kong Dolphinwatch** (☎ 2984 1414; www.hkdolphinwatch.com; 1528A Star House, 3 Salisbury Rd, Tsim Sha Tsui) includes information on the plight of the endangered Chinese white dolphin, of which between 100 and 200 inhabit Hong Kong's coastal waters. Departures are at 8.50am from the Kowloon Hotel in Tsim Sha Tsui every Wednesday, Friday and Sunday.

HKTB offers visitors a one-hour ride ($100) two days a week on a sailing junk called the *Duk Ling*. Boarding is at 2pm and 4pm on Thursday and 10am and noon on Saturday at the Tsim Sha Tsui public pier next to the Star Ferry terminal (Map p107, B4) in Tsim Sha Tsui. Visitors should register with any HKTB branch in advance.

If you're after faster, thrill-based water tours, the four-hour tour ($740) from **Kayak and Hike** (☎ 9300 5197; www.kayak-and-hike.com) of the harbour around Sai Kung in the New Territories takes you by unique 'fast pursuit craft' (FPC) to the otherwise inaccessible Bluff Island and the small fishing village of Leung Shuen Wan. Tours depart from Sai Kung pier at 9am; book in advance.

Learn all about t'ai chi, feng shui and Chinese tea with a 4-hour tour ($298) from **Sky Bird Travel** (☎ 2736 2282; www.skybird.com.hk). Tours depart at 7.30am from the Excelsior Hong Kong Hotel in Causeway Bay and at 7.45am from the Salisbury YMCA in Tsim Sha Tsui on Monday, Wednesday and Friday.

PHOTOGRAPHY & VIDEO

Any photographic accessory you could possibly need is available in Hong Kong. Stanley St (Map p41, D2) on Hong Kong Island is the place to look for reputable camera stores; Photo Scientific (p60) is especially recommended.

TELEPHONE

Hong Kong boasts the world's highest per-capita usage of mobile telephones, and they work everywhere – even in tunnels and the MTR. Any GSM-compatible phone can be used in Hong Kong.

Retail outlets **PCCW** (☎ 2888 0008; www.pccw.com) and **Hong Kong CSL** (☎ 2888 1010; www.hkcsl.com) rent and sell mobile phones, SIM cards and phone accessories. Handsets can be rented from $35 per day. A SIM card with prepaid call time can be as cheap as $50. You can buy phonecards at 7-Eleven and Circle K stores.

USEFUL PHONE NUMBERS

There is no Hong Kong area code.

Country code ☎ 852
Local directory assistance ☎ 1081
International directory assistance ☎ 10015
International access code ☎ 001
Reverse-charge (collect) ☎ 10010
International credit card ☎ 10011
Time & weather ☎ 18501

TIPPING

Hong Kong is not a particularly tip-conscious place; taxi drivers only expect you to round up to the nearest dollar. Tip hotel staff $10 to $20, and if you make use of the porters at the airport, $2 to $5 a suitcase is expected. Most hotels and many restaurants add a 10% service charge to the bill (see boxed text, p65).

TOURIST INFORMATION

The very efficient and friendly **Hong Kong Tourism Board** (HKTB; www.discoverhongkong.com) produces reams of useful pamphlets and publications. Its website is also a good point of reference.

There are HKTB branches at **Hong Kong International Airport** (Map p141, B2; 7am-11pm), the **Star Ferry Concourse** (Map p107, B4; 8am-8pm) in Tsim Sha Tsui and the **Peak Piazza** (Map p75, C6; 9am-9pm). Alternatively, call the **HKTB Visitor Hotline** (2508 1234; 8am-6pm).

TRAVELLERS WITH DISABILITIES

Disabled people will have to cope with MTR stairs as well as pedestrian overpasses, narrow footpaths and steep hills. People whose sight or hearing is impaired must be cautious of Hong Kong's demon drivers. On the other hand, some stairs in MTR stations and most buses are now accessible by wheelchair, taxis are never hard to find and most buildings have lifts (many with Braille panels). Wheelchairs can negotiate the lower decks of most of the ferries, and almost all public toilets now have access for the disabled.

Contact the **Joint Council for the Physically and Mentally Disabled** (Map p79, C3; 2864 2931; Room 1204, 12th fl, Duke of Windsor Social Service Bldg, 15 Hennessy Rd, Wan Chai).

>INDEX

See also separate subindexes for See (p204), Shop (p205), Eat (p206), Drink (p208) and Play (p208).

000 map pages

SEE

Architecture

Art Galleries

Artist Communes

Beaches & Caves

Churches, Mosques & Synagogues

Forts

Historic Buildings

Islands

Markets

000 map pages

SHOP

EAT

000 map pages

DRINK

PLAY

000 map pages